# Test Your English Vocabulary in

Advanced **Use**

# Michael McCarthy
# Felicity O'Dell

CAMBRIDGE
UNIVERSITY PRESS

CAMBRIDGE UNIVERSITY PRESS
Cambridge, New York, Melbourne, Madrid, Cape Town, Singapore, São Paulo, Delhi

CAMBRIDGE UNIVERSITY PRESS
The Edinburgh Building, Cambridge CB2 8RU, UK

www.cambridge.org
Information on this title: www.cambridge.org/9780521545341

First published 2005
3rd printing 2007

Printed in the United Kingdom at the University Press, Cambridge

A catalogue record for this publication is available from the British Library

ISBN 978 0 521 54534 1 paperback

# Contents

## Functional vocabulary

## Idioms and phrasal verbs

## Aspects of variation

## Answer key

# Acknowledgements

We are grateful to the following teachers who commented on the materials and made many helpful suggestions:
Ian Chitty, UK
Joy Godwin, UK
Ludmila Gorodetskaya, Russia
Magdalena Kijak, Poland
Jacky Newbrook, UK

We would also like to thank our editors at Cambridge University Press, in particular Nóirín Burke and Martine Walsh, whose expert advice has been invaluable throughout the production of these tests.

We also owe a great deal to our domestic partners for their tolerance while we were absent at our computer screens and their constant support throughout the writing of this book.

# Introduction

## Why test vocabulary?

Research has shown that you need to meet a word at least 7 times before you know it properly. Doing exercises like these, that practise words and expressions that you have already encountered, is, thus, a useful way of helping yourself to fix the vocabulary you are working on in your long-term memory.

## What vocabulary is tested?

This book provides a series of tests on different aspects of English vocabulary at an advanced level. It is based on the vocabulary presented and practised in the units of *English Vocabulary in Use: Advanced* and the test numbers correspond to the units of *English Vocabulary in Use: Advanced*. You can do the test immediately after doing the unit in *English Vocabulary in Use: Advanced* or you can wait a week or so.

You can, of course, use these tests even if you have not been working with *English Vocabulary in Use: Advanced* but are simply interested in assessing your knowledge of the vocabulary area covered by the test.

## How do I score my tests?

Each test is scored out of 40 and a key, with information about how many marks each item gets, is given at the back of the book. It should be clear from the key what you need to write to get each mark and so you should be able to score your work without a teacher, if you wish to.

The first exercise in each test generally offers a maximum score of ten and it is recommended that you do this exercise first. If your score for this exercise is less than half, then we suggest that you do a bit more work in the language area covered by the test before doing the rest of it.

Although the tests are all scored out of 40, you will probably feel that some tests are easier than others. This is partly because everyone is more familiar with some vocabulary areas than others. However, because certain vocabulary areas are particularly dense, it is also true that in a few cases you need to show that you know more words and expressions in these areas than you do elsewhere to get the same number of marks.

Finally, if you write your answers in pencil or on a sheet of paper rather than in this book, it is possible to do each test more than once and try to improve your score at a later date.

## How long do the tests take?

Each test should take 20 to 30 minutes to complete.

We hope that you enjoy using these tests and that they will help you to learn the vocabulary that you want and need to master at this level.

# Abbreviations and acronyms

**1.1**

10 marks

**What do the abbreviations in bold mean?**

*Example:* He's addicted to **sci-fi** comics. *science fiction*

1 I would appreciate it if you could reply to this invitation **asap**.
2 To go hiking you will need good equipment, **e.g.** strong boots and a raincoat.
3 Doors open at 7.30. **NB**: all tickets must be booked in advance.
4 You have to be a qualified driver, **i.e.** you must have passed your driving test.
5 Several **EU** countries introduced the new euro currency in 2002.
6 He thought he saw a **UFO** but it was only a bird.
7 The temple ruins date from about 200 years **BC**.
8 **VAT** was first introduced in 1973 as a tax on goods and services.
9 In many countries, everyone has to carry an **ID** card.
10 Nowadays millions of people have a **PC** at home.

**1.2**

10 marks

**In each of these sentences it is possible to change one word or phrase into an abbreviation or acronym. Rewrite the sentences making any other necessary changes.**

*Example:* The speed limit here is 30 miles per hour.
　　　　　**The speed limit here is 30 mph.**

1 I'd prefer to watch a good documentary rather than a situational comedy any day.
2 I've loved science fiction ever since I was a kid.
3 The city was founded about 500 years after Christ.
4 Accommodation is expensive. Even an apartment which is just a bedroom and sitting room combined will cost you 600 pounds a month.
5 The information leaflet had a useful list of frequently asked questions.

**1.3**

12 marks

**Rewrite these small ads without using the abbreviations and acronyms in bold.**

> <u>For Sale</u>
> Large family house in pretty village **8m** from Cambridge. Garden, **d/g**.
> Tel: 0132 56374 for details.

> <u>To let</u>: 2-bedroom **s/c** flat near city centre. **Ch** and all **mod cons**. Rent £800 **pcm excl**.

> Room to let in shared **f/f** flat.
> Suit **ns prof** female.
> £100 **pw incl**.

**1.4**

5 marks

**The letters of the abbreviations or acronyms in these sentences have got mixed up. Write them in the correct order.**

1 **IDAS** is a terrible disease which has killed millions of people.
2 **ONAT** was formed after the Second World War as a mutual defence organisation.
3 At the bottom of the invitation it said **RPVS**, so I replied immediately.
4 **TPO** for further information on how to make a reservation.
5 For sale: Lumina digital camera. $280, **OON**.

**1.5**

3 marks

**Write the abbreviations in bold in these text messages as full words.**

1 HI JOEL! **CU** AT THE MATCH TOMORROW?
2 NO WAY. **FYI** I'M BROKE. BUY ME A TICKET?
3 **UR** JOKING!

Your score

/40

# 2 Prefixes: creating new meanings

**2.1**

10 marks

Use your knowledge of the underlined prefixes to help you answer these questions.

1  This hotel is nice but rather <u>over</u>priced.
   What does the speaker think about the hotel's prices?
2  The problems at the hospital are because it's <u>under</u>staffed.
   What staff problem does the hospital have?
3  It is good for young people to experience some kind of <u>cross</u>-cultural exchange.
   What kind of exchange do you think the speaker is thinking of?
4  I was <u>up</u>graded on the flight home!
   What happened to this airline passenger?
5  The children are staying <u>over</u>night at their grandparents'.
   When are the children coming home?
6  I think Tim behaved in a very <u>under</u>hand way.
   What is the speaker suggesting about Tim's behaviour?
7  The business is currently experiencing a bit of an <u>up</u>turn.
   Has the business improved or got worse?
8  We can't solve the problem of crime without dealing with the <u>under</u>lying causes.
   What do you think might be an underlying cause of crime?
9  Don't <u>under</u>estimate Helen. She'll surprise you one day.
   What does the speaker suggest about the other person's opinion of Helen?
10 <u>Cross</u>-border shootings take place on a regular basis.
   Where are the people who are shooting each other?

**2.2**

10 marks

Match the examples on the left with the correct meaning of the underlined prefixes on the right.

| | | |
|---|---|---|
| 1  <u>under</u>funded, <u>under</u>stated, <u>under</u>paid | a) | out, off |
| 2  <u>con</u>dolences, <u>con</u>versation, <u>con</u>taminate | b) | outside, beyond the usual |
| 3  <u>e</u>ject, <u>e</u>mit, <u>e</u>vict, <u>e</u>radicate | c) | with |
| 4  <u>ad</u>jacent, <u>ad</u>join | d) | forward |
| 5  <u>pro</u>mote, <u>pro</u>create, <u>pro</u>liferate, <u>pro</u>crastinate | e) | less, too little |
| 6  <u>ab</u>sence, <u>ab</u>dicate, <u>ab</u>scond, <u>ab</u>duct | f) | to |
| 7  <u>a</u>blaze, <u>a</u>float, <u>a</u>sleep | g) | away from |
| 8  <u>extra</u>terrestrial, <u>extra</u>ordinary, <u>extra</u>curricular | h) | like '–ing' form of verb |
| 9  <u>Inter</u>net, <u>inter</u>related, <u>inter</u>national | i) | within, inside |
| 10 <u>intra</u>net, <u>intra</u>venous, <u>intra</u>departmental | j) | between, connected |

**2.3**

20 marks

Choose a word from the examples in exercise 2.2 to fill each gap. Write it in the correct form.

1  We were all surprised when the king ............................................ in favour of his son.
2  I was so sad to hear of your uncle's death. Please give your aunt my ............................................ .
3  After his operation, the patient was fed ............................................ for several days.
4  After four years in the company, he was finally ............................................ to senior manager.
5  If the pilot presses this button, he ............................................ himself from the plane.
6  We asked for ............................................ rooms at the hotel but they actually put us on different floors.
7  It's such a small island that most of the families there are ............................................ .
8  The machine has started ............................................ a strange, high-pitched sound.
9  A lot of small businesses these days are finding it hard to stay ............................................ .
10 Do you believe that there are ............................................ beings in outer space?

# 3 Suffixes: productive suffixes and word classes

**3.1**

20 marks

Match the roots from box A with suitable suffixes from box B to create new words. Use each root and suffix once only.

A:
| sound | additive | fibre | like | crime |
|---|---|---|---|---|
| news | wash | stress | student | health |

B:
| -able | -minded | -conscious | -related | -led |
|---|---|---|---|---|
| -free | -proof | -ridden | -rich | -worthy |

**3.2**

10 marks

Complete these sentences using the suffixes from box B in exercise 3.1. Use each suffix once only.

1  She's a highly ambitious, career-............................ young woman.
2  If you want to go swimming with a watch on it will have to be water............................ .
3  He was guilt-............................ when he realised it was all his fault.
4  Hilary's a trust............................ person. I can think of no one better for the job.
5  The British are thought to be more class-............................ than the Americans.
6  Three staff-............................ protests have taken place in the company in the last few months.
7  Sugar-............................ chewing gum is better for your teeth than the sugary stuff.
8  Athletes often follow a protein-............................ diet to help build their muscles.
9  I don't want to discuss work-............................ issues outside of office hours.
10  I don't really think the new plan is work............................ .

**3.3**

10 marks

Are these words nouns, verbs, adjectives or adverbs? Tick (✓) the correct box.

| | noun | verb | adjective | adverb |
|---|---|---|---|---|
| occupant | | | | |
| moisten | | | | |
| costly | | | | |
| golden | | | | |
| heavily | | | | |
| relevant | | | | |
| sweeten | | | | |
| lively | | | | |
| claimant | | | | |
| warmly | | | | |

Your score

/40

# Word-building and word-blending

**4.1**

12 marks

Add one of the word parts from the box to complete the words.

| auto | bio | cyber | de | graph | graphy | |
|------|-----|-------|-----|-------|--------|---|
| ics | ology | post | pre | retro | ~~techno~~ | tele |

*Example:* There's a story in the paper today about someone who was so ....**techno**....phobic that he wouldn't go near a computer.

1 He went to a psychologist who taught him some ........................suggestive techniques to help him deal with stress.
2 Scientists have proved there are ........................pathic links between pets and their owners.
3 The civil war has ........................stabilised the whole economy.
4 A woman has got 20 years in jail for the ........................meditated murder of her husband.
5 There's going to be a big international conference on ........................degradable packaging.
6 The new taxation regulations will not be ........................active.
7 Writers of detective stories can do a new course in crimin........................ .
8 Here's a review of that new bio........................ of King Edward VIII.
9 Linguist........................ is the study of the structure and development of languages.
10 He spends all his time e-mailing friends from his local ........................café.
11 The professor has now published a mono........................ on child psychology.
12 After his first degree he went on to do a ........................graduate course in computing.

**4.2**

18 marks

What blend or combination of two well-established words matches each of these definitions? Which two words does each blend come from?

*Example:* a CD-ROM or TV programme that is both educational and entertaining
    *edutainment   from education + entertainment*

1 a place where helicopters take off and land
2 a device for analysing the amount of alcohol in someone's breath
3 a burger that can be eaten by vegetarians
4 a hotel for motorists
5 pollution caused by smoke and fog
6 a meal that is a combination of breakfast and lunch

**4.3**

10 marks

Use your knowledge of word parts in English to explain what the basic meanings of the underlined words in these sentences are.

*Example:* More and more people are <u>teleworking</u> now.
    *working at home rather than in a central office   tele = over a distance*

1 I saw a famous pop star at the airport and managed to get her <u>autograph</u>.
2 I bought my son some <u>prepaid</u> phone cards so he can ring home while he's away.
3 He's a specialist in <u>climatology</u> and global warming.
4 Nurses on surgical wards have to watch out for <u>post-operative</u> complications in their patients.
5 The government claims that it wants to pursue a policy of <u>decentralisation</u>.
6 The aim of the conservation agency is to preserve the country's <u>biodiversity</u>.
7 In <u>retrospect</u> it's easy to see where the business went wrong.
8 The growth of the Internet has inevitably led to the development of a range of <u>cybercrimes</u>.
9 My flatmate is quite a <u>techno-wizard</u> and he's set up a great sound system for us.
10 We've made a lot of <u>progress</u> with the project this week.

**Your score**

/40

# 5 Global contact and language enrichment

**5.1**
16 marks

Circle the correct underlined word.

1 The word stick/store/stock of English includes a lot of borrowings/loanings/lendings from other languages.
2 Over 120 different languages are listed as supplies/sources/originals of words in English.
3 The everyday wording/lexicon/dictionary of English consists of around 2,000 words.
4 Words from other languages have grown/added/enriched English over the centuries.
5 English has many words which come from the classical/classy/classic languages.
6 Borrowings is another term for lend/loan/lean words.
7 The linguistical/linguist/linguistic consequences of centuries of overseas exploration, colonisation and trade can be observed in present-day English.

**5.2**
12 marks

The jumbled words in the second column are examples of words that have entered English from the languages in the left-hand column. Find the words by putting the letters in the correct order. The right-hand column gives you some clues.

| language | jumbled word | word | clue |
| --- | --- | --- | --- |
| German | skrcuakc | rucksack | bag you wear on your back |
| Russian | nllegtsniiaite | | intelligent people in society |
| Spanish | mockmah | | hanging bed |
| German | kicmmig | | trick to sell something |
| Greek | cinto | | makes you feel better |
| Portuguese | vealarp | | fuss and bother |
| Arabic | braem | | jewellery is made from it |
| Japanese | ahar-irik | | suicide |
| Hindi | oct | | bed |
| Icelandic | spmum | | infectious disease |
| Farsi | batby | | type of cat |
| Dutch | storer | | list of people's turns for jobs |
| Turkish | nabrut | | headware |

**5.3**
12 marks

Use the words from exercise 5.2 to fill the gaps in these sentences.

1 She was wearing a beautiful ............................................. bracelet.
2 Giving a free mouse-pad with every copy of the book was just a sales ............................................. .
3 Many warriors were willing to commit ............................................. for love of their country.
4 All that fuss and bureaucracy for such an unimportant thing! What a ............................................. !
5 My old uncle always took some sort of ............................................. if he was feeling unwell.
6 We looked at the ............................................. to see if it was our turn to do the cleaning.
7 They have two gorgeous cats, a black one and a ............................................. .
8 Did you ever have ............................................. as a child? Or measles, or chickenpox?
9 The Spanish ............................................. in the 19th century often wrote about national identity.
10 When they had their first baby, we bought them a ............................................. as a present.
11 I've always wanted to sleep in a ............................................. in my garden on a sunny day.
12 The police officer wore a ............................................. instead of a helmet because of his religion.

# 6 Similar but different: words easily confused

**6.1**
10 marks

**Complete the words in these sentences.**

1 This traffic jam is terrible – we've been station.................... for ten minutes.
2 It was lovely sitting in the shad.................... of the big garden umbrella reading a novel.
3 I hate the way he contin.................... complains about anything and everything.
4 Do you think the government should inter.................... to try to stop the strike?
5 The professor compl.................... me on my first-class exam marks.
6 Please stop inter.................... ! It's none of your business!
7 As the sun goes down, the shad.................... of the trees in the garden grow longer.
8 I think that strawberries and cream compl.................... each other perfectly.
9 I usually buy pens, notebooks and other station.................... before term begins.
10 It's better to take a break than to work contin.................... all day long.

**6.2**
15 marks

**Complete these sentences with a word from the box. Write the verbs in the correct form.**

| | | | | | | | |
|---|---|---|---|---|---|---|---|
| alter | arouse | avoid | change | damp | end up | evade | lookout |
| moist | outlook | rouse | serial | theme | topic | upend | |

1 Water your plants regularly but keep the soil ............................................ rather than wet.
2 Can we change the ............................................ of conversation, please? I'm fed up with football!
3 If you ............................................ the sofa it'll be easier to get it down the stairs, I think.
4 Politicians often manage to ............................................ difficult questions from journalists.
5 Don't sit on the grass – it's ............................................ .
6 Len sleeps very heavily – it's really hard to ............................................ him.
7 We must watch the next episode of the ............................................ . I really want to know who the heroine ............................................ marrying.
8 I always enjoy talking to Fiona – she has such a positive ............................................ on life.
9 Tom chose rock and roll as the ............................................ for his birthday party.
10 The inquiry into the minister's financial affairs has ............................................ a lot of interest.
11 The dress may be a little big for you but you can always get it ............................................ .
12 Ricky is always trying to find ways to ............................................ doing any work.
13 I got soaked in the downpour – I must go and ............................................ my clothes.
14 Matt stood at the door as ............................................ in case a teacher came along.

**6.3**
15 marks

**Answer these questions.**

1 Complete these two sentences with words beginning with 's'.
  a) A ............................................ officer is responsible for preventing accidents.
  b) A ............................................ officer is responsible for protecting property.
2 Which of these would you rehearse and which would you revise for?
  play      exam      concert      test
3 Circle the two words which frequently go with 'outbreak'.      flu/glass/rioting
4 What might cause a train to be held up? What happens if a decision is upheld?
5 Which of these things would you pick and which would you pick up?
  flowers      a pen that's fallen on the ground      a friend from the airport      strawberries
6 Is a breakout more likely to happen from a prison or a china shop?

**Your score**
/40

# At work: colleagues and routines

**7.1**

*6 marks*

Decide which paraphrase best describes the meaning of the underlined expression.

1 I'm pretty low down in <u>the pecking order</u> in the company.
   a) system of choosing people to do particular jobs in rotation
   b) hierarchy or order of importance
2 I'd prefer not to <u>talk shop</u> at the moment.
   a) talk about work matters outside of working hours
   b) talk about problems on the shop floor
3 Charles is my <u>opposite number</u> in the Singapore office.
   a) Charles does the same job as me in the Singapore office
   b) Charles does a completely different job to mine in the Singapore office
4 I don't want to get <u>stuck in a rut</u>.
   a) be in a situation where I can't see a solution to a problem
   b) be trapped in a job I cannot escape from
5 I don't like having to <u>meet deadlines</u>.
   a) get things finished by a fixed time
   b) meet dull, boring people
6 I usually <u>knock off</u> around five on Fridays.
   a) I usually do about five jobs on a typical Friday
   b) I usually finish work about five o'clock on a typical Friday

**7.2**

*12 marks*

Find these words by putting the letters in the correct order. You are given clues.

| teskrowma | ............................... | people you work with |
| onsmoontuo | ............................... | boring and always the same |
| enin-to-vefi | ............................... | regular office hours |
| lowdroka | ............................... | amount of work |
| lanfreece | ............................... | not directly employed by a company |
| lefs-pledemoy | ............................... | you are your own boss |

**7.3**

*10 marks*

What do you call ...?

1 ... a job where two people have a 50% contract each to do the same job?
2 ... the system where employees may start and finish work at times which suit them?
3 ... a worker who works days one week, then nights the following week, etc.?
4 ... a job with no prospects of promotion?
5 ... work which involves a lot of forms, letters, reports, invoices, etc., beginning with
   p........................... ?

**7.4**

*12 marks*

Complete the words in these sentences. You are given the first letter.

1 I don't mind working different hours each week, but I hate the night s........................... .
2 The job is so r........................... , just the same thing day after day, week after week.
3 Doctors work very i........................... hours. They never know what their schedule will be.
4 A career in the hotel industry traditionally involves very a........................... hours such as evenings and weekends.
5 I don't want to spend thirty years stuck b........................... a desk. I want a challenging job.
6 I gave up my teaching job. The stress l........................... were too high.

# At work: career and promotion

**8.1**
10 marks

Complete these sentences with a word from the box.

| career | entitlement | experience | glass | overworked |
|--------|-------------|------------|-------|------------|
| passed | paternity | shortlisted | snowed | turned |

1 In some countries new fathers are allowed ........................................... leave.
2 Women sometimes complain of a ........................................... ceiling which stops them getting promotion.
3 I can't come out tonight – I'm ........................................... under with work.
4 Dom has been ........................................... for the job – he's got an interview next week.
5 The salary for Nell's job is excellent but the holiday ........................................... is not very good.
6 Bella is always complaining of being ........................................... and underpaid.
7 If you are looking for a rewarding ........................................... in journalism, send us your CV.
8 We are looking for people who already have some sales ........................................... .
9 Kay was disappointed when she was ........................................... down for the job she'd applied for.
10 Vita was ........................................... over for promotion again this year.

**8.2**
8 marks

Correct the eight spelling mistakes in this job reference.

I would certainly recommend John Geddes for a job in your company. He is a very
dinamic and ambiciou young man and I am sure he could be a high acheiver in any
carear he chooses. The job description you sent me is a little ambigguous but it looks as
if you are seaking someone with very divers abilities. John has many of these and I am
sure he would be willing and eeger to acquire any other skills that the position requires.

**8.3**
8 marks

Match these definitions with the words that were wrongly spelt in exercise 8.2.

1 can be interpreted in different ways
2 energetic and forceful
3 series of jobs you do in your working life
4 keen to do well and get to the top
5 keen or enthusiastic
6 looking for
7 someone determined and able to succeed
8 varied or different

**8.4**
14 marks

Complete these texts. You are given the first letters of the words.

1
For me, j............... s............... is
more important than a large salary. As I'm
not particularly money m..............., I'm
looking for a c............... that I will find
r............... in itself. I would certainly
far rather work in a close-k...............
team than have a very prestigious and
l............... position in a company where
I felt isolated.

2
When Don was d............... to
being just a middle manager, he
lost a lot of the p............... he
had previously enjoyed as a top
manager and he also no longer
received a large salary i...............
each year.

3
■ Are you r...............? We need people
who can find imaginative ways of doing
things.
■ And are you self-r...............? We need
people who can do things independently.

■ Do you think you might f...............
this description?
■ If you also have an a...............
spirit and enjoy challenges, then call or
write today!

Your score

/40

# 9 Business 1

**9.1**

10 marks

**Match the halves of these expressions, then use them to complete the sentences below.**

a) hard       marketing
b) niche       leader
c) confusion    selling
d) inertia      market
e) loss        sell

1 Computers that you wear on your wrist may become popular in the future, but for now they only appeal to a ......................................................... of people who love computers and gadgets.

2 They are selling CDs as a ............................................................ to attract more customers into the store.

3 The ..................................................... doesn't always work with everybody; a lot of people don't like to feel they are being pushed into buying things.

4 There's a lot of ..................................................... going on right now; it's not surprising that people get mixed up over who can offer the best products or the best price.

5 It was an example of ..................................................... ; we were forced to buy travel insurance just because we didn't explicitly say 'no' on the travel agent's form.

**9.2**

20 marks

**Rewrite the underlined parts of these sentences, using expressions from the box. Make any other necessary changes.**

| | | | |
|---|---|---|---|
| shop around | cold calling | red tape | on approval |
| swallow up | brand loyalty | have first refusal on sth | |
| come/go under the hammer | highest bidder | hammer out a deal | |

1 Business leaders are always complaining about too much <u>bureaucracy</u>.
2 <u>Surprise phone calls from people trying to sell you things are</u> extremely annoying.
3 It's a good idea to <u>look at different stores and compare prices</u> before buying household goods.
4 The country estate of Lord Blethercomb <u>was sold at auction</u> in 1998.
5 The estate will be sold to the <u>person who offers the most money</u>.
6 Unfortunately our local bookshop has been <u>taken over</u> by a big high street chain.
7 Car manufacturers often rely on <u>people's liking for their product and their tendency to buy the same again</u> in order to make further sales.
8 Gerald is selling his computer and he said he would let me <u>have the first chance to buy it before selling it to anyone else</u>.
9 The two companies <u>finally reached a business agreement</u> after 18 hours of negotiations.
10 We bought the bicycle <u>with the right to return it if it wasn't suitable</u>.

**9.3**

10 marks

**Answer these questions. You are sometimes given the first letters.**

1 What expression means a small, specialised group of customers? n.......................... m.........................
2 What are the noun forms of the verb *to bid*? ............................................ , ..............................
3 What phrase means all the buildings and machines owned by a company?
c............................................ a..........................................
4 An *entrepreneur* is a person who gets involved in businesses and business risks. What is the related noun form which refers to this type of activity? ............................................
5 Which adjective means producing a lot of money? l............................................
6 Which verb means to join together to form one company? ............................................
7 Complete this sentence with an appropriate verb:
The unions and the bosses ............................................ a compromise after many days of negotiation.

**Your score**

/ 40

**10.1**

*10 marks*

Match words from box A with words from box B to make ten expressions.

*Example:* to conduct business

A:
| a lack | a penalty | an outstanding | low | the survival | to acknowledge |
| to amass | ~~to conduct~~ | to default | to miss | to submit | |

B:
| a deadline | a fortune | a tender | account | ~~business~~ | clause |
| morale | of resources | of the fittest | on a payment | receipt | |

**10.2**

*20 marks*

Use the collocations from exercise 10.1 to rewrite these sentences, without changing the meaning.

*Example:* I don't approve of his business style.

*I don't approve of the way he conducts business.*

1 Henry had already made a lot of money by the time he was thirty.
2 Please let us know when you receive the parcel.
3 Unfortunately, you have failed to complete your report by the agreed date.
4 The staff are suffering from a lack of confidence in the company.
5 In business just as in the natural world, it is the case that the strongest will be the most successful.
6 Please note a point in the contract that states what happens if you do not do what you agreed to do.
7 The firm's problem is that it doesn't have enough staff, equipment or materials.
8 If you are interested in doing the work, you should send in a proposal by 1 June.
9 We no longer do business with that company because they have failed to pay a bill.
10 The company still has a bill from us that they have not yet paid.

**10.3**

*10 marks*

Complete the sentences below to solve the crossword.

Across

2 Although he's the boss, he's willing to turn his ............................................. to anything that needs doing.
4 Every new ........................................... in the company has a three-month probation period.
6 We won't order parts from that company again as they never ........................................... our deadlines.
7 The most successful businesses always pay attention to the human ........................................... .
8 Is this passport still valid? When is the ........................................... date?
9 On 1 April we shall decide which company has ........................................... the tender.

Down

1 Customs officials found drugs hidden in a ........................................... of bananas.
3 Tony's not very good at ........................................... – he prefers to do things on his own.
5 I like doing business with Taylor's. They always give you a square ........................................... .
7 No one is perfect – everyone has at least one character ........................................... .

# 11 Cramming for success: study and academic work

**11.1** Rewrite the underlined parts of these sentences using expressions based on the words in brackets.

10 marks

1 <u>Learning to recite texts word for word</u> is a strong tradition in some cultures. (ROTE)
2 I had several little <u>tricks</u> when I was preparing for my exams <u>to help me remember things</u>. (MNEMONIC)
3 After studying geography for ten years, I feel I know the subject <u>thoroughly</u>. (OUT)
4 Some things just have to be <u>committed to memory</u> when you study for exams. (HEART)
5 I have an exam next week. I'll just have to <u>concentrate completely on</u> my books. (BURY)

**11.2** Choose a word from the box that is most closely associated with each sentence and write it in the table. Sentence seven is associated with two words. Use all the words from the box.

8 marks

| portfolio | paper | assignment | project |
| composition | article | dissertation | thesis |

| | | |
|---|---|---|
| 1 | He's only nine but he's already writing little stories at school. | |
| 2 | It's 100,000 words long and breaks new ground in genetics. | |
| 3 | It's 5,000 words long and I have to hand it in at the end of term. | |
| 4 | It's 10,000 words long and it was part of her Master's degree. | |
| 5 | I submitted a selection of my work for assessment. | |
| 6 | It was on local history; I did interviews and made videos. | |
| 7 | It was published in the *Journal of Zoological Sciences* in 1994. | |

**11.3** Cross out six more vocabulary mistakes in this text and write the correct word above each mistake.

12 marks

                *do*

I have a lot of essays to ~~make~~ this term. I usually make a first draught and then I write it under

in its final form a day or two before I have to remit it to my tutor. I'm always nervous when I'm

waiting for backwash from him, but he always asserts our work very fairly and I've had some

quite high notes so far this term.

**11.4** Answer these questions.

10 marks

1 What do you call exam papers from previous years?
2 Which phrasal verb with the particle *out* means 'to withdraw from a course before you have finished it'?
3 Which phrasal verb goes with the noun *research* and means 'do or conduct'?
4 What do you call the system where one library borrows a book from another library?
5 What are academic articles usually published in?
6 What is the verb form of the noun *revision*?
7 What word means 'the last exams students take before getting their degree'?
8 What verb means 'to copy material from other people's work and pretend it's yours'?
9 What do you call diagrams that help you organise your ideas?
10 What word means 'the final date' for handing in an essay or assignment?

**Your score**

/40

# 12 Education: debates and issues

## 12.1
**10 marks**

Are these statements true or false? If they are false, correct them.

*Example:* Numeracy is the ability to read.
> False   Numeracy is the ability to count and do basic maths.

1  A comprehensive school is one that chooses pupils on the basis of their ability.
2  When major changes are made to the educational programme this is called 'curriculum reform'.
3  The three Rs are rubbers, rulers and rucksacks.
4  Equality of opportunity means that all children have the same chances of a good education.
5  A well-endowed school is one that has good facilities and plenty of money.
6  A two-tier educational system educates boys and girls together.
7  Elitism in education is when a small privileged group is favoured.
8  Special needs education is for children whose parents live abroad.
9  Bullying is when big children behave cruelly to smaller, weaker children.
10  Illiteracy means the ability to read and write.

## 12.2
**10 marks**

Match the words on the left with the words on the right to make ten collocations.

| | | |
|---|---|---|
| 1 | continuing | Association |
| 2 | league | class |
| 3 | lifelong | education |
| 4 | mature | education |
| 5 | one-to-one | governor |
| 6 | Parent–Teacher | school |
| 7 | peripatetic | students |
| 8 | school | tables |
| 9 | selective | teacher |
| 10 | supply | teacher |

## 12.3
**10 marks**

Answer these questions about the collocations in exercise 12.2.

1  Which two phrases are synonyms?
2  Where does a peripatetic teacher teach?
3  How many people are there in a one-to-one class?
4  What do children have to do before entering a selective school?
5  What key information about schools is usually published in league tables?
6  What is special about mature students?
7  When is a supply teacher needed?
8  What is the role of the school governors?
9  Is a Parent–Teacher Association associated with one town or one school?

## 12.4
**10 marks**

Write the letters in the correct order to complete the text. You are given some letters.

A surprising number of adults have managed to go through British VERIMOCPHENSE
(1) c........................... education without acquiring good basic skills and this of course
SEDREPSES (2) d........................... their chances of getting a good job. Educationalists
VIREPECE (3) p........................... this to be less of an issue in TEBRET-FOF (4) ..........................-
..........f areas, so problems of inequality are REPPTETADEU (5) p........................... . In an attempt
to deal with this, primary schools are now paying much more attention to RALECITY
(6) ...........................y and MACERUNY (7) ...........................y. The problem of LUBLINGY
(8) ...........................g unfortunately seems to be THERENIN (9) i........................... in all
schools regardless of how LLEW-FOF (10) ...........................-...........f the pupils are.

# 13 Talking about yourself

**13.1** Fill the gaps in this personality questionnaire, based on the meaning clues.

10 marks

### Popular or unpopular?

*Answer this questionnaire to find out.*

| | | | |
|---|---|---|---|
| 1 Are you d...............t and conscientious? | YES ☐ | NO ☐ |
| 2 Are you always ob........................ to your workmates? | YES ☐ | NO ☐ |
| 3 Would you call yourself al........................c? | YES ☐ | NO ☐ |
| 4 Do you have a p........................d temperament? | YES ☐ | NO ☐ |
| 5 Does the word sag........................s apply to you? | YES ☐ | NO ☐ |
| 6 Do you tend to be op........................c? | YES ☐ | NO ☐ |
| 7 Do you often pro........................te? | YES ☐ | NO ☐ |
| 8 Are you ever t........................ss? | YES ☐ | NO ☐ |
| 9 Do you ever make ch........................ comments? | YES ☐ | NO ☐ |
| 10 Are you a bit of a fl........................y dresser? | YES ☐ | NO ☐ |

1 hard-working
2 ready to help
3 thinking of others more than yourself
4 calm, not easily angered
5 wise
6 using situations for your own benefit
7 delay doing things
8 say things that upset or offend people
9 too patriotic
10 expensive/ impressive

**13.2** Match each word from box A with the word from box B it is most closely related to in meaning.

10 marks

*Example:* stubborn – mulish

A: | sharp-tongued astute cunning morose generous dogged |
| frugal extravagant ~~stubborn~~ tolerant diligent |

B: | unstinting shrewd ~~mulish~~ resolute broad-minded terse |
| industrious thrifty immoderate sly sullen |

**13.3** Correct the vocabulary mistake in each of these sentences.

10 marks

1 Edward is an old-fashioned, gallon gentleman.
2 Don't take any notice of Jack; he gets carried off sometimes.
3 A lot of politicians are basically inscrupulous and obsessed with power.
4 Arthur is very industrial and hard-working.
5 Tim is very self-searching, always trying to gain every advantage for himself.

**13.4** Rewrite the underlined parts of these sentences using a word from the box. Make any other necessary changes.

10 marks

| witty stingy work-obsessed sober naïve |
| pithy superficial workaholic intuitive magnetic |

1 Why am I so <u>inexperienced and trusting of others</u>? Some people seem to be much more <u>instinctive and understanding</u> and can see when trouble is coming.
2 My parents are so <u>mean with money</u>! I like spending money on clothes and going out, but my parents say I <u>don't care about serious things</u>.
3 I don't think I have a personality <u>that attracts people</u>, and I think people find me too <u>serious and calm</u>.
4 My colleagues at work are all so <u>good at making humorous remarks</u> and always seem able to come out with <u>quick, clever</u> comments that are just right for the situation.
5 I think I'm <u>a person who is obsessed with work</u>.

Your score

/ 40

# Relationships: positive aspects

**14.1**

10 marks

Complete the sentences using the correct form of the words in brackets.

*Example:* The company is famous for publishing ...*romantic*............... novels. (ROMANCE)

1 Relationships may become less ........................................... as time goes by. (PASSION)
2 The twins are always together – they're quite ........................................ . (SEPARATE)
3 It is very important that couples should be ........................................ to one another. (FAITH)
4 I could never work for anyone who was not ........................................ . (TRUST)
5 Ben and Christina swear that their relationship is totally ........................................ . (PLATO)
6 Ian insists on complete ........................................ from his staff. (LOYAL)
7 A true friend will always be ........................................ when you have problems. (SUPPORT)
8 Ken has a great ........................................ for Italy – he spends every summer holiday there. (FOND)
9 Pupils should always behave in a ........................................ way to all members of staff. (RESPECT)
10 Please be more ........................................ and keep the music down when I'm studying. (CONSIDER)

**14.2**

10 marks

Fill the gaps in this e-mail.

> Hi, Anna,
>
> Two new people have started working in our office. There's a fantastic new man – all the girls have fallen head over (1) ..................... in love with him. In fact I'm quite besotted (2) ..................... him myself. Unfortunately, he's only (3) ..................... eyes for Nicola in the canteen. Nicola says she's fond (4) ..................... him but she's not as infatuated (5) ..................... him as the rest of us. The other newcomer is a girl called Zoe. She and I get on like a house on (6) ..................... – we (7) ..................... it off immediately. As we seem to see things in exactly the same way, she's a woman after my own (8) ..................... . You must meet her. I think you'll find you're kindred (9) ..................... . Do e-mail me soon. How did your blind date go? Was it love at first (10) ..................... ?
>
> Best,
> Georgia

**14.3**

10 marks

Find and correct the five mistakes in this e-mail.

> Hi, Georgia,
>
> The blind date was OK, though I wouldn't say he was a man for my own heart. He was quite amiable but I'm not sure that amiableness is what I'm really looking for in a man. He talked a lot about his family – he's obviously devoted with them and he talked in a very affectionful way about his sisters, which I liked. But I really don't think we were very good-matched. Oh well, better luck next time.
> Anna

**14.4**

10 marks

Put the letters in the correct order.

*Example:* romantically obsessed with ~~IFTNAUADET IWTH~~ *infatuated with*

1 strong connection  LOCES DONB  ...........................................
2 close friends  SMOOB DIBUDSE  ...........................................
3 a person who has been with you all your life  LGENFOIL NIMCAPONO  ...........................................
4 connections because of a blood relationship  YIMALF ESIT  ...........................................
5 to share the same attitude to life  OT EB OASTMELUS  ...........................................

# Relationships: problems

**15.1**

Fill the gaps in these sentences with appropriate words. You are given some letters.

1 She always showed uns_ _ _ _ _ _ _ loyalty to her boss.
2 He has been scr_ _ _ _ _ _ _ _ honest and returned the overpayment.
3 You're a t_ _ _ friend, always there when I need you.
4 He's not a friend; he's just a c_ _ _ _ _ acquaintance.
5 Anne and Mark have always been bi_ _ _ _ rivals. They never could work together.

**15.2**

Fill the gaps with the correct form, as instructed.

1 honesty:    (adjective) ............................................. ; (opposite adjective) ............................................. .
2 contentment:    (adjective) ............................................. ; (opposite adjective) ............................................. .
3 welcome:    (adjective) ............................................. ; (opposite adjective) ............................................. .
4 support:    (adjective) ............................................. ; (opposite adjective) ............................................. .
5 criticise:    (adjective) ............................................. .
6 alliance:    (noun – person) ............................................. .

**15.3**

Correct five more mistakes with prepositions.

Friends don't always see eye ~~at~~ to eye. I hate it when people talk under my back. I've always been loyal at my friends, but some of them have been critical in me and said things to other people which are not true. I've always tried to be honest for them, and I've never been disloyal on them.

**15.4**

Read Hilda's private diary, then answer the questions opposite.

**WED 23**

My relationship with Harry has been rather bumpy lately. Perhaps we should split up.

**THU 24**

I hate being on bad terms with a colleague, but Gemma has been impossible lately. A bit of discord is normal now and again in offices, but things seem to have really turned sour.

**FRI 25**

So many ups and downs this week. Harry, Gemma, and now Jane and Sarah don't see eye to eye.

**SAT 26**

Bit of a rift developing between Auntie Edna and cousin Bob. This could become a real family feud. Edna's side seem to hate Bob's guts and don't like his wife either.

1 Are Bob and Edna becoming closer to each other? Give a reason.
2 Name one person Hilda works with.
3 On what day did Hilda consider ending a relationship?
4 Which is correct? Jane and Sarah (a) have stopped seeing each other (b) do not agree.
5 Which people are running the risk of a long-term quarrel with their relations?
6 Hilda thinks physical fights are normal among colleagues. True or false?
7 Which two people does Hilda have a difficult relationship with?
8 Edna's family dislike Bob, but only slightly. True or false?
9 When things 'turn sour', it means (a) there are problems, but only for a few minutes (b) people get very angry (c) relations which were good become bad.
10 'Ups and downs' means a mix of good moments and bad moments. True or false?

# 16 Passions: reactions and emotions

**16.1** Complete these sentences using the correct form of a word from the box. Use each word once only.

10 marks

| appease | bliss | conciliate | covet | defuse |
| exult | hanker | jubilant | placate | rapture |

1 All my attempts at ............................................ the tension between Sam and Paul failed.
2 Don't you ever have a ............................................ for a more interesting life?
3 Ray is ............................................ unaware of his wife's unfaithfulness.
4 Sophie's family were in an ............................................ mood after her success in the competition.
5 The Prime Minister managed to avoid a war but his critics blamed him for opting for
............................................ .
6 The protesters were not ............................................ by the minister's empty promises.
7 Clive keeps casting ............................................ eyes on my new sports car – I don't know why, as his own car is at least as good.
8 There was much ............................................ when Jock scored the winning goal in the last minute of the match.
9 He was in ............................................ when she said she'd marry him.
10 After forgetting their anniversary, Martin bought his wife a magnificent bunch of flowers as a
............................................ gesture.

**16.2** Complete these sentences.

5 marks

1 Film star Angelica Pretty says she is ............................................ to bits with her new baby.
2 The captain of Liverpool United said he was ............................................ the moon at the match result.
3 New mum Anita Howley said she was floating on ............................................ .
4 Ever since she was a child Julia has yearned ............................................ her father's approval.
5 Nora Parker has always had a thirst ............................................ adventure.

**16.3** Explain how each of the people in exercise 16.2 are feeling.

5 marks

**16.4** Match the beginnings of the sentences with their endings.

10 marks

| | |
|---|---|
| 1 Jim looks miserable but Rosa looks full of the joys | hatred for injustice. |
| 2 Ever since we moved to the country I've felt on top | after my mum's cooking. |
| 3 I've lived abroad for years now but I still hanker | the tense situation. |
| 4 I stick to my diet but I still have occasional cravings | on air. |
| 5 Biddy did her best to defuse | for sick children. |
| 6 They have appointed an officer to conciliate | of spring. |
| 7 I feel great pity | of his poor marks. |
| 8 Josh's parents were blissfully ignorant | of the world. |
| 9 Alicia has an implacable | for chocolate. |
| 10 Since I got the job, I feel as if I've been walking | between the two sides. |

**16.5** Match the words in the box to make five collocations.

10 marks

*Example:* blissfully unaware

| a prize | ~~blissfully~~ | appease | covet | defuse | exultant | hatred |
| implacable | mood | ~~unaware~~ | tension | the enemy | | |

**17.1** Rewrite these sentences by replacing the underlined words as instructed. Make any other necessary changes.

20 marks

1 She scorned my attempts at writing poetry. (Use the adjective form.)
2 The sight of so much rotting food and filth everywhere filled me with revulsion. (Use the verb form.)
3 Her comments were full of antipathy. (Use a related adjective form.)
4 I have no aversion to the idea of renting a flat in the city centre. (Use the adjective form.)
5 He had a loathing for people who lacked moral courage. (Use the verb form.)
6 Some modern buildings fill people with repulsion. (Use the adjective form.)
7 I abhor violence. (Use the adjective form.)
8 His table manners fill me with revulsion. (Use the adjective form.)
9 I don't understand his hostility towards the plans. (Use the adjective form.)
10 I abhor war. (Use the noun form.)

**17.2** Find a more negative word to replace each of the underlined words in these sentences. You are given some letters.

10 marks

1 Mr Peabody acted in a very authoritative manner.  of............................
2 Everyone commented on his rather childlike behaviour.  p............................
3 People tend to become rather traditional as they grow older.
   f............................-d............................
4 Eric has a meticulous attitude to detail when he reads our reports.
   n............................-p............................
5 She responded to our complaint in a rather casual way.  o............................-h............................
6 I suppose you could say Rory has a somewhat colourful personality.  br............................
7 Lara is a bit changeable; she'll think one thing one day and the opposite the next.
   f............................
8 The apartment was terribly dirty when we took it over.  s............................
9 Why does she always wear such dull clothes?  d............................
10 He had a very careless attitude to the job.  s............................y

**17.3** Write the letters in the correct order to complete these sentences.

10 marks

1 General Romano was one of the most XSOUNOBIO ............................ tyrants in history.
2 I have a pet NIOVEASR ............................ to mobile phones, especially when people use them on trains.
3 I also hate the TOSTNETIOSUA ............................ way people show off their latest models and ring tones.
4 He made a TITRE............................ remark that everyone had heard before.
5 I felt an STINANT ............................ aversion to him the moment we met.
6 He's the most SPNGIRAG ............................ and greedy director I've ever met.
7 The article about university reforms was LDABN ............................ and innocuous.
8 He has such a TENEPROSIUT ............................ , self-important manner.
9 Don't be so MPPOOSU ............................ and arrogant.
10 I can't stand the OSBSEUQIUO ............................ way he tries to please his boss.

# Observing others: appearance and mannerisms

**18.1**

Complete the words in these sentences. You are given some letters.

1  My boss has a d........................................ chin and a rather pale, sa........................................ complexion.
2  Paula is far too thin; in fact, I'd call her s........................................ .
3  Kristy never has a hair out of p........................................ .
4  Henry always has an angry expression on his face, but although he looks as if he's sc........................................ , it doesn't necessarily mean that he's in a bad mood.
5  When Ian's angry he t........................................ his fingers on his desk or c........................................ his fist.
6  Pete has a bad habit of b........................................ his nails and he also p........................................ his nose if he thinks no one is looking.
7  I hate the way Ron can't stop himself le........................................ at the pretty young women in the office.

**18.2**

Read the descriptions then write the correct names under the pictures.

Bill is a gangly youth.
Dick is shrugging his shoulders.
Glyn has folded his arms.
Harry always looks unkempt.
Mark is clenching his fists.
Nick is scratching his head.
Robbie is scowling.
Sean is portly.
Tom is looking very haggard.
Tony has crossed his legs.

3

..........................

7

..........................

4

..........................

8

..........................

1

..........................

5

..........................

9

..........................

2

..........................

6

..........................

10

..........................

**18.3**

Put the words and phrases in the box into one of the four categories below.

| | | | |
|---|---|---|---|
| portly | unkempt | complexion | corpulent | tap your fingers |
| clench your fist | scowl | gangling | grimace | scruffy | lanky |
| leer | overweight | pout | sallow | raise your eyebrows |
| not have a hair out of place | shrug | stout | swarthy | |

- *words relating to skin*
- *words relating to build*
- *words relating to tidiness of appearance*
- *gestures and facial expressions*

**19.1**
*10 marks*

**Rewrite these sentences using an appropriate word from the box, using the word in brackets.**

| pushy | taciturn | impulsive | garrulous | impetuous |
|---|---|---|---|---|

1 He always acts without thinking and makes a lot of mistakes.
2 She always promotes her own interests in a selfish way.
3 He talks all the time, never stops.
4 He does things without thinking and can't help spending money on other people.
5 She hardly ever says a word.

**19.2**
*18 marks*

**Complete the words in these horoscopes with words that match the definitions.**

**Virgo 23 Aug–22 Sep** ✳✳✳✳✳✳✳✳✳✳✳✳✳✳✳

Some people find you ¹re.......................... and ²un.......................... , and a bit of an ³i.......................... , but this week you'll have a chance to present a new image.

You will meet someone who is an ⁴ex.......................... and very ⁵ef.......................... but don't be fooled by appearances. Tread carefully. If you are too ⁶gu.......................... you'll end up getting hurt.

¹ not immediately sociable
² distant and difficult to start a conversation with
³ inward-looking and quiet
⁴ outward-looking and sociable
⁵ gives exaggerated expressions of pleasure
⁶ easily deceived

**Capricorn 22 Dec–19 Jan** ✳✳✳✳✳✳✳✳✳✳✳✳

Someone at work will act in a very ⁷ha.......................... and ⁸al.......................... manner towards you. But there's no need to be ⁹dif.......................... . Tell them it's not acceptable and they'll respect you more.

⁷ unfriendly, thinks they're better than others
⁸ unfriendly, not sociable
⁹ lacking in confidence

**19.3**
*5 marks*

**Rewrite these sentences by replacing the underlined words as instructed. Make any other necessary changes.**

1 I've always found Georgina quite easy to <u>approach</u>. (Use the adjective form.)
2 She's a child who gets easily <u>excited</u>. (Use the adjective form.)
3 Liam loves <u>flirting</u> so much! (Use the noun form for a person.)
4 If he hadn't <u>pushed</u>, he would never have got his promotion. (Use the adjective form.)
5 Iris always looks at you with <u>disdain</u> if you say something mildly funny. (Use the adverb form.)

**19.4**
*7 marks*

**Answer these questions. Sometimes you are given some letters.**

1 Give a synonym for *stubborn* which begins with the letter O. ..............................................
2 Which is correct: *inscrupulous* or *unscrupulous*? ..............................................
3 Which opposite adjectives starting with the letters given mean:
   (a) think yourself to be wonderful? c..........................
   (b) prefer not to talk about your personal qualities and achievements? m..........................
4 Give an adjective for a person who has an exaggerated sense of their own importance
   s..........................-..........................
5 What adjective could describe a person willing to believe simple things? n..........................
6 What adjective describes a person who puts a lot of effort into their work? con..........................

**Your score**

/ 40

# Birth and death: from cradle to grave

**20.1**

10 marks

Rewrite these sentences without changing the meaning, using the word in the brackets.

1  I'm afraid his grandfather died last night. (PASSED)
2  She may be ninety but she still has a very good brain. (WITS)
3  This flu is awful – I feel as if I'm dying. (DOOR)
4  Rob received a large sum of money from his late grandmother. (INHERITANCE)
5  I inherited a small house in the country from my uncle. (BEQUEATHED)
6  The accident looked very serious but fortunately no one died. (FATALITIES)
7  There were legal problems because the old man died intestate. (WILL)
8  Funeral services can help mourners to deal with their grief. (BEREAVED)
9  My old aunt quite enjoys living in special housing for old people. (SHELTERED)
10  Dan lives in his deceased father's house. (LATE)

**20.2**

20 marks

Fill the gaps in these sentences. You are given the first letters.

1  When a woman is pregnant, the f............................ in her u............................ is nourished by the p............................ .
2  Due to complications the doctors decided to d............................ her baby by c............................ s............................ .
3  The funeral is going to be a c............................ , not a burial. The family will then s............................ the a............................ on the dead man's favourite hillside.
4  In an ectopic p............................ the fertilised egg develops in the f............................ t............................ rather than in the w............................ .
5  Jill wanted to get pregnant but she failed to c............................ naturally so the doctor prescribed some f............................ d............................ .
6  The mother m............................ medical h............................ by giving birth to eight babies, all of whom survived.
7  She w............................ into l............................ and the baby was born before they reached the hospital.

**20.3**

10 marks

Read these newspaper headlines and answer the questions.

## HUNDREDS PERISH IN EARTHQUAKE
1  What simpler word could replace 'perish'?
2  Why was the word 'perish' chosen instead of the simpler word?

## Valuable animals slaughtered
3  What simpler word could replace 'slaughtered'?
4  What does 'slaughtered' suggest that the simpler word does not?

## SMOKING INCREASES RISK OF MISCARRIAGE
5  What will the story under this headline be about?
6  What is the difference between a miscarriage and an abortion?
7  What is another word beginning with T that means abortion?

## RAILWAY NETWORK ON LAST LEGS
8  What does this headline suggest about the railway network?

## Deceased driver's will
9  What happened to the driver?

## FAMOUS SINGER'S OBITUARY – see page 10
10  What will you read on page 10?

# 21 Free time: relaxation and leisure

**21.1**
10 marks

In these dialogues speaker B repeats the underlined parts of speaker A's remarks using a different word. Complete the dialogues. You are given the first letters.

1 A: I spend hours every week on committee work. It <u>takes up so much time</u>.
   B: Yes, it's very t...............................-................................ .
2 A: Kate is <u>making a lot of money</u> out of her new Internet company.
   B: Yes, it seems to be very l............................ .
3 A: The collaboration between our two clubs has <u>had many positive results</u>.
   B: Yes, it's been very f............................ .
4 A: I <u>get a lot of personal satisfaction</u> out of the voluntary work I do.
   B: Yes, it sounds very r............................ .
5 A: Just lying here in the sauna <u>reduces the stress and tension</u>, doesn't it?
   B: Yes, it's very r............................ .

**21.2**
5 marks

Correct the spelling or vocabulary mistake in each of these sentences.

1 Jane's a shipaholic. Her wardrobe is full of new clothes she's never worn.
2 Martin's a real dabber. He took up the guitar, then basketball, then joined a poetry club, but none of them lasted longer than a couple of weeks.
3 Barbara's a real culture eagle. She's always going to the opera and art exhibitions.
4 After a hard week in the office, Carla always finds gardening at the weekends very therapist.
5 Pam is quite lazy, but her sister Roxanne is such a maker; she just never stops!

**21.3**
20 marks

Rewrite the underlined parts of these sentences using expressions based on the word or prefix in brackets.

1 I've <u>become very involved in</u> scuba diving these days. (INTO)
2 What do you normally <u>do</u> on Saturday mornings, anything special? (GET)
3 I value my <u>time when I'm not working</u> very much. (OFF)
4 A lot of people get <u>addicted to</u> the Internet and spend hours online. (HOOK)
5 I have a <u>very busy schedule</u> next week, so we'd better meet the week after. (DIARY)
6 She divides her time <u>half and half</u> between London and Frankfurt. (FIFTY)
7 I <u>came to dislike</u> football because of all the violence and hooliganism. (OFF)
8 <u>The use of machines to make things</u> has transformed factory work. (AUTO-)
9 Since I retired I've become <u>incredibly lazy</u>. (POTATO)
10 Jack <u>isolates himself from the world</u> for days on end when he's writing poetry. (LOCK)

**21.4**
5 marks

Answer these questions.

1 Give two expressions with the word *time* meaning 'periods when you aren't working'.
2 What expression means 'making a large number of goods all at once'? m............................
   p............................
3 Which is correct? A dishwasher is a <u>labour-saving/work-saving</u> machine.
4 Why do you think a vulture is a suitable metaphor to refer to people's consumption of culture?

Your score

/40

# 22 All the rage: clothes and fashion

**22.1**
10 marks

Match words from box A with words from box B to make ten expressions.

A:
| dress | casual | a slave | to set a | off the | ahead of your |
|---|---|---|---|---|---|
| up to the | on the | to be dressed | all the | | |

B:
| time | trend | minute | rage | codes | to fashion |
|---|---|---|---|---|---|
| to kill | peg | clothes | high street | | |

**22.2**
10 marks

Write a word from the box under the correct picture.

| seams | cloak | cuff | shoestring | feather |
|---|---|---|---|---|
| frill | straitjacket | dagger | hem | glove |

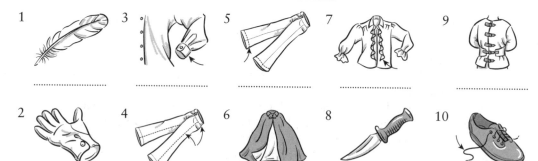

1 ......................... 3 ......................... 5 ......................... 7 ......................... 9 .........................

2 ......................... 4 ......................... 6 ......................... 8 ......................... 10 .........................

**22.3**
10 marks

Explain the meaning of the underlined expressions by rewriting the sentences in simpler English.

1  The bus was <u>bursting at the seams</u>.
2  Was it really necessary to <u>cloak everything in such secrecy</u>?
3  It's not fair to ask Tim to speak <u>off the cuff</u>.
4  The book tells you how to cook delicious meals <u>on a shoestring</u>.
5  It was <u>a real feather in Hanna's cap</u> to win the essay competition.
6  The service on the train is <u>without frills</u> but it is perfectly adequate.
7  Vincent refused to let his bosses <u>put him in a straitjacket</u>.
8  They've been having a lot of <u>cloak-and-dagger</u> meetings at work.
9  Lisa will leave Ben if she starts to feel that she is <u>hemmed in</u>.
10  Mel <u>is hand in glove with</u> Victor.

**22.4**
10 marks

Answer these questions.

1  Are baggy trousers tight or loose?
2  How much material does a skimpy top need?
3  If a company has a dress-down day, what sort of clothes should employees wear?
4  Would a woman be pleased if she was told that she looked frumpy? Why?
5  If a style catches on, does it become more or less popular?
6  If an invitation says 'smart-casual clothes', what would you wear?
7  If you say that person X wears the trousers in a marriage, is X more likely to be the husband or the wife?
8  If a friend asks if a party is going to be 'a dressy do', what do they want to know?
9  If someone says to you, 'That's a very snazzy outfit', how would you feel?
10  If a woman wears a power outfit to work, what is she probably wearing?

# 23 Homestyles, lifestyles

**23.1**

10 marks

**Fill in the missing words using the meaning clues.**

1 The City Council has announced plans to build new ª.......................................................... to replace
   ᵇ.......................................................... due for demolition.
2 The police arrested three people in connection with drugs offences during a raid on a
   ᶜ.......................................................... in the city centre yesterday.
3 The pop star Len Dussaquid bought himself a ᵈ.......................................................... apartment in a fashionable
   part of London. He wanted a ᵉ.......................................................... in the capital city.

   ª houses provided by the state for poorer people
   ᵇ tall, modern buildings with many flats
   ᶜ empty building where people live without permission
   ᵈ luxury flat at the top of a building
   ᵉ small second home in a city, used for short visits

**23.2**

12 marks

**Read what these people say, then answer the six questions below by writing the correct names in the boxes.**

TANYA: Careful design of your living space makes a huge difference to your well-being.
JAMES: All a living room needs is a sofa, a bookshelf and a small table, and everything should be
       white or near-white.
LARA: I have purple drapes and astrological charts on the walls, and plants everywhere.
KAREN: I visited a drug addict called Lucas. His house was in a state of total disrepair.
IRIS: It's nice being near my son and his family but still having my independence.
DAVID: Well it was built in the 1980s and has design features from various periods.

| | | |
|---|---|---|
| 1 | Who lives in a granny flat? | |
| 2 | Who is keen on Feng Shui? | |
| 3 | Who lives in a minimalist environment? | |
| 4 | Whose home is an example of post-modernism? | |
| 5 | Who seems to be a New Age person? | |
| 6 | Who lives in a hovel? | |

**23.3**

18 marks

**Rewrite the underlined words using fixed expressions based on the words in brackets.**

1 Barry was fed up with <u>all the intense competition</u> and went off to live in the country. (RAT)
2 When I told the waiter I had worked in the restaurant five years ago he brought me a drink
  <u>which I didn't have to pay for</u>. (HOUSE)
3 I know Glenda got upset, but it's about time someone told her a few <u>unpleasant facts about
  herself and the way she behaves</u>. (HOME)
4 <u>Farmers growing just enough to live on</u> is the typical pattern in the northern part of the
  country. (SUBSISTENCE)
5 The hotel was OK, but it was <u>nothing very special</u>. (WRITE)
6 That lovely old building on the corner has <u>been transformed into something fresh and new</u>
  since it was converted into an art gallery. (LEASE)
7 She led <u>an unhappy and hard life</u> for twenty years as a servant to Lady Trollop. (DOG)
8 Within two years of its launch, the new product had become <u>something everyone knew
  about</u>. (HOUSEHOLD)
9 Whenever I meet a handsome man it turns out he's already married – <u>it's just typical</u>! (STORY)

Your score
/40

# Socialising and networking

**24.1**
20 marks

Rewrite the underlined parts of these sentences using expressions based on the words in brackets.

1  Joe was supposed to be taking me out last night but he <u>didn't turn up</u>.  (STOOD)
2  As she works in PR, Sally is used to <u>mixing socially</u> with the rich and famous.  (SHOULDERS)
3  I hope I haven't <u>stayed too long with you</u>.  (WELCOME)
4  Who does Amal <u>spend his time with</u> these days?  (HANG)
5  Dave decided to <u>end his relationship with</u> Pam when he heard she'd been dating another man.  (DROP)
6  Is the wedding going to be a <u>formal</u> occasion?  (TIE)
7  Tristram got his job through <u>a friend he was at Oxford University with</u>.  (NETWORK)
8  My sister says she has much more fun when she <u>goes out with her female friends</u>.  (GIRLS')
9  Hugh is not particularly interested in <u>getting a promotion</u>.  (LADDER)
10 Do you fancy having a night <u>out</u> this evening?  (TOWN)

**24.2**
5 marks

What kinds of parties are these?

1  COME TO CELEBRATE THE PUBLICATION OF THE NEW HENRY BARKER BOOK

4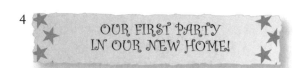
OUR FIRST PARTY IN OUR NEW HOME!

2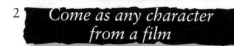
*Come as any character from a film*

5  Help Steve enjoy his last night as a bachelor – men only!

3  *Help me celebrate my last night before I become a married woman!*

**24.3**
10 marks

Explain the difference between:

1  *a party animal* and *a party pooper*
2  *to be pally with* and *to be an item*
3  *to hobnob with* and *to knock around with* people
4  *socialising* and *networking*
5  a wedding *reception* and a wedding *party*

**24.4**
5 marks

Complete this e-mail using words from the box.

| cliquey | lunch | bash | clubbing | get-together |
| --- | --- | --- | --- | --- |

Hi, Lucy

I went to a great ............................................ last night. I enjoyed it because it gave me a chance to mix with my new colleagues. They're nice – much less ............................................ than I thought at first. Hope we can do ............................................ some time soon. Or do you fancy going ............................................ one night? Shall I see you at that ............................................ that Julie's organising for her cousin from Australia?

Shelley

**25.1**

10 marks

Rewrite the underlined parts of this text using adjectives from the box. Make any other necessary changes.

| | | | | | |
|---|---|---|---|---|---|
| moving | risqué | far-fetched | gripping | harrowing | disjointed |
| memorable | hackneyed | impenetrable | overrated | | |

*Fields of Darkness* was a film <u>which excited me and kept my attention</u> and <u>which I shall remember for a long time</u>, even though the plot was in some ways <u>difficult to believe</u>. Some critics have said it's <u>not as good as people say it is</u> and <u>the story is boring because it has been done so often</u>, but I disagree. I found it <u>emotional</u> and even <u>extremely upsetting</u> at times.

On the other hand, another film I saw recently, *Three Delicate Balances*, had a plot <u>which was complex and impossible to understand</u> and <u>lacked a clear order</u>. I also feel that the director thought that if he threw in a few <u>slightly immoral and shocking</u> scenes it would make a good movie, but it just didn't work.

**25.2**

10 marks

Change the underlined words in these sentences to produce the opposite meaning.

1 It was what I'd call a very <u>forgettable</u> performance.  m.............................
2 Didn't you think the plot was all a bit <u>overstated</u>?  u.............................
3 The critics <u>condemned</u> Ferly's new play.  l.............................
4 The play <u>triumphed</u> on Broadway and in London's West End.  b.............................
5 The soloist got <u>no applause</u> at the end of the concerto.  a s............................. o.............................

**25.3**

4 marks

Complete these sentences using a word from the box.

| | | | |
|---|---|---|---|
| portrayal | rendition | version | interpretation |

1 Which ............................. of 'New York' do you prefer, Frank Sinatra's or the 1996 cover by Nick Riverstone?
2 I disagree with Professor Morton's ............................. of Shakespeare's *Twelfth Night*; I think he has completely misunderstood the play.
3 It was a beautiful play; the actor's ............................. of the mother was very touching.
4 Her ............................. of Wordsworth's *Daffodils* poem at the party last night just made everyone laugh, even though she was deadly serious.

**25.4**

16 marks

Choose the correct answer.

1 No actor likes to feel that he or she is becoming (a) cast-type (b) type-cast (c) a caste-type.
2 All actors love to receive (a) awards (b) rewards (c) premiums such as Oscars and young actors love to be named best up-coming actor of the year.
3 It was a very (a) harassing (b) horroring (c) harrowing film about torture in a prison.
4 The film was a real (a) cliff-hanger (b) cliff-end (c) cliff-top; the suspense was incredible.
5 Hobarth's new movie is tipped to become this year's (a) blasterblock (b) blockbuster (c) blastblock.
6 *The Hit Gang* is a (a) police-and-thieves (b) cops-and-robbers (c) cops-and-thieves drama with great high-speed car chases.
7 Many critics have called her latest play a (a) masterpiece (b) masterwork (c) masterclass.
8 The band got three (a) agains (b) mores (c) encores; the audience loved them.

Your score

/40

# 26 The plastic arts

**26.1**

10 marks

Are these sentences true or false? If they are false, correct them.

1  The Tate Modern is an art gallery in London.
2  If you pull the wool over someone's eyes, you show them something beautiful.
3  Cubism is a style of painting from the 20th century.
4  A philistine is someone who loves art.
5  If people vote with their feet, they show they like something by coming to see it.
6  Surrealism is a style of art which depicts things in a strange or impossible way.
7  If someone is visually literate, they read a lot about visual art.
8  An impressionist painting depicts its subject in a rather imprecise way.
9  'Fad' means fashion and it suggests that the speaker likes the fashion in question.
10  The Renaissance (14th–16th centuries) was a period of new interest in the arts in Europe.

**26.2**

10 marks

All the adjectives below can describe works of art. Match an adjective from box A with its opposite from box B.

A:  evocative     colourful     highbrow     peerless     impenetrable     exquisite
    pedestrian     tongue-in-cheek     sophisticated     undemanding     dreary

B:  challenging     clumsy     primitive     uninspiring     dazzling     earnest
    lowbrow     run-of-the-mill     transparent     intriguing     drab

**26.3**

10 marks

Answer these questions and try to explain your answer.

1  Which is more highbrow: a tabloid newspaper or a broadsheet?
2  Which would you say is more sophisticated: an opera or a nursery rhyme?
3  Which is more likely to be intriguing: a detective story or a computer manual?
4  What would you be more likely to call exquisite: a piece of jewellery or a table?
5  Which would be more likely to be called evocative: a carpet or a painting?
6  Which is more likely to be tongue-in-cheek: a comedy sketch or a TV ad?
7  Which is more likely to be run-of-the-mill: an ancient Greek vase or a watercolour?
8  Which is more likely to be challenging: a book on philosophy or a comic?
9  Who is more likely to behave in a clumsy way: an athlete or a clown?
10  Whose performance is more likely to be dazzling: a ballerina or a drummer?

**26.4**

10 marks

Underline the words or phrases which are used metaphorically in each sentence. Then replace the metaphors using the word in brackets. Make any other necessary changes.

1  Carla paints her ex-husband in a very bad light.  (NEGATIVE)
2  The characters in the novel are rather black-and-white.  (COMPLEXITY)
3  I would certainly recommend this article – I found it very illuminating.  (INSIGHTS)
4  We are all moulded by the things that happen to us in our youth.  (INFLUENCED)
5  Although Paul Hart usually plays quite colourful people, his character in this play is a rather ordinary person.  (PERSONALITY)

# Talking about books

**27.1**

10 marks

In these dialogues speaker B repeats the underlined parts of speaker A's remarks using a different word. Complete the dialogues. You are given the first letters.

1 A: That vampire novel was <u>full of scenes of cruelty and death</u>.
  B: Yes, it was a bit ma............................ , wasn't it?

2 A: The plot was <u>really powerful and kept me interested throughout</u>.
  B: Yes, it was really co............................ .

3 A: What a story! <u>All those dark, gloomy streets and shadowy places</u>.
  B: Yes, the settings were a bit lu............................ , to say the least.

4 A: I thought the mother in his first novel was a <u>mysterious</u> character, didn't you?
  B: Yes, she was en............................ .

5 A: The plot was just so <u>sad and moving</u>, wasn't it?
  B: Yes, it was very po............................ .

**27.2**

15 marks

Answer these questions. You are sometimes given the first letters.

1 What adjective goes before *humour* and means 'in the face of bad circumstances'?
  w............................

2 Complete this sentence using a noun meaning a book which makes you want to go on reading:
  It was a brilliant book, a real p............................-t............................ .

3 Complete this sentence to produce a similar meaning to the sentence above:
  It was a brilliant book. I just ............................ put ............................ ............................ .

4 What formal adjective goes before the noun *reading* and means 'difficult to stop once you've started'? c............................

5 What expression can refer to a book which is good to read just before going to sleep?
  ............................ ............................

6 What word means the same as *story*? t............................

7 What do we call the type of book often written by politicians and military figures when they retire? m............................

8 What word means the scene or place where a story occurs? s............................

9 What do you call a book that records events and times, e.g. all the journeys made by a lorry or a ship? l............................

10 What do we call a technical book which tells you how to use a piece of equipment, e.g. a computer? m............................

**27.3**

10 marks

Rewrite the underlined parts of these sentences using expressions based on the words in brackets.

1 Her first novel was <u>difficult to read</u>. (HEAVY/GO)
2 I tried his latest novel but just couldn't <u>become engaged with</u> it. (GET)
3 It was an absolutely <u>terrifying</u> narrative. (CHILL)
4 His new novel is a <u>fantastic and staggering</u> achievement. (BREATH)
5 I have to say I think his poetry was <u>not complex or deep</u>. (WEIGHT)

**27.4**

5 marks

Match the words on the left with their definitions on the right.

1 chronicle      short text on the back cover of a book saying what it is about
2 journal      account of a sequence of events
3 blurb      collection of poems or stories by different authors
4 anthology      collection of detailed information about a subject
5 compendium      written record of what someone has done each day

**Your score**

/40

# 28 We are what we eat

## 28.1
10 marks

Write down two words that are often used with the given words.

*Example:* reduced ..*fat, sugar*...........................................

| | |
|---|---|
| 1 wholemeal | ................................................ |
| 2 organic | ................................................ |
| 3 free range | ................................................ |
| 4 low fat | ................................................ |
| 5 vegetarian | ................................................ |
| 6 genetically modified | ................................................ |
| 7 to dilute | ................................................ |
| 8 cherry flavoured | ................................................ |
| 9 wholesome | ................................................ |
| 10 juicy | ................................................ |

## 28.2
18 marks

In this e-mail the writer has used nine food metaphors. Underline them and then explain in your own words what each one means.

Hi, Mike,

I must tell you about this party Pete organised the other night. He wanted to spice up our social life a bit as it's been a bit dreary recently. It had all the ingredients for success – good friends, good music, plenty to eat and drink – but things began to turn a bit sour when Ray arrived bringing some rather unsavoury characters with him. They started telling everyone about some half-baked scheme they have for making loads of money. Rhona, who wants to join the police, started grilling them about it. Pete and I decided it was beginning to feel like a recipe for disaster so we went for a short walk and left the others to it. You won't believe what had happened by the time we got back … But I won't tell you the really juicy bits until we meet up! Suffice it to say that Rhona is going to let Ray stew for quite some time.

Love,

Emma

## 28.3
12 marks

Find one word that could fill all three gaps in each set of sentences.

1 He's a ........................................ sleeper.
   The baby's getting quite ........................................ .
   Do you like ........................................ metal music?

2 Potatoes are full of ........................................ .
   Don't eat too much ........................................ if you want to lose weight.
   In the past people used to ........................................ their sheets and shirt collars.

3 This throws some new ........................................ on the situation.
   The artist has a pleasantly ........................................ touch.
   If you think hard enough, you will probably ........................................ on the right answer.

4 Would you like a bowl of ........................................ for breakfast?
   Take a ........................................ bar to have with your coffee.
   Wheat, barley and oats are types of ........................................ .

5 You're reading a very ........................................ book. It must be at least 1000 pages!
   Do you think he'll pass his exams? ........................................ chance!
   The ........................................ content of a hamburger is enormous.

6 You should ........................................ the wheels regularly.
   They use genetically modified ........................................ in this dressing.
   Is it an ........................................ painting or a watercolour?

Your score

/40

# 29 Dinner's on me: entertaining and eating out

**29.1** Circle the correct underlined word or phrase.

10 marks

1 The waiters here are incredibly nice. They go <u>over their way/out of their way/away out</u> to be helpful.
2 I always have a dessert. I have quite a sweet <u>tongue/taste/tooth</u>.
3 The loud music in the restaurant was very <u>off-putting/put offing/putting-off</u>.
4 I always enjoy Ritchie and Margaret's dinner <u>feasts/parties/meals</u>.
5 The film starts at seven. We could <u>grab/grasp/grip</u> a bite to eat before that perhaps.
6 You're welcome to eat with us tonight as long as you don't mind taking <u>the lucky pot/a pot lucky/pot luck</u>.
7 It's not a proper party, just a family <u>go-together/get-together/come-together</u>.
8 No, please, let me <u>have/take/get</u> this. You paid last time. I insist.
9 My great aunt never drinks alcohol. She's <u>teatotal/teetotal /totalty</u>.
10 That snooty head-waiter always addresses customers in a very <u>breeze/braise/brusque</u> manner.

**29.2** Rewrite these sentences using the words in brackets.

10 marks

1 Put your credit card away. I am paying for this meal. (ON/ME)
2 I was taken out to restaurants every night when I visited our headquarters in Seville. (DINED/WINED)
3 Shall we pay half of the bill each? (SPLIT)
4 Do you mind if Maria comes with us for dinner tonight? (JOINS)
5 Mark, I'd like to pay for your dinner tonight. (GUEST)

**29.3** Read these people's comments about eating and entertaining, then answer the questions below.

6 marks

> The service is generally courteous at the Golden Bengal restaurant.

> The service was a bit sluggish the last few times we were at the Green Bough.

> Why are the waiters always so sullen at the Sea View?

> We were wined and dined by John's boss at the Panorama last night. It was fantastic!

> The waiters at the Lobster House are always too overbearing for my liking.

> Have you ever eaten at the Pittsburgh? The service is just impeccable.

1 Where is the service unfriendly and unsmiling?
2 Where is the service more or less perfect?
3 Where is the service too imposing, telling people what to do?
4 Where is the service polite?
5 Where has the speaker experienced slow service?
6 Where was the speaker treated to a fine meal?

**29.4** Rewrite the underlined parts of these sentences using expressions based on the words in brackets.

14 marks

1 Would anyone like <u>some more of this food</u>? (SECOND)
2 I've put on a bit of weight so I've started to <u>look at how many calories everything has</u>. (COUNT)
3 Does anyone in your group have any <u>special things they can't eat</u>? (REQUIREMENT)
4 I won't have any dessert, thanks. I don't want to <u>be excessive</u>. (DO)
5 Sally <u>has rather particular demands when it comes to food</u>; she won't eat this, she won't eat that. (EATER)
6 Would you like some <u>nuts and crisps</u> before we eat? (NIBBLE)
7 I don't feel like cooking tonight. Shall we get a <u>meal from a restaurant to bring home</u>? (TAKE)

**Your score**

/ 40

# 30 On the road: traffic and driving

## 30.1
**10 marks**

Complete the words in these sentences.

1 Chris has been charged several times with reck............................ driving.
2 I had to pay an on-the-............................ fine for parking on double yellow lines.
3 The accident has caused major tail............................ in both directions of the A14.
4 You mustn't drive the car until a mechanic has told you that it is road............................ .
5 There was a terrible pile-............................ on the motorway this morning.
6 The traffic in the city has got so bad that if there is an accident there can be total grid............................ .
7 It was a head-............................ collision so it's amazing that everyone survived.
8 You must stop at a give-............................ sign.
9 I didn't realise I'd parked in a tow............................ zone so I thought my car had been stolen.
10 I think ............................-and-run drivers should be banned from driving for life.

## 30.2
**5 marks**

Match words from the box to make five compound nouns.

| | | | | |
|---|---|---|---|---|
| rage | back-seat | bags | points | penalty |
| exhaust | road | air | emissions | driver |

## 30.3
**5 marks**

Match the compound nouns you found in exercise 30.2 to their definitions below.

1 official notes made on a driving licence if the driver commits an offence
2 a passenger who has the irritating habit of telling the driver how to drive or where to go
3 aggressive anger, even violence, caused by bad driving or bad driving conditions
4 the waste gases produced by a vehicle
5 protective balloons which automatically inflate to protect the people in the front seats of the car if there is a collision

## 30.4
**20 marks**

Complete these sentences using a verb from the box. Write the verb in the correct form.

| | | | | |
|---|---|---|---|---|
| clamp | collide | conk out | divert | jump |
| pull over | skid | sound | ban | tow |

1 In some countries I believe you can be fined for ............................ your car horn late at night.
2 The car must have ............................ on the icy roads causing it to crash.
3 Hey, look at that red car – it just ............................ those traffic lights!
4 Will's car broke down on the motorway and he had to get it ............................ back home.
5 Jim's in trouble with the police for shouting at a traffic warden who ............................ his car.
6 Because of the pile-up all traffic is being ............................ via the B289.
7 He was ............................ for six months for speeding.
8 The car made a strange hissing noise before it finally ............................ .
9 I saw the blue light flashing behind me and realised the police wanted me to ............................ .
10 In the darkness the two cyclists ............................ with each other at the crossroads.

**31.1** Fill the gaps in speaker B's replies.

**10 marks**

1 A: Can you get your money back if you cancel the flight?
   B: No, the ticket is ................-............................ .
2 A: Can you break your journey between London and Melbourne?
   B: Yes, the ticket allows one ........................................ .
3 A: Was it one of those holiday flights?
   B: No, it was a proper ........................................ flight, full of business travellers.
4 A: If you cancel, do you have to pay anything?
   B: Yes, there's a ........................................ ........................................ of 25 per cent.
5 A: Will you have to pay for taxis from the airport to the hotel and back?
   B: No, the cost of the holiday includes all ........................................ .
6 A: Are you getting your meals provided at your holiday apartment?
   B: No, we have to cook for ourselves; it's ..................-......................... .
7 A: Do you have to pay per mile you drive with your rental car?
   B: No, they give you ........................................   ........................................ .
8 A: Did you eat all your meals at the hotel?
   B: No, just lunches; we only had ........................   ........................ . We ate out every night.
9 A: Did you have to pay for the flight and the hotel separately?
   B: No, it was ........................   ........................ .
10 A: Did you fly first class?
   B: No, we could only afford ........................................ class.

**31.2** Match words from box A with words from box B to make five travel-related collocations.

**10 marks**

A: | upper    guest    charter    full    fare |

B: | board    type    deck    flight    house |

**31.3** Rewrite these sentences using expressions based on the words in brackets.

**16 marks**

1 I don't want to go with an organised group. I want to make my own decisions. (BOSS)
2 I like to travel to a different place each day when I'm on holiday. (KEEP)
3 It really was a very special holiday that I'll never forget. (LIFETIME)
4 I don't mind staying in basic, low-standard accommodation. (ROUGH)
5 It was a trekking holiday where you slept in the open every night. (STARS)
6 Low-cost airlines offer a lot for what you pay. (MONEY)
7 Our trip to Japan cost us a huge amount of money. (FORTUNE)
8 We spent a week very far away from civilisation; it was wonderful. (WILDS)

**31.4** Match a word from the box with the sentence it is most closely associated with.

**4 marks**

| cruise    chalet    B and B    inn |

1 They have these small cottages for holiday-makers all along the lake shore.
2 It's fun to stay in someone's private home and be served by them.
3 Just lazing on deck or relaxing in the cabin, that's all we ever did.
4 Well, it's like a pub, but they do accommodation too.

**Your score**

**/40**

**32.1** Complete these sentences with one word.

10 marks

1 Nigel always likes to spend his holidays off the ........................................... track.
2 The National Park is renowned for its varied ........................................... and fauna.
3 Janice gets very annoyed about having to pay a single room ........................................... when she goes on holiday alone.
4 In this adventure brochure you'll find holidays for people who are looking for something out of the ........................................... .
5 Being a city dweller, when I go on holiday I'm always keen to get back to ........................................... and lead a more simple, uncomplicated life.
6 Bookings are, of course, ........................................... to availability.
7 When I visit a new city, I like to do a guided ........................................... first.
8 Usually hotels have babies' cots and high chairs ........................................... on request.
9 Our company prides itself on offering unbeatable ........................................... for money.
10 When we go on holiday, we usually go for the fly-........................................... option and collect a hire car at the airport.

**32.2** Correct the vocabulary mistake in each of these sentences.

10 marks

1 The view of the mountains from our hotel balcony was wow-inspiring.
2 Ego-tourism is becoming increasingly popular.
3 You will find a great deal of wildlove in the forest.
4 Waterfront, auto-catering villas are very popular at all times of the year.
5 The region offers unriveting opportunities for water and other sports.
6 The centreland of the country is a wild and spectacular bush area.
7 The church is built on the sighting of a Roman temple.
8 If you would like us to arrange a customised tour for you, tell us what you want and we will give you a quota.
9 There is no need to have a two-by-two vehicle for driving in town.
10 Flora refers to plants and florid refers to animals.

**32.3** Circle the correct underlined word.

10 marks

1 Travel to the Amazon and experience the rainforest/bush for yourself!
2 The tourism tract/sector is very important to Thailand's economy.
3 Golden Bay is the perfect destination for the stunning/discerning traveller.
4 We went for a lovely little trek/ramble this morning down by the lake.
5 Sit in a pavement café and enjoy watching the wealth/hordes of people passing by.
6 It's easy to unwind/savour on a desert island.
7 The region seeks/boasts some of the best ancient sites in the country.
8 I'd love to go on a hike/an itinerary in the mountains this Saturday.
9 The country has the largest expanses of virgin/promising forest in the world.
10 Escape/Recharge your batteries lazing by the villa's private pool.

**32.4** Write your own definitions of the ten words not used in exercise 32.3.

10 marks

Your score

/40

# 33 Describing the world

**33.1**

*10 marks*

Find one word to replace the underlined words in these sentences. You are given the first letter.

1  The south has suffered a severe <u>long period without rain</u> this year. d............................
2  The <u>plant life</u> in the north is very dense and almost tropical. v............................
3  As you head towards the desert region, the landscape becomes <u>totally dry</u>. a............................
4  The southern region is <u>subject</u> to earthquakes. p............................
5  Many of the forests in Northern Europe are <u>always green and produce cones</u>. c............................

**33.2**

*10 marks*

Read what these people say about their family histories, then answer the questions below by writing the correct names in the boxes.

PACO:       My great-great-grandparents and their parents before them worked on the land.
JEESHA:     I am the son of a young couple who arrived in this country forty years ago with no money or possessions.
CIARAN:     My great-grandparents and grandparents lived in the same village all their lives.
LUCINDA:    My parents travelled from country to country looking for a better life.
THOMAS:     My mother and father were heartbroken at having to leave their native land.

| | | |
|---|---|---|
| 1 | Whose parents were migrants? | |
| 2 | Whose ancestors never moved away from home? | |
| 3 | Who is descended from farmers? | |
| 4 | Whose parents were emigrants? | |
| 5 | Whose parents were immigrants? | |

**33.3**

*10 marks*

Cross out the five vocabulary or spelling mistakes in this text and write the correct word above each mistake.

The farmers in the north grow serials such as maize and wheat, and trend their sheep and cattle in small fields. In the south, padded fields can be seen where the farmers grow rice. The central area is dominated by prayers where cattle graze on the rich grasslands. The north is a cold area of frozen tandra.

**33.4**

*10 marks*

Complete the words in these sentences using the clues in brackets.

1  The economy was once dominated by m............................g industries but now tourism has taken over. (producing goods in large numbers)
2  For many years, the country was at the f............................t of the international rubber industry. (in an important position)
3  Explorers who s............................d on the coast found the climate very pleasing. (made their homes)
4  The hydro-electric plant g............................s 12% of the country's total electricity needs. (produces, often used of electricity)
5  Federico was a d............................t of rich 18th-century landowners. (someone who is related to someone who lived a long time ago)

**Your score**

/40

# Weather and climate

**34.1**

10 marks

Write these weather words in the correct column or columns.

| ~~chilly~~ | clammy | deluge | stifling | freezing |
| sweltering | muggy | nippy | roasting |

| hot | cold | wet or damp |
|-----|------|-------------|
|     | chilly |           |

**34.2**

10 marks

Circle the underlined word which collocates with the bold word or words in each sentence.

*Example:* I'm rained/snowed/hailed **under** with work.

1 Maggie looked misty/foggy/hazy-**eyed** at her new baby.
2 Bob has written a fascinating book on the **current political** weather/climate/time.
3 The orchestra received stormy/thunderous/thundery **applause** after the concert.
4 Over the summer Jana and Pedro enjoyed a thundery/windy/whirlwind **romance**.
5 Amanda **has a very** sunny/oppressive/muggy **disposition**.
6 The breezes/winds/tornados **of change** are blowing through the civil service.
7 Our proposal **met with a** snowy/wet/frosty **reception**.
8 A rain/hail/snow **of bullets** hit the military convoy.
9 Henry left **under a** cloud/storm/frost **of suspicion**.
10 I hadn't slept all night so I **was in a** mist/cloud/haze all day.

**34.3**

10 marks

Complete the words in these sentences. You are given the first letter and number of letters.

1 The climate there is very a _ _ _ . Hardly any rain falls there at all.
2 In the mountains most p _ _ _ _ _ _ _ _ _ _ _ _ falls in the form of snow rather than rain.
3 The UK has a m _ _ _ _ _ _ climate – it is usually neither very hot nor very cold.
4 The rainfall in June this year was higher than the m _ _ _ for this time of year.
5 As the town is in a hollow and there is little movement of air there, it can feel terribly o _ _ _ _ _ _ _ _ _ on a hot day.
6 I don't mind the heat if it's dry but I really hate this humid, s _ _ _ _ _ weather.
7 The island is located at a l _ _ _ _ _ _ _ of sixty degrees north.
8 The roof panels help to create energy by trapping s _ _ _ _ radiation.
9 The climate of the UK is maritime while that of central Russia is c _ _ _ _ _ _ _ _ _ _ _ .
10 The village lies at an e _ _ _ _ _ _ _ _ of over 1000 metres.

**34.4**

10 marks

Put what the speaker means into simpler English.

*Example:* It's very blowy today. It's very windy today.

1 It's chucking it down!
2 What a stifling day!
3 It's nippy today, isn't it!
4 Economic prospects look sunny.
5 The train thundered down the track.
6 The prevailing winds are westerly.
7 Katie is snowed under!
8 She looked at me icily.
9 I've only a hazy idea of his plans.
10 Karl's political views sometimes cloud his judgement.

# 35 Buildings in metaphors

**35.1**
16 marks

Complete these sentences using expressions associated with buildings.

1 James was a t............................ of strength when we were going through difficulties at work.
2 I feel I've come up against a g.................... c........................ in my job and can't progress any further.
3 I tried to find out why they hadn't promoted me but just came up against a b........................ w............................ .
4 Sue h........................ the r........................ when she heard we'd missed the deadline for the report. I've never seen her so angry.
5 The merging of the company names and logos will finally c........................ the partnership which has existed informally for ten years.

**35.2**
4 marks

Complete these sentences with a preposition.

1 The key ..................... good health is a balanced diet and plenty of exercise.
2 The price of computer chips went ..................... the roof because of a world shortage of silicon.
3 The business is ..................... ruins thanks to bad management.
4 I don't want to get locked ..................... an argument over who was right and who was wrong.

**35.3**
8 marks

Complete each pair of sentences with the same word.

*Example:* Nuclear weapons were a ..key.......................... issue in the general election.
Professor Pit played a ..key.......................... role in the discovery of galactic flixons.

1 He's an academic; he tends to live in an ivory ........................... .
My sister was a ........................... of strength when my husband died.
2 I've never seen him so angry. He just went through the ........................... .
The ........................... fell in on our grand plan and we had to think again.
3 The company was ........................... in a damaging and expensive lawsuit for five years.
His eyes were ........................... on Sally's as he told her how much he loved her.
4 She got the job through the ........................... door; she knew someone high up in the company.
We should clean up our own ........................... yard before we criticise other countries for polluting the atmosphere.

**35.4**
12 marks

Answer these questions.

1 Which part of a building is used in a metaphor involving the word 'silence': wall, window or door? What is the exact metaphor?
2 Write this sentence in a different way using a word based on the root 'gate':
A college degree gives you access to a better-paid job.
3 Give two verbs which could fill this gap:
Apes ........................... the key to understanding our own evolution.
4 What type of building would you live in, metaphorically, if you wanted to ignore the unpleasant and everyday things in life?
5 Which building activity means, metaphorically, 'creating the right conditions for something to develop': (a) building the roof (b) laying the floor (c) laying the foundations?
6 Find a word to replace 'ceiling' in this sentence:
They imposed a ceiling of £100 on parking fines.

Your score
/ 40

# Trees, plants and metaphors

**36.1**
10 marks
Rewrite the underlined parts of these sentences using an expression based on the word in brackets.

1 It's time <u>to get rid of</u> some of our less efficient employees. (WEED)
2 It's a journalist's job <u>to discover</u> interesting facts about celebrities' lives. (DIG)
3 At his age, it's time to think about <u>settling down</u>. (ROOTS)
4 John's been <u>living a very luxurious life</u> for some years. (CLOVER)
5 At last Paul <u>is enjoying the results of</u> all his hard work. (REAPING)
6 Pat seems to be getting a bit snobbish; we'd better <u>put a stop to that</u>. (NIP)
7 The idea had been around for many years before it really <u>became accepted</u>. (ROOT)
8 Her problems <u>have their origins in</u> her childhood. (STEM)
9 Becky was always <u>the teacher's favourite</u>. (APPLE)
10 She <u>got a lot thinner</u> when she started walking to work. (SHED)

**36.2**
10 marks
Complete these sentences with a word from the box.

| budding | grass | mushrooming | potato | flourishing |
| fading | seeds | shed | shrivelling | withering |

1 The .............................................. of revolution were sown long before the French Revolution.
2 Pauline is a ........................................... poet – she wrote her first sonnet at the weekend and it was fantastic!
3 When we started giggling the teacher gave us a ........................................... look.
4 The course helped him to ........................................... some of his inhibitions about speaking in public.
5 Our business had problems at first but it's ........................................... now.
6 Joey lies around all day; he's such a couch ........................................... .
7 Funding for the building project is ........................................... up.
8 The Prime Minister depends for his support on the ........................................... roots of the Party.
9 Mobile phone masts are ........................................... all over the country.
10 Sadly her hopes of ever gaining a seat in Parliament are ........................................... .

**36.3**
20 marks
Underline the ten metaphors based on trees and plants in this paragraph. Then explain the meaning of the metaphors. Refer to the literal meaning of each expression in your answer.

Daisy's idea for opening a clothes shop was germinating while we were on holiday in Spain one year ago and she had some very fruitful discussions with some Spanish businessmen she happened to meet there. So you could say that the seeds of her success were planted on a Spanish beach. Her first shop flourished and soon she was branching out into interior furnishings as well. Shops with the Daisy name sprouted up all over the country. Last year when the economy was generally wilting, she had to prune back a bit. She had to shed some employees but now things seem to be looking up again.

**Your score**

/ 40

**37.1**

10 marks

**Write down the nouns which fit these definitions.**

1 animal that eats meat ...........................................
2 animal that gives birth to babies and feeds them on its own milk .............................................
3 animal that hunts and eats other animals, e.g. shark .............................................
4 cold-blooded animal that lays eggs, e.g. snake .............................................
5 animal that eats grass and other plants .............................................

**37.2**

10 marks

**Complete these sentences. For sentences 1–5 the answers are from exercise 37.1. For the other missing words you are given the first letter.**

1 Deer don't eat meat, they're ........................................... .
2 A whale is a ........................................... , not a fish.
3 I couldn't give up meat. I think humans are natural ........................................... .
4 There were lizards, alligators and other ........................................... basking on the river bank.
5 Small birds fear large ........................................... such as eagles and vultures.
6 The birds were so t........................................... that they took food from our hands.
7 The place was infested with r........................................... , both mice and rats. We had to call in a specialist to exterminate them.
8 P........................................... have shot so many gorillas that they have brought these lovely animals to the brink of extinction.
9 Cats were d........................................... thousands of years ago and have lived with humans ever since.
10 W........................................... birds should never be kept in cages. It is so cruel.

**37.3**

10 marks

**Rewrite the following sentences by changing the underlined words into a different word class, as instructed. Make any other necessary changes.**

1 Large <u>carnivores</u> roamed the earth millions of years ago. (change to adjective)
2 The elephant showed such <u>docility</u> when his keeper approached him. (change to adjective)
3 These animals are <u>predators</u> with regard to small mammals. (change to verb)
4 He's very <u>active</u> in animal rights. (change to noun)
5 The dog exhibited an incredible <u>fierceness</u> when cornered. (change to adjective)

**37.4**

5 marks

**Underline where the stress falls on these words.**

*Example:* <u>pre</u>datory

1 herbivorous     4 carnivore
2 reptile              5 domesticated
3 predator

**37.5**

5 marks

**Complete these sentences using a word from the box.**

| habitat | sanctuary | ivory | blood | shelter |
|---------|-----------|-------|-------|---------|

1 This beach is now a bird ........................................... . 10,000 birds visit it every year.
2 ........................................... sports such as foxhunting have been banned in many countries.
3 The illegal ........................................... trade has caused the death of thousands of elephants.
4 The cliffs are the natural ........................................... of more than twenty species of sea bird.
5 We got a dog from an animal ........................................... ; the poor thing had been abandoned.

Your score

/ 40

**38.1** Complete these sentences.

10 marks

1 In the worst ............................................. scenario, the species will survive only in captivity.
2 Many argue that it's mainly the car which is to blame for the greenhouse ............................................. .
3 Laurence is very miserable company – he's such a prophet of ............................................. and gloom.
4 ............................................. warming has caused glaciers to melt and sea ............................................. to rise.
5 There are laws which aim to protect endangered ............................................. .
6 Coal and oil are examples of fossil ............................................. .
7 If forests are cut down, this affects the amount of carbon ............................................. in the atmosphere.
8 Large urban populations exert severe ............................................. on limited resources.
9 Development that can be maintained without seriously depleting natural resources or having negative effects on society is called ............................................. development.

**38.2** Complete the word puzzle.

10 marks

1 A solution dealing with only part of the problem is a ............................................. solution.
2 The World Wildlife Fund is an international organisation concerned with the ............................................. of plant and animal species.
3 We should try to maintain the ecological ............................................. .
4 pure, unspoilt
5 Experts ............................................. that the average income will rise by 5% next year.
6 You ............................................. pressure on something.
7 Another expression for 'the worst possibilities for the future' is 'the worst case .............................................'.
8 another word for endangered (species)
9 a person who predicts the future
10 the colour that suggests being eco-friendly

**38.3** Correct the ten spelling mistakes in these phrases.

20 marks

1 a pristine enviroment
2 exhaust emitions
3 profits of doom
4 uncontrolled defforestation
5 climattic changes
6 finite ressources
7 project sustenability
8 shrinking habbitats
9 in a peacemeal fashion
10 demografic projections

Your score

/40

**39.1**

10 marks

Look at this magazine survey on the quality of service of three computer companies, Zigma, Panther and Q-Mark. Then answer the questions below.

### Computer firms: our survey

★ poor   ★★ adequate   ★★★ good   ★★★★ excellent

| | Zigma | Panther | Q-Mark |
|---|---|---|---|
| impeccable after-sales service | ★★ | ★★★★ | ★★★ |
| responsive to complaints | ★★★ | ★ | ★ |
| able to satisfy queries | ★★ | ★★★ | ★ |
| accommodating and obliging | ★★ | ★ | ★★★★ |
| prompt dispatch | ★★★ | ★★★ | ★★★★ |

| | | |
|---|---|---|
| 1 | Which firm is most willing to understand and help? | |
| 2 | Which firm is best at following up problems once you have bought something? | |
| 3 | Which firm sends goods quickest to customers? | |
| 4 | Which firm deals best with dissatisfied customers? | |
| 5 | Which firm gives the best answer to people's individual questions? | |

**39.2**

10 marks

Complete the words in these sentences using the clues in brackets. You are given some letters.

1  That company sells sh............................ imported goods; I don't recommend it.  (poor quality)
2  She said the delay was due to a b............................g of orders.  (number waiting to be dealt with)
3  Those people at the car insurance company are totally inc............................ !  (unable to do their job properly through lack of skill or training)
4  Their level of service is su............................d for a big company.  (below the expected standard)
5  My CD player broke down, but as it was under g............................ I didn't have to pay for the repair.  (written promise to repair or replace faulty goods)

**39.3**

10 marks

Cross out the five vocabulary mistakes in the text and write the correct word above each mistake.

I hate the unpersonal service you get when you phone a big company. You usually get an automated voice, but even if you get a human, they are often incooperative and just put you on waiting for hours. They have no sense of urgentness. It's often easier to deal with things online, but if it's not a secure sight it can be dangerous to give personal information.

**39.4**

10 marks

Answer these questions. You are given some letters.

1  What expression means 'The set of principles a company follows to protect your personal information'?  p............................ p............................
2  What verb means 'to look at the various goods available before buying'?  b............................
3  What adjective goes with 'delivery' to mean 'covering the whole country'?  n............................
4  What do we call a sale of goods on the Internet where people can bid different prices? o............................ a............................

Your score

/40

5  What word connected with death is sometimes used with 'bargains' to mean 'extremely good special offers'?  k............................

# 40 Authorities: customs and police

**40.1**
10 marks

Complete these sentences using one word per gap.

1 The police used sniffer .......................... to locate the drugs.
2 Surveillance .......................... now film our behaviour in many public places like airports or shopping centres.
3 Some people who want to live in another country are .......................... seekers while others are economic .......................... .
4 If you have information about a crime the police will ask you to make a .......................... .
5 Customs .......................... regularly carry out spot .......................... on people's luggage.
6 The police cannot search a suspect's home without a search .......................... .
7 If you commit a traffic .......................... , you may have to pay an on-the-spot .......................... .

**40.2**
10 marks

What do you call police or officials who ...

1 wear ordinary clothes rather than a uniform?    p.......................... c.......................... police
2 are specially trained to combat the drug problem?    d.......................... s..........................
3 check that cars are not illegally parked?    t.......................... w..........................
4 focus on combating bribery?    a..........................-c.......................... s..........................
5 help the armed forces in their work?    p.......................... p..........................

**40.3**
5 marks

Match the words on the left with a suitable word on the right.

1 photofit      operations
2 surveillance      restrictions
3 random      picture
4 entry      police
5 undercover      checks

**40.4**
5 marks

Complete these sentences using the expressions from exercise 40.3.

1 Customs officers routinely carry out .......................... at immigration.
2 Suspected drugs gangs have been infiltrated by .......................... .
3 The police have produced a .......................... of the wanted man.
4 .......................... have been taking place at a number of city locations overnight.
5 There are .......................... on people coming into the UK from certain places of origin.

**40.5**
10 marks

Circle the correct underlined word.

1 The police have the right to halt/stop and search any suspicious person.
2 The police set up roadblocks/streetblocks hoping to catch the getaway car.
3 John would like a career of some kind in the security/safety forces.
4 When you go to India, remember to take your injection/vaccination certificate.
5 Before landing in a foreign country, you are usually given a landing ticket/card and a customs/custom declaration form.
6 Most foreign visitors to the island come through the same port of entry/entrance.
7 My plane lands at 2 p.m. but it'll take an hour or so to pass/clear customs.
8 There are strict laws about tapping/knocking people's phones.
9 Joe had to take a breathalyser test/exam because the police thought he'd been drinking.

Your score

/40

# 41 World views: ways of thinking

**41.1**
Complete these letters to a newspaper editor, using words from the box. Change the form of the words if necessary.

| adherent | fanatic | eradicate | bigot | convert |

Dear Editor,

I am a recent (1) .......................... to green politics, but I would not call myself a radical. Your article condemning Green Party activists as (2) .......................... was unfair and biased.

Vick Bolsher

Sir,

(3) .......................... of a fair justice system will have been horrified to read in your columns that the government thinks it can (4) .......................... crime by increasing prison sentences. This government simply plays into the hands of the (5) .......................... in our society who believe that criminals should be beaten or hanged.

Les Birchemall

**41.2**
Rewrite the underlined parts of these sentences using a word from the box in exercise 41.1. Make any other necessary changes.

1  I don't think all my ideas are right and everyone else is wrong, but I do have strong principles.
2  I'm not a person who supports communism, but I do believe in workers' rights.
3  I believe in animal rights, but I'm not a person of obsessive or extremely strong views.
4  Every politician promises to rid us of poverty, but no one ever succeeds.
5  He became a new believer in Buddhism in 1994.

**41.3**
Answer these questions. You are sometimes given letters.

1  Give two adjectives beginning with *cred...* connected with believing.
   .......................... , ..........................
2  What is the opposite of *plausible*? ..........................
3  Give a synonym for the verb *ascribe*.  att..........................
4  What is the verb form of the noun *postulate*? ..........................
5  What word means 'trusting, sincere, often in a naïve or foolish way'?  ing..........................
6  Complete the missing word: The revolution u..........................d in a new era of democracy.
7  What noun connected with beliefs begins and ends in 't'?  t..........................t
8  If you take something with a pinch of salt do you believe (a) none (b) not much (c) all of it?
9  What expression means 'accept that someone is telling the truth even though you can't be certain'?  Give someone the b.......................... of the d.......................... .
10  Is a 'likely story' (a) probably true (b) probably false (c) probably nice?
11  What can you ask someone to pull if you don't believe them?
    Pull the o.......................... o.......................... !
12  Complete the expression involving *born* which means you don't believe someone.
    I wasn't born .......................... !
13  What adjective means 'easily tricked into believing untrue things'?  g..........................
14  What is the jumbled word in this sentence?
    This report lends RDCEECNE .......................... to the idea that prison simply does not work.
15  What word beginning with 'r' means 'someone who believes in extreme political change'?
    r..........................
16  What abstract noun is made from the word 'bigot'? ..........................

**42.1**

10 marks

Complete these sentences using a word based on the word in brackets.

1 The ceremony ........................... the lives of soldiers from the local regiment. (MEMORY)
2 Many people have ........................... beliefs about New Year. (SUPERSTITION)
3 When you get your PhD, the family will organise a ........................... meal. (CELEBRATE)
4 It was very ........................... in the town on carnival day. (ATMOSPHERE)
5 The tribe's traditional wedding ........................... last for several days. (FESTIVE)
6 At the end of the golden jubilee, there was a ........................... pageant. (SPECTACLE)
7 You must go and watch the ........................... procession in the evening. (CEREMONY)
8 There are big ........................... on this hill every Midsummer Day. (CELEBRATE)
9 Every finisher in the marathon received a ........................... medal. (MEMORY)
10 People enjoy the spring celebrations as a time of ........................... . (NEW)

**42.2**

10 marks

Match the words in the box with the definitions 1–10 below.

| | | | | |
|---|---|---|---|---|
| bi-centenary | flamboyant | harvest | lantern | pagan |
| penance | raucous | sombre | fast | symbolise |

1 serious, heavy and sad
2 a lamp that can be held or carried
3 go without food
4 colourful in an exaggerated way
5 very noisy
6 represent
7 time when fruit is picked
8 200th anniversary
9 an act that demonstrates regret
10 having ancient, pre-Christian beliefs

**42.3**

10 marks

Answer these questions.

1 If someone is fasting what are they not doing?
2 Does someone do penance if they want to celebrate or if they've done something wrong?
3 Which bird is more flamboyant – a pigeon or a peacock?
4 Why do people sometimes celebrate at harvest time?
5 Charles Dickens was born in 1812. When will his bi-centenary be?
6 Does a lantern provide warmth or light?
7 Does a white dove symbolise peace or good health?
8 Are people more likely to wear sombre clothes at a wedding or a funeral?
9 Are pagan beliefs connected to one of the world's major religions?
10 If you say someone has a raucous voice, do you like the sound of their voice?

**42.4**

10 marks

Circle the correct underlined word.

1 The origins of Hallowe'en can be traced/tracked back to pre-Christian times.
2 I don't really like the way they celebrate their National Day here – it somehow seems very raucous/sombre and gloomy for a day of festival/celebration.
3 Davis wrote a fascinating book about the origins of suspicions/superstitions.
4 The statue recalls/commemorates a battle that took place here.
5 People associate/symbolise Lent and Ramadan with feasting/fasting.
6 The Rio Carnival is a world-famous spectacle/spectacular.
7 The focus/aim of the festival is the evening parade.
8 For luck Kay always uses the same pen on an exam day – she's very flamboyant/superstitious.

**Your score**

/ 40

# Talking about languages

### 43.1
**10 marks**

Circle the incorrect word in these underlined lists.

1 The <u>Chinese, Russian and Vietnamese</u> languages belong to a morphological type called isolating.
2 I studied Slavic languages at university – <u>Polish, Italian and Russian</u>.
3 <u>Latin, Spanish and Chinese</u> are examples of inflected languages.
4 <u>Malay, Hindu and Farsi</u> are all Indo-Arian languages.
5 Germanic languages often contain compounds such as <u>soulmate, clampdown and clumsy</u>.
6 The Celtic languages of Britain, which include <u>Welsh, English and Gaelic</u>, are very ancient.
7 <u>Greek, Arabic and Hebrew</u> share the label 'Semitic'.
8 I read somewhere that <u>Malay, Tagalog and Japanese</u> are Austronesian languages.
9 She studied Romance languages, including <u>Spanish, Dutch and French</u>.
10 <u>Swedish, Turkish and English</u> belong to the Germanic family.

### 43.2
**5 marks**

The underlined words are in the wrong sentences. Put them in the correct sentences.

1 The Chinese languages belong to a morphological type called <u>Germanic</u>.
2 The <u>Semitic</u> words in English are often long and difficult.
3 Latin was an example of an <u>isolating</u> language.
4 Arabic and Hebrew are both members of the <u>Graeco-Latin</u> family.
5 Swedish and English both belong to the <u>inflected</u> family.

### 43.3
**5 marks**

The left-hand column of the table contains rules of English. Complete the right-hand column using words from the box which explain which aspect of language each rule refers to.

| orthography | phonology | syntax | morphology | lexicon |
|---|---|---|---|---|

| 1 | Phrasal verbs often have more formal single-word equivalents. | |
| 2 | Adverbs rarely come between a verb and its object. | |
| 3 | Some words begin with the sound 'tr', but no words begin with 'gf'. | |
| 4 | English letters are only written with accents in words borrowed from other languages, e.g. risqué, from French. | |
| 5 | The prefix un- is used to create opposites. | |

### 43.4
**16 marks**

Match the terms on the left with the correct examples on the right.

1 modal verb    keyboard, windscreen
2 umlaut    <u>impolite, helpful</u>
3 character    España, puño
4 acute accent    boil, now
5 diphthong    might, could
6 compound noun    g, w, z
7 morpheme    passé, café
8 tilde    naïve, Noël

### 43.5
**4 marks**

Complete the table with the missing adjective or noun form and underline the stressed syllable.

| noun | le<u>xi</u>con | | or<u>tho</u>graphy | |
|---|---|---|---|---|
| adjective | | <u>mo</u>dal | | pictographic |

**44.1** Circle the correct underlined word.

10 marks

1 When his father died, Prince Dick was too young to become king, so a regent/pretender ruled in his name.
2 The heir to the throne is the first in line of success/succession.
3 Victoria was only eighteen when she was proclaimed/acclaimed queen.
4 A pretender is a person who lays/puts claim to the throne.
5 The rebels wanted to oppose/depose the president and claim power for themselves.
6 A politician who uses power for evil purposes can be said to usurp/abuse power.
7 In the past in Europe the monarch had absolute/absolutist power.
8 Kings and queens accede/succeed each other to the throne.
9 Princess Sophia is fifteenth in queue/line to the throne.
10 As the King's eldest son, Prince Carlos is the pretender/heir apparent.

**44.2** Choose one of the words from the box to complete the gaps in these quotations.

10 marks

| throne | crown | govern | history | monarchy |
|--------|-------|--------|---------|----------|
| politics | power | presidency | reign | stagecoach |

1 Here I and sorrows sit; Here is my ............................................ , bid kings come bow to it. (*William Shakespeare*, 1564–1616, playwright)
2 A ............................................ is merely a hat that lets the rain in. (*Frederick the Great*, 1712–1786, King of Prussia)
3 The US ............................................ is a Tudor ............................................ plus telephones. (*Anthony Burgess*, 1917–1993, English novelist)
4 The king ............................................s but does not ............................................ . (*Jan Zamoyski*, 1542–1605, Polish Chancellor and army leader)
5 The Labour Party is like a ............................................ . If you rattle along at great speed, everybody is too exhilarated or too seasick to cause any trouble. But if you stop, everybody gets out and argues about where to go next. (*Harold Wilson*, 1916–1995, British Labour Prime Minister)
6 There are no true friends in ............................................ . We are all sharks circling and waiting for traces of blood to appear in the water. (*Alan Clark*, 1928–1999, British Conservative politician)
7 Apart from the occasional saint, it is difficult for people who have the smallest amount of ............................................ to be nice. (*Anthony Clare*, 1942–, Irish psychiatrist and broadcaster)
8 ............................................ teaches us that men and nations behave wisely once they have exhausted all other possibilities. (*Abba Eban*, 1915–2002, Israeli diplomat and politician)

**44.3** Decide which is the odd word out in each set of three and explain your answer.

14 marks

1 galleon, serf, stagecoach
2 cavalry, infantry, armour
3 medieval, feudal, chariot
4 legion, Victorian, Renaissance

5 stagecoach, jester, medieval
6 cart, chariot, galleon
7 highwayman, regent, pretender

**44.4** Which words from exercise 44.3 describe these pictures?

6 marks

1   2   3 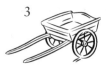  4   5   6

**45.1**
8 marks

Match the types of poverty on the left with the correct definition on the right.

1 human poverty     poor only in connection to other people around you
2 absolute poverty     less money than the defined minimum in your country
3 relative poverty     below a universally accepted, objective standard
4 income poverty     includes other factors, e.g. life expectancy

**45.2**
4 marks

What do these initials stand for?

1 GNP ................................................     2 GDP ................................................

**45.3**
8 marks

In these dialogues speaker B repeats the underlined parts of speaker A's remarks using a different word. Complete the dialogues.

1 A: A lot of the villages lack <u>proper waste water systems</u>; that's why there's so much disease.
   B: Yes, s............................ is very poor.
2 A: Some of those people <u>have no homes, no money, no possessions, nothing</u>.
   B: Yes, they're absolutely d............................ . It's tragic.
3 A: A lot of the poorer inhabitants <u>can't read or write</u>.
   B: Yes, there is a high level of i............................ .
4 A: <u>Ill health caused by lack of food</u> is rife in the poorer regions.
   B: Yes, there is widespread m............................ in those areas.

**45.4**
5 marks

Match words from box A with words from box B to make five expressions.

A: | trade    debt    overseas    poverty    life |

B: | line    aid    deals    expectancy    servicing |

**45.5**
5 marks

Use the expressions from exercise 45.4 to complete these sentences.

1 The government has reduced its ................................................ budget. Poor countries will suffer.
2 ................................................ in Europe increased dramatically during the 20th century; Europeans can now anticipate living well into their 80s.
3 International ................................................ are often unfair and only benefit rich, powerful countries.
4 20% of the population live below the ................................................ .
5 ................................................ swallows up a lot of aid received by countries. They have to use it to try to lower their national debt.

**45.6**
10 marks

Cross out the five vocabulary or spelling mistakes in this text and write the correct word above each mistake.

When I first tried to make my living as a sculptor I spent several years living in perjury.

I did earn some money as time passed, but I was still living by hand and mouth and money

was pressed. I kept reminding myself that life for many people living in depraved areas

was worse than mine and that whole families were living beyond the bread line. Then I

sold a major work and my life was transformed.

Your score

/40

# British politics

**46.1**

10 marks

**Complete the words in these sentences.**

1 It'll be hard to stop the development plans but we could ask people to sign a p............................n.
2 An MP's first responsibility is to his or her c............................s: the people who elected him or her.
3 UK government is less c............................d than in the past: there are more government departments in the regions now.
4 Cabinet ministers are always being pressured by l............................s trying to influence decisions.
5 The charity sent a d............................n to the Prime Minister to plead their cause.
6 The government is planning to introduce some interesting new l............................n relating to education and the health service.
7 A prisoner who has a g............................e against the prison authorities can a............................l to a special arbitration committee, which will decide if the complaint is justified or not.
8 Industrialists have more political power because they are the p............................s of goods, whereas the rest of us are merely the c............................s of their products.

**46.2**

10 marks

**Match words from box A with words from box B to make ten expressions.**

A:

| tax | civil | paid-up | Chancellor of the | mass- |
|-----|-------|---------|-------------------|-------|
| close- | well- | Friends of the | annual | Child Poverty |

B:

| servant | knit | Action Group | Earth | member |
|---------|------|--------------|-------|--------|
| funded | budget | produced | Exchequer | concession |

**46.3**

10 marks

**Answer these questions about the expressions in exercise 46.2.**

1 Which two expressions are names of charity organisations?
2 Which expression is closely connected with manufacturing things?
3 Which five expressions are very closely connected with money?
4 Which expression describes an administrative job in a government department?
5 Which expression implies having many connections and interrelationships?

**46.4**

10 marks

**Complete the word puzzle.**

1 a large company
2 someone who speaks on your behalf
3 try to persuade someone forcefully
4 to go against
5 another name for the Treasury or Finance Ministry
6 groups that try to influence government
7 an area of the country which elects a politician
8 to pass laws
9 formal request signed by lots of people
10 complaint about unfair treatment

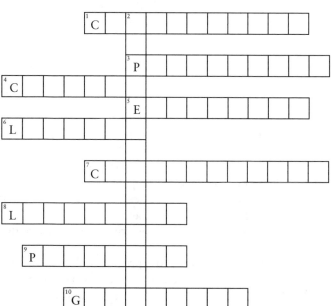

# 47 The language of law

**47.1**

10 marks

Match the verbs on the left with the nouns on the right to make ten expressions.

| | | |
|---|---|---|
| 1 | lodge | a precedent |
| 2 | quash | a treaty |
| 3 | contravene | an appeal |
| 4 | impeach | a marriage |
| 5 | abrogate | a law |
| 6 | overturn | custody |
| 7 | set | a conviction |
| 8 | infringe | a verdict |
| 9 | grant | a president |
| 10 | annul | on someone's rights |

**47.2**

10 marks

Use the verbs from the left-hand column in exercise 47.1 to complete these sentences. Write the verbs in the correct tense.

1 The State Legislature voted by a majority of fifty to ............................................ the governor.
2 The construction of the flats ............................................ the 1998 building regulations.
3 The harsh new laws ............................................ on people's basic human rights.
4 In this case, the father was ............................................ custody of the children.
5 This case has ............................................ a precedent for all such cases in the future.
6 The law was ............................................ in 1973 as it was outdated.
7 The defendant's lawyers decided to ............................................ an appeal against the conviction.
8 The verdict was ............................................ by the Supreme Court, which ruled it unconstitutional.
9 The agreement was ............................................ by the High Court, which found it contained flaws.
10 His conviction for murder was ............................................ by a panel of three appeal court judges.

**47.3**

12 marks

Rewrite these sentences by changing the word class of the underlined word as instructed. Make any other necessary changes.

*Example:* I think it is wrong to <u>discriminate</u> against women. (change to noun)
         I think *discrimination against women is wrong.*

1 The President was <u>impeached</u> in 1993. (change to noun)
2 There are <u>statutory</u> laws which protect children's rights. (change to noun)
3 That human rights are <u>infringed</u> is unacceptable in a civilised society. (change to noun)
4 Ms Carter said she had been sexually <u>harassed</u> at work. (change to noun)
5 The court ruled that Jones was guilty of a <u>perversion</u> of the course of justice. (change to verb)
6 The company was found guilty of <u>embezzlement</u> of large sums of money. (change to verb)

**47.4**

8 marks

Answer these questions. You are given some letters.

1 What verb apart from *grant* goes with *custody* and has the same meaning? a............................
2 What is the opposite of 'to *overturn* a verdict'? u............................ a verdict
3 Complete these expressions meaning 'buying or selling shares illegally based on specialist knowledge of a company'. i............................ trading/dealing
4 What verb is used with *rules* to mean 'break them in a way which is not harmful'? b............................ the rules
5 What do we call the crime where people drive around for enjoyment in stolen cars? j............................
6 If you walk across private land, you may be guilty of t............................ .
7 If you lie when you are under oath, what crime are you guilty of? p............................
8 What is the name of the crime where money is moved illegally to disguise its origins? m............................ l............................

Your score

/ 40

# War and peace

## 48.1
10 marks

Rewrite the underlined parts of these sentences using expressions based on the word in brackets.

1  The government is trying <u>to overcome</u> drug trafficking in this country.  (WAR)
2  It's regrettable if politicians resort to warfare <u>to achieve what they want</u>.  (ENDS)
3  If only we could <u>make war illegal</u>.  (OUTLAW)
4  The guerrillas threw <u>a fire bomb</u> at the building.  (DEVICE)
5  Why not <u>call everyone together</u> and explain the situation to them?  (RALLY)
6  A nuclear war could result in <u>all mankind being killed</u>.  (ANNIHILATION)
7  <u>Using germs to cause disease among the enemy</u> is internationally banned.  (BIOLOGICAL)
8  England <u>was heavily beaten</u> by Australia in the final match.  (ROUTED)
9  Hostilities often <u>begin</u> for some petty reason.  (BREAK)
10  There are international troops there <u>to help keep the peace</u>.  (PEACEKEEPING)

## 48.2
10 marks

Explain the difference between these expressions.

1  *a truce* and *a ceasefire*          4  *to break out* and *to cease*
2  *a siege* and *an ambush*           5  *to place an incendiary device* and *to set off an incendiary*
3  *hostilities* and *warfare*              *device*

## 48.3
10 marks

Complete these sentences using a word based on the root in brackets.

1  Some people argue that possessing weapons of mass destruction may act as a
   ............................................ .  (DETER)
2  We all experienced feelings of ............................................ against the atrocities committed in the war.
   (REVOLT)
3  During the war the city was ............................................ for over two years.  (SIEGE)
4  Greg and his three old friends formed the ............................................ of the new theatre company.
   (NUCLEAR)
5  Two ............................................ tribes have been fighting for control of the area for years.  (WAR)
6  The new law ............................................ the police to arrest suspected terrorists.  (POWER)
7  No one has really proved whether there is a ............................................ relationship between
   watching violent films and behaving in a violent manner.  (CAUSE)
8  The museum is devoted to the history of ............................................ from Roman times to the present
   day.  (WAR) (2 answers)
9  Military ............................................ are understood to have begun in the area last night.  (OPERATE)

## 48.4
10 marks

Which word can fill the gaps in both phrases?

1  to ............................................ with anger; bombs ............................................
2  the ............................................ of war; an ............................................ of flu.
3  to visit a holiday ............................................ ; the last ............................................
4  to ............................................ a campaign; to ............................................ a ship
5  ............................................ warfare; a TV ............................................ on the roof
6  the great ............................................ ; to have supernatural ............................................
7  to give money to a good ............................................ ; to ............................................ a war
8  the ............................................ to an end; a ............................................ of transport
9  to ............................................ a bomb; to ............................................ on a trip
10  to ............................................ war; to earn the minimum ............................................

# 49 Economy and finance

**49.1** Fill the gaps in these extracts from the financial pages of a newspaper, using the clues 1–10.

**10 marks**

The Minister announced new development g...............¹ totalling 250 million pounds for Africa. She also stressed the need to reduce the debt b...............² for the poorest countries. Sanitation and other health-related p...............³ were to be given the highest priority.

In his speech, Mr Luziano pointed to the need for s...............⁴ development in poorer countries. Poverty could only be a...............⁵ if there was genuine, l...............⁶ development, not just short-term measures.

¹ money given
² heavy weight someone has to carry
³ schemes, plans

⁴ which does not destroy the economy or environment
⁵ made less oppressive
⁶ which continues for a long time

Prime Minister Dowaka said there were e...............⁷ signs that the country was r...............⁸ from the d...............⁹ in its exports, and that he was optimistic that the Republic would a...............¹⁰ positive economic growth over the next five years.

⁷ positive, giving reasons for optimism
⁸ improving after a negative state of affairs
⁹ drop, fall
¹⁰ reach, accomplish

**49.2** Complete these pairs of sentences using the same word.

**8 marks**

1 a) Free ............................................ often only benefits large, powerful countries.
   b) ............................................ wars may happen if countries try to protect their internal markets.
2 a) Millions of human beings live in abject ............................................ .
   b) As countries emerge from crippling ............................................ , they have new challenges to face.
3 a) Poor countries often incur ............................................ which they can never hope to eradicate.
   b) Repaying international ............................................ is a huge problem for many poor countries.
4 a) The embargo was ............................................ in 1995, and continues to the present day.
   b) The United Nations ............................................ economic sanctions on the country in 1998.

**49.3** Rewrite the underlined parts of these sentences so that they have the same meaning. Use expressions based on the words in brackets and make any other necessary changes.

**16 marks**

1 Many countries <u>which have debts</u> are trapped in an impossible situation. (DEBTOR)
2 <u>Uniting the currency and financial systems</u> is a controversial issue in the EU. (UNION/MONEY)
3 <u>The placing of unfair restrictions</u> has a negative impact on poorer countries. (PRACTICES)
4 The economies of countries <u>that have suffered from wars</u> take years to recover. (TEAR/WAR)
5 The currency was <u>lowered</u> last week; before, one Fadal was worth 50 US cents, now it is worth only 35. (VALUED)
6 A recession lasting three years <u>has now ended</u> for the Kingdom of Gwatana. (EMERGE)
7 A recession <u>has begun in</u> the Lubanian economy. (GO INTO)
8 <u>There are no longer</u> trade sanctions on Pergania. (LIFT)

**49.4** Complete the missing words.

**6 marks**

1 The euro is Europe's si............... cu............... .
2 There was a sl............... in prices last year, but they have stabilised this year.
3 Fis............... measures are often needed to bring the economy back on course.
4 Taxes were lowered in an attempt to bo...............t the economy.
5 The Minister announced measures to rescue the ai............... economy.
6 The new lower tax rates will ea............... the tax burden for millions of workers.

# 50 Personal finance: balancing your books

## 50.1
**12 marks**

Answer these questions.

1 If a friend says 'I'm skint', how much money have they got?
2 If someone gives you a cheque which bounces, how do you feel?
3 What does the expiry date on a credit card indicate?
4 When you are writing a cheque and you are unsure whose name to put on the cheque as the payee, what do you ask?
5 If you read that credit card fraud is on the increase, how would you feel?
6 What kind of company might try to sell you health cover?

## 50.2
**8 marks**

Match the two halves of these compound nouns.

| | |
|---|---|
| 1 store | sum |
| 2 lump | portfolio |
| 3 golden | claim |
| 4 life | shark |
| 5 share | handshake |
| 6 loan | card |
| 7 pension | savings |
| 8 insurance | plan |

## 50.3
**8 marks**

Match the compound nouns from exercise 50.2 to their definitions below.

1 a large amount of money paid out at one time, e.g. to someone who is made redundant
2 a person who lends money to others at huge rates of interest
3 a piece of plastic that lets you buy goods on credit from one particular shop
4 a present or money paid by the company to a person who is leaving
5 a request for compensation made to an insurance company
6 all the money a person has managed to put aside over a long period
7 an arrangement to make regular payments so you have an income after your retirement
8 an individual set of investments

## 50.4
**12 marks**

Fill the gaps in these letters from the financial advice pages of a magazine. You are given the first letter of each word.

As a single parent, I'm finding it very hard to make (1) e............... meet and always seem to be (2) s............... for cash. I manage by (3) c............... everything to my credit card but money is always very (4) t............... at the end of the month. What advice can you give me?

An (5) e............... that I took out fifteen years ago has now matured and I now have a large (6) l............... s............... available to invest. Would you recommend turning to the stock market and expanding my (7) s............... p............... or would it be better to invest in property?

I thought my car was fully insured – I have always paid my p............... regularly – but now I want to make a (9) c............... , I'm told that I have to pay the first £250 and they will only pay anything in (10) e............... of that. Can this be correct?

**Your score**

/40

**51.1**
10 marks
Complete these sentences with words which refer to different parts of newspapers.
You are given the first letter.

1 I read Princess Magda's o............................ and it made me cry. She was a wonderful person.
2 The *Sunday Clarion* did an excellent f............................ on Ireland recently. Did you see it?
3 We've bought an old boat. We spotted it in the c............................ ads in our local paper.
4 The e............................ in the *Daily Times* today made me angry. It's such a reactionary paper.
5 Some of the letters in the a............................ column are unbelievable. People give the most intimate details of their lives.

**51.2**
6 marks
Answer these questions.

1 What adjective means 'published every three months'?
2 What word beginning with 'f' means 'an exact reproduction in every detail' of a book?
3 What do we call the narrow side of the cover of a book where the title is usually displayed?
4 What do we call an extra magazine which comes with, for example, a weekend newspaper?
5 Give at least one typical example of what a flyer can be used for.
6 What is the difference between a book and a booklet?

**51.3**
20 marks
Circle the correct underlined word.

1 The laptop computer prospectus/manual/pamphlet explained that you should charge the battery for 24 hours before using it.
2 We're thinking of a holiday in Portugal next year. We've got some pamphlets/prospectuses/brochures from the travel agent's.
3 There were people giving out leaflets/booklets/pamphlets advertising the free rock concert in the park.
4 I asked the university to send me a manual/leaflet/prospectus so that I could choose a course.
5 The Liberal MP Hilda Swaine has published a controversial brochure/pamphlet/manual on family morality.
6 Celebrities often do not write their autobiographies but have spirit/ghost/phantom writers to do it for them.
7 I could never imagine myself writing to a(n) misery/agony/anxiety aunt.
8 I took out a prescription/description/subscription to a computer magazine but I think I'll cancel it.
9 The coat/jacket/vest was a bit torn so the bookshop took a pound off the price of the book.
10 That website is very good if you want the updown/highdown/lowdown on the latest books and films.

**51.4**
4 marks
Use words from exercise 51.3 in their literal sense to complete these sentences.

1 They said the old house was haunted, but I don't believe in .................................... , so I wasn't afraid.
2 When I broke my ankle I was in .................................... for several hours until I got some painkillers from the hospital.
3 This .................................... and trousers look like a suit, but in fact the colours are slightly different.
4 It's a .................................... coffee grinder – you have to turn the handle. I used to have an electric one, but it broke.

**52.1**

10 marks

**Are these statements true or false? If they are false, correct them.**

1  If you want to undelete something, you have got rid of something by mistake.
2  When you buy some new software, you first have to uninstall it.
3  If you upload data, you want to take it from a website to your own computer.
4  Bookmarking favourite web pages helps you to find them again more easily.
5  If you want to get a long document to someone electronically, you can send them an e-mail with an attachment.
6  If you visit a chat room, you can see the people you meet there.
7  If you are working offline, you are connected to the Internet.
8  If you update some software, you get a more recent version of some software that you already have.
9  If you change your ISP, you buy a new computer.
10  If you screen out spam, you use a special filter program that stops you receiving so many junk e-mails.

**52.2**

16 marks

**Write the jumbled words in these sentences in the correct order.**

1  Could you resend me that attachment – when I opened it, it was just a EDBLARG ............................................. set of weird symbols.
2  My son and his schoolfriends have really got into ANNTIST SMEAGISGN ...................................
..................................... and spend ages at the computer every evening.
3  There are lots of interesting groups you can join on the Internet. I've BEBRISCUDS
............................................. to a really useful ORGUSPWEN ......................................... for students of English.
Do you want the url?
4  I'd really recommend this program if you want to work with CARPIGH SMEAGI ...................................
..................................... . It's great for handling any kind of visual material.
5  Ken spends ages GWOBNSIR ......................................... the Web every night.

**52.3**

14 marks

**Cross out the seven vocabulary mistakes in this e-mail and write the correct word above each mistake.**

Someone packed into our computer at work yesterday and managed to disrupt the whole

system. We thought the ante-virus software would have prevented this from happening but it

didn't. When we logged on to our e-mail this morning we were all bombarded with ham and

had to spend ages deleting a lot of offensive and unwanted messages. Moreover, a lot of the

messages we had sent jumped back to us, which was extremely annoying. They called

someone in to sort it out but that meant the system was up for ages and we couldn't get any

work done. I was supposed to be swimming the Web all day to get information for a report

I'm writing on trends in e-commercial and what's happening these days to dotcoms. I couldn't

do it of course so I'm going to have to go in and do some work at the weekend, I'm afraid.

Your score

/40

# 53 Advertising

**53.1** **Answer these questions.**

10 marks

1 If product X leaves product Y standing, does it (a) collapse because Y is better, or (b) do what it is designed for much better than Y?
2 What is the adjective form of the noun innovation?
3 If a product is unsurpassed, is it (a) better than all its rivals, or (b) unapproved or uncertified by the authorities?
4 If product X puts product Y in the shade, does it (a) sell more than Y, or (b) make Y seem insignificant?
5 What are 'sizzling summer sales' and 'crazy cash competition' examples of?

**53.2** **Complete the missing words in these sentences. You are given some letters to help you.**

8 marks

1 Some of the new dresses were very eye-c..................... .
2 They were advertising digital cameras at r.....................-bottom prices so we bought one.
3 Every evening the hotel had a most sum..................... buffet with all kinds of wonderful food.
4 It's a five-star hotel with the most op..................... décor you can imagine.
5 This medicine is pro.....................n to be 100% effective in most cases.
6 My computer was s.....................-of-the-a..................... just a year ago. Now it seems ancient.
7 The documentary gave a tanta..................... glimpse of the life of a sports megastar.
8 Would you like to have a smooth, all..................... complexion? *Novana* cream is the answer.

**53.3** **Decide which word is the odd one out and explain your answer.**

12 marks

1 bargain   discount   appeal
2 pamper   fetch   indulge
3 billboard   sandwich board   whiteboard
4 fetching   grasping   alluring
5 discount   trailer   sky-writing
6 plug   advertise   prove

**53.4** **Read these people's comments about six different shops then answer the questions below.**

5 marks

MIRIAM:   There were bargains galore in the sale at Gifford's.
HARRY:   I think Doran's leaves other stores in the shade.
MONA:   Lapford's have got furniture fit for a king.
JOSH:   Everyone likes to pamper themselves occasionally; you can do that at Kaplan's.
LEAH:   They've slashed the prices of carpets at Threadgold's.

| | | |
|---|---|---|
| 1 | Which store sells extremely good quality items? | |
| 2 | Where would you find lots of things to buy at very good prices? | |
| 3 | Which shop is much better than its competitors? | |
| 4 | Which store has drastically reduced prices? | |
| 5 | Where could you give yourself a special treat now and then? | |

**53.5** **Rewrite the underlined parts of these sentences using the correct forms of the words in brackets.**

5 marks

1 Zapemall makes other weedkillers look inferior. (LEAVE/STANDING)
2 The hotel was fabulous – we were living in a luxurious situation for two weeks. (LAP/LUXURY OF)
3 She gave several TV and radio interviews to get publicity for her new novel. (PLUG)
4 With Ekta sunglasses you'll really be noticed among all the other people. (STAND OUT/CROWD)
5 I think these shoes are really excellent value at 35 euros. (OUTSTAND)

Your score

/40

# 54 The news: gathering and delivering

**54.1**
10 marks

Complete these sentences.

1 The famous couple have issued a press ........................................... explaining why the wedding is off.
2 The story is hot off the ........................................... .
3 Of all the newspapers, *The Guardian* devoted most column ........................................... to the story.
4 If you order a back ........................................... of the April 2003 issue of the magazine, you'll have a complete set.
5 The Prime Minister is very good at producing a sound ........................................... for any occasion.
6 The President was abroad when the story about him hit the newspaper ........................................... .
7 The football match was delayed by a couple of hours so the results only made it to the ........................................... press column.
8 The Minister is going to sue the paper for defamation of ........................................... .
9 The gutter ........................................... goes in for a lot of ...........................................-raking in its quest for stories about celebrities and royalty.

**54.2**
10 marks

Find the words which match the definitions. You are given the first letters to help you.

1 an expensive magazine printed on shiny good-quality paper:  a g...........................
2 the crime of publishing an untrue negative story about someone:  l...........................
3 the time by which material to be published has to be ready:  the d...........................
4 a special story which only one newspaper manages to publish:  an e...........................
5 material produced by journalists or advertisers for publication:  c...........................
6 a colloquial and negative word for a tabloid newspaper:  a r...........................
7 an old issue of a magazine or newspaper:  a b................... c...........................
8 people who work together to try to influence the government:  a p................... g...................
9 a brief memorable extract from a politician's statement quoted on TV or radio:  a s................... b...................
10 a different expression for the crime in item 2:  d........................... o............. c...........................

**54.3**
10 marks

Circle the correct underlined word.

1 The Prime Minister will be <u>doing/making/having</u> a statement later today.
2 Politicians love to get the chance to <u>issue/provide/air</u> their views in public.
3 All newspapers <u>put/take/give</u> their own spin on a story.
4 Journalists have to <u>observe/notice/monitor</u> news agencies for interesting stories for their papers.
5 The <u>silly/stupid/foolish</u> season is the time of year when politicians and other public figures are on holiday and there tends to be little serious news for newspapers to write about.

**54.4**
10 marks

Match the beginnings of the sentences with their endings.

1 A press conference was held at      a lot of coverage.
2 Inevitably the story received      gloss on events.
3 The newspaper has to go to      that you could tap for your story.
4 The actor collected all the press      the end of the summit meeting.
5 All politicians want to put their      when the story broke.
6 The Managing Director will issue      press by 9 p.m.
7 I know some useful sources      publicity for its fund-raising events.
8 The actor was out of the country      public knowledge soon.
9 The charity is seeking      cuttings where he was mentioned.
10 I think the scandal will become      a statement this afternoon.

Your score

/40

# 55 Health and illness I

**55.1**

10 marks

**Read these comments, then answer questions 1–10 below.**

JIM: I've been feeling a little unwell these last few days.

SUE: I can't get an appointment at my national health dentist so I think I'll go to one where I can pay for it myself.

ROB: I'm struggling against a cold at the moment. I've been taking hot lemon drinks.

ANNE: I was quite ill last week, but I have come through the most serious phase now.

JASON: I became ill with a cold a couple of weeks ago.

MIKE: I get colds now and then, but I usually recover from them quickly.

JACKIE: I was in hospital but I'm fully active again now.

SARAH: I was sick for a couple of weeks, but I'm gradually recovering now.

DANNY: I think I'm beginning to suffer from a cold! I'd better take some medicine.

ROSE: I find it hard to sit for a long time with the pain. I have to get up and walk around.

1 Who usually gets over things quite easily? ............................

2 Who's on the mend? ............................

3 Who's been feeling poorly? ............................

4 Who's trying to fight something off? ............................

5 Who is over the worst? ............................

6 Who went down with a minor illness a few weeks ago? ............................

7 Who's suffering from backache? ............................

8 Who is back on her feet again? ............................

9 Who's thinking of going private? ............................

10 Who's coming down with something? ............................

**55.2**

6 marks

**What do these initials mean?**

1 NHS    2 GP    3 TB

**55.3**

6 marks

**Complete each sentence with three different words. You are given the first letters.**

       (a) d............................

1 Heart (b) a............................ is/are a very common cause of death in western societies.

       (c) f............................

       (a) l............................

2 She is suffering from (b) b............................ cancer.

       (c) s............................

**55.4**

6 marks

**Match the illnesses on the left with their definitions on the right.**

1 hepatitis — inflammation of the breathing system; causes coughing

2 tuberculosis — intestinal disease; can be caused by bad drinking water

3 typhoid — inflammation of the liver

4 bronchitis — the body does not properly absorb sugar and starch

5 diabetes — highly infectious disease in the lungs

6 cholera — fever, with red spots on the chest and abdomen

**55.5**

12 marks

**Match the words in the box to make six expressions.**

| doctor | prescription | sore | blood | insurance | fever |
| throat | charge | family | national | transfusion | hay |

Your score

/ 40

# Health and illness 2

**56.1**
**10 marks**
Complete what the person on the left says about their symptoms. Then match the symptoms with an appropriate response on the right.

1  I feel a bit f............................ .            You should lie down in a darkened room.
2  My head is t............................ .             Take these travel sickness pills.
3  I'm a............................ to nuts.            Take an aspirin to reduce your temperature.
4  I feel n............................ in a car.        Try inhaling steam.
5  My nose is b............................ up.          Don't eat that cake then.

**56.2**
**20 marks**
Make ten expressions by matching words from box A with words from box B. Then write an appropriate definition for each expression.

A:
| aches and | donate | contact |
| cuts and | herbal | off- |
| out of | sick | stiff |
| under the | | |

B:
| lenses | medicine | colour |
| sorts | weather | note |
| blood | bruises | pains |
| neck | | |

**56.3**
**10 marks**
Complete the word puzzle.

Clues
1  set of medicine used to treat an illness
2  using perfumed oils to help with medical or other physical problems
3  the medical problems that indicate an illness, e.g. high temperature, cough, rash
4  injection that prevents you from getting a specific disease
5  what a bee or wasp may do to you
6  shake, usually because of nervousness or fear
7  the paper the doctor gives you so you can get medicine from the chemist's
8  the amount of medicine that you need to take
9  traditional Chinese form of medicine using needles
10  how you feel when your head spins

**Your score**
/40

# 57 Health and illness 3

**57.1** Rewrite these sentences using the word in brackets.

10 marks

1 Her pregnancy began five months ago. (PREGNANT)
2 Babies who experience breastfeeding have more immunity to certain diseases. (BREASTFED)
3 I was feeling extremely dehydrated. (DEHYDRATION)
4 This is symptomatic of a deeper problem. (SYMPTOM)
5 The doctor's diagnosis was bronchitis. (DIAGNOSED)

**57.2** Fill the gaps in these newspaper extracts with health-related words. You are given the first letters.

6 marks

1

### NEW HEART DRUG UNVEILED

A new drug, said to be 95% effective in preventing blood c........................ and with no visible s........................ e........................ has been developed by Danish scientists.

2

### ECONOMIC FORECAST GOOD

The Minister said the p........................ for the next five years was very positive, with growth expected in all sectors.

3

### FOOTBALL FRENZY GROWS

Excitement over the forthcoming world cup has reached f........................ p........................ , with TV channels offering 24-hour coverage.

**57.3** Complete these pairs of sentences using the same word.

20 marks

1 a) My skin is very s........................ to the sun.
  b) A good teacher is always s........................ to the needs of her students.
2 a) I had a r........................ on my arm where I'd brushed against a prickly plant.
  b) There has been a r........................ of news stories about football violence lately.
3 a) These inner city estates, s........................ by crime and violence, offer little hope.
  b) His face was horribly s........................ after the terrible accident.
4 a) You have all the s........................ of flu: headache, high temperature, aching limbs.
  b) We have seen the first s........................ of economic recession in the last six months.
5 a) His face had taken on a yellowish, j........................ hue.
  b) Why do you always take such a j........................ view of everything? You're so negative.
6 a) The disease has no cure and is f........................ in most cases.
  b) I made the f........................ mistake of not saving my work before the computer crashed.
7 a) He became p........................ from the waist down after a road accident.
  b) The economy was p........................ by the years of civil war. Now it can grow again.
8 a) He visited his a........................ mother, who was being looked after by a private nurse.
  b) The World Bank lent the country 10 billion dollars to boost the a........................ economy.
9 a) Health workers have to protect themselves from c........................ diseases.
  b) He has a c........................ laugh; when he starts laughing everyone starts laughing.
10 a) She is ill, but the p........................ is good, and she should get better in the next few weeks.
   b) The Minister said the p........................ was good, and that the economy would grow.

**57.4** Answer these questions.

4 marks

1 Give three words meaning 'solid human waste': give (a) a formal word often used by doctors, (b) a general formal word and (c) a word often used when talking to children.
2 What do you call a painful, infected area which you can get in your mouth or stomach?

**Your score**

/40

# 58  Diet, sport and fitness

**58.1**

10 marks

**Answer these questions.**

1 Would you feel proud or embarrassed if you scored an own goal?
2 If you sail through an interview, does the interview go well or badly?
3 If you are in the running for a promotion, what may happen?
4 If someone moves the goalposts, do you feel pleased or annoyed?
5 If a politician skates around a subject, what are they trying to do?
6 If Rob and Jimmy are neck and neck in a race, who is winning?
7 What sport does the idiom 'neck and neck' come from?
8 What kind of playing field is an expression used to mean a fair situation?
9 If you do cardiovascular exercise, what will you be benefitting?
10 What verb most frequently goes with *calories* meaning to use them up?

**58.2**

20 marks

**Find the words that match the definitions 1–10. You are given some clues in the box.**

```
p _ _ _ e      g _ _      m _ _ d e _ _ _ _ _ _ r
o _ _ _ l      gl u c o se      i _ _ _ _ n      p _ _ _ d
f _ _ e      d _ _ _ _ _ c      c _ _ _ _ _ _ _ _ l
e _ _ _ _ e
```

*Example:* another word for sugar – *glucose*

1 internal organs of animals that can be eaten as food (heart, kidneys, liver, etc.)
2 a person whose body does not produce enough insulin
3 an unwanted substance on the surface of teeth or arteries
4 substance in food that travels through the body as waste and improves digestion
5 a more colloquial word for intestine
6 fatty substance that can cause problems if there is too much of it in our arteries
7 medical term meaning to get rid of waste from the body
8 a drug that improves your mood, makes you more cheerful
9 a British measurement of weight equal to 0.454 kilos
10 hormone controlling the level of sugar in the body

**58.3**

10 marks

**Which one word can fill each of the gaps in these sets? Explain the connection between the different uses of the word.**

1 blood ............................ ; to go out in a fishing ............................; an earthenware ............................
2 to ............................ to Hinduism; to ............................ from pounds to kilos; to ............................ a loft
3 to suffer from postnatal ............................ ; a ............................ over the Atlantic; a severe economic ............................
4 religious ............................ ; my ............................ of heat is not very high; ............................ to medical drugs
5 ............................ to disease; to take the line of least ............................ ; wind ............................

**59.1** Write the jumbled words in these sentences in the correct order.

10 marks

1 OLW-EHTC ............................. industries are more suitable for countries with a large pool of unskilled labour.
2 In Britain, the railways receive massive BIDSISUES ........................... from the government.
3 NIVATRISIATOP ........................... of state-owned industries has taken place in many countries in the last decade.
4 Foreign corporations were given TEWSEREENS ........................... to persuade them to build factories in the poor regions of the north.
5 RECSIVE ........................... industries such as tourism have become the mainstay of many European economies.
6 Most of the workers are on WIPEKEORC ........................... ; they get paid only for what they produce.
7 The government launched a campaign to encourage WINDAR ........................... investment.
8 The company decided to TRELEOCA ........................... to another country in order to boost profitability.
9 SRELKILING ........................... is crucial in modern economies where the workforce has out-of-date skills.
10 NINFAMUACTRUG ........................... industry has suffered badly during the recession.

**59.2** Match the words on the left with their collocations on the right.

10 marks

| | | |
|---|---|---|
| 1 | heavy | laws |
| 2 | public- | cutting |
| 3 | industrial | labour |
| 4 | money | representation |
| 5 | infringe | tape |
| 6 | child | duck |
| 7 | red | industry |
| 8 | cost- | private |
| 9 | union | espionage |
| 10 | lame | laundering |

**59.3** Now use the collocations from exercise 59.2 to fill the gaps in these sentences.

20 marks

1 ........................... industries are left to decline and die in the capitalist system.
2 The United Nations held a conference to tackle the problem of ........................... and other forms of industrial exploitation.
3 A squad of detectives was set up to investigate ........................... by drug cartels.
4 The government has promised to reduce ........................... to enable companies to implement their plans more quickly.
5 The decline in ........................... is best exemplified by the closure of the shipyards in the major ports.
6 Many employers are unwilling to allow ........................... on company boards.
7 The government believes in ...........................-........................... partnerships as a way of expanding public services.
8 They were guilty of ........................... the copyright ........................... by publishing the article without the author's permission.
9 There was a serious case of ........................... when one company stole designs from another company in 1998.
10 ...........................-........................... measures were put in place to try to save the firm from bankruptcy.

# Technology and its impact

**60.1**

20 marks

Circle the correct underlined word.

1 A portable computer can be called a <u>handtop/laptop/tabletop</u>.
2 A mobile phone that allows you to use it while you are driving is called a <u>handless/ handy/hands-free</u> phone.
3 Hospital doctors usually carry a <u>caller/ringer/pager</u> so that they can easily be contacted when they are needed.
4 A rather negative word for someone who is very interested in computers is a <u>technique/ nerd/weird</u>.
5 A rather positive word for someone who is knowledgeable about computers is a <u>technique/technical/techie</u>.
6 Some modern portable computers allow users to move the cursor by using a <u>trackpad/ touchpad/rollpad</u>.
7 PDA stands for <u>private/personal/palmtop</u> digital assistant.
8 Digital technology is more advanced than <u>analogue/analytical/analogous</u> technology.
9 A very small pocket computer can be called a <u>fingertop/palmtop/handtop</u>.
10 The little pictures on your computer screen that you can click on are called <u>icons/ symbols/pictograms</u>.

**60.2**

15 marks

Complete the words in these sentences. You are given the first letters.

1 E............................ is the study of human environments in order to improve effectiveness and design things in a more efficient way.
2 Scientists working in A............................ I............................ would like to create computers that behave like humans.
3 The G............................ P............................ S............................ in modern cars helps drivers to navigate.
4 B............................ are scientists who work on things like producing disease-resistant crops.
5 In a modern workplace workers may have to use a s............................ card to get in and out of the building.
6 If you are a photographer, one advantage of a d............................ c............................ is that you don't need to keep buying film.
7 A s............................ is useful because it helps to protect your computer screen when you are not working.
8 One advantage of having a hands-free e............................ and m............................ for your mobile phone is that you can talk on the phone while you're driving.
9 S............................ communications depend on transmitters sent up into space to orbit the earth and organise communications.
10 Click on the th............................ of the picture to see the image in full size.

**60.3**

5 marks

What is each of these things called?

**Your score**

/40

# 61 Future visions

**61.1**

10 marks

**Complete the words in these sentences.**

1 One day int_ _ _ _ _ _ _ _ _ry travel will be possible and we'll go for holidays on Mars.
2 It was a v_ _ _ _l reality program where you could train as an airline pilot. It was so realistic I forgot it was just a computer program.
3 With in_ _r_ _ _ve TV you can sit at home and press the remote control to vote, answer quizzes, buy things, and so on.
4 Nowadays more and more people buy things on the Internet. E-c_ _ _ _ _c_ has really become popular.
5 Our office is in a s_ _ _t building: the lights and heating come on automatically when someone enters a room and go off when they leave.

**61.2**

12 marks

**Complete these sentences with appropriate expressions. You are given some letters.**

1 The complete description of the hu........................... ge........................... is one of the greatest scientific developments ever. It could be of enormous value to medical science.
2 Robert Tyler's book *The Last Humans* portrays a do........................... sc........................... of a violent, polluted, decadent society in the future.
3 Every student is to be issued with a sm........................... c........................... which will record their ID and their registration details. It can also be used to make purchases in campus shops.
4 Consumers may have to accept ge........................... mo........................... fruit and vegetables because farmers will want to grow them to get increased crops, even though the risks are unknown.
5 The nu........................... f........................... , with mother, father and two children, may no longer be the core social unit in the 21st century.
6 In the future, in big cities, traffic will be gr........................... most of the time, and travelling to work may take hours.

**61.3**

8 marks

**Complete the table. Do not write in the shaded boxes.**

| noun | verb | adjective |
|------|------|-----------|
| globe | | |
| | | genetic |
| modification | | |
| | | wide |
| | | therapeutic |
| designer | | designer |

**61.4**

10 marks

**Use words from the table in exercise 61.3 to fill the gaps in these sentences.**

1 The gulf between rich and poor continues to ........................... , despite efforts to close it.
2 It may be possible for parents to have ........................... babies within a decade or so.
3 ........................... communications via the Internet have revolutionised international commerce.
4 Scientists have genetically ........................... this crop to make it disease resistant.
5 Attempts to ........................... industry and commerce have met with huge protests and demonstrations across the world.

Your score

/40

# Space: expanse and confinement

**62.1**

10 marks

Circle the correct underlined word. Then explain why you rejected the other word.

*Example*: Our new car is nice and (roomy)/rambling.
*Rambling is normally used about a building or a village, e.g. a rambling farmhouse.*

1  Jo suffers from claustrophobia/agoraphobia and hardly ever goes out of the house.
2  The roads were cramped/congested with holidaymakers heading for the beaches.
3  I bought this printer because it is compact/poky and doesn't take up much room on my desk.
4  Extensive/excessive drinking can cause health problems.
5  Little white clouds were scattered/crammed across the sky.

**62.2**

10 marks

Divide these words into two groups: those which have negative associations and those which have positive associations.

bustling    poky    roomy    extensive    spacious
incarcerated    compact    rambling    congested    cramped

**62.3**

10 marks

Fill the gaps in these sentences. You are given the first letter.

1  During the rush hour on the London Underground everyone is packed in like s........................ .
2  She s........................ some clothes into a bag and rushed to the airport.
3  Sanjeev's been i........................ in his room all day preparing for his test tomorrow.
4  Maria's room in the student accommodation is very p........................ but she may be able to move into a more spacious one next year.
5  The shanty town s........................ out for miles to the west of the city.
6  When Oleg came to England from rural Russia, he missed the w........................ open spaces of his homeland.
7  The town is usually b........................ with activity on market day.
8  When we were first married we lived in a rather dark, c........................ flat, so I love having more space now.
9  If everyone moves up a bit along the bench, then I can s........................ in next to you.
10  There isn't enough room to s........................ a cat in Nina's study.

**62.4**

10 marks

Complete the table. Do not write in the shaded boxes.

| noun | adjective | verb |
|---|---|---|
|  | congested |  |
|  | cramped |  |
|  | spacious |  |
|  | extensive |  |
| claustrophobia |  |  |
|  | wide |  |

# 63 Time: sequence and duration

**63.1** Fill in the missing words in these informal time expressions. The meanings are given in brackets.

10 marks
1 for d.....................'s years (for many years)
2 at a rate of k........................ (very fast)
3 once in a b........................ m........................ (very rarely)
4 since the y........................ d........................ (since a very long time ago)
5 till the c........................ come h........................ (forever)
6 in l........................ than no t........................ (very soon/quickly)

**63.2** Use the expressions in exercise 63.1 to complete these conversations. Use each expression once.

6 marks
1 JEFF: How often do you see your cousins?
   ROGER: Oh, hardly ever. It's really only ........................................ .
2 CARRIE: When was the last time you saw Ulla?
   SUE: Ulla? Oh, gosh, ages and ages! I haven't seen her ........................................ .
3 WINNIE: Has Dan worked at Briscoe's for a long time?
   PAUL: Oh yes! He's been working there ........................................ .
4 TIM: Barry left rather suddenly, didn't he?
   IAN: Yes, I don't know what the problem was, but he drove away
   ........................................ .
5 RON: Wow! You got all those leaflets printed so fast!
   GEMMA: Yes, they're an excellent firm. They did it all ........................................ .
6 DORIS: Do you think I should go on trying to persuade Joe to stop smoking?
   TONY: Well, you can try ........................................ , but I don't think you'll succeed.

**63.3** Rewrite these sentences using expressions based on the words in brackets.

12 marks
1 I'm on the phone at the moment. I'll be with you soon. (SEC)
2 Just because I'm in my 50s, it doesn't mean I'm too old. (HILL)
3 Mary Swann spent her entire life in the tiny village of Hickenbower. (DAYS/BORN)
4 He was a famous rock star in the 1980s, but now he's just not famous any more. (BEEN)
5 I will keep protesting forever. I will never give up. (HELL/FREEZE)
6 I managed to contact him just before it was too late. (NICK)

**63.4** Match the words from box A with words from box B to make six expressions.

6 marks

A: 
| fleeting | pristine | inexorable | protracted | persistent | transient |

B:
| negotiations | cough | decline | glimpse | population | environment |

**63.5** Answer these questions.

6 marks
1 Complete these two expressions meaning 'very soon': (a) in a t........................k
   (b) in a j........................y.
2 Complete this synonym for the expression 'for donkey's years': for y........................ .
3 Give another way of saying the second half of this sentence: 'You can have this CD *and keep it forever*.'
4 Complete this expression meaning 'very quickly': in a f........................ .
5 Complete this sentence with a rather formal adjective meaning 'just beginning': He sensed signs of i........................ anger among the protesters.
6 Complete this expression with an adjective meaning 'taking a long time to disappear': a li........................ perfume.

Your score
/40

# Motion: nuances of pace and movement

**64.1**

20 marks

Explain what the underlined words suggest in these sentences.

*Example:* When the doors opened, people <u>poured</u> into the hall.

*Poured suggests that the people moved quickly and in large numbers.*

1 We had a wonderful time <u>meandering</u> through the old town.
2 Bill <u>staggered</u> across the room and fell at Ginny's feet.
3 The children <u>chased</u> each other round the garden.
4 People are beginning to <u>trickle</u> into the theatre.
5 Sadie <u>sidled</u> up to me at the party.
6 Mickey <u>trampled</u> on his sister's toys.
7 Patrick did <u>staggeringly</u> well in his oral exams.
8 During the Industrial Revolution people <u>flooded</u> into the towns from the countryside.
9 Suzie <u>strode</u> into the shop and asked to see the manager.
10 At the interval everyone <u>spilled</u> into the bar for drinks.

**64.2**

10 marks

Match the best verb of motion from the box for each of these people.

| ambles | glides | hobbles | limps | lurches |
|--------|--------|---------|-------|---------|
| stamps | struts | stumbles | tiptoes | trudges |

1 a proud person
2 someone with one shorter leg
3 someone anxious not to be heard
4 a drunk
5 a very tired person
6 someone who nearly falls
7 a very elegant person
8 a slow, relaxed person
9 someone with aching feet
10 an angry person

**64.3**

6 marks

Write the jumbled letters in the correct order to find the words which collocate with step or steps.

1 Moving back home to live with his parents after working abroad for three years felt like a DAWBCARK ............................................. step to Jake.
2 Walking on the moon for the first time was said to be a TAGIN ............................................. step for mankind.
3 George took the, for him, DECENTURPEDEN ............................................. step of being the first to apologise.
4 With today's elections the new republic took its STRIF ............................................. steps towards democracy today.
5 Paul would never have become a star had he not taken the ASINFICTING ............................................. step of moving to New York.
6 Resigning from his job was a SIEVEDIC ............................................. step for Tim, but it was the right thing to do.

**64.4**

4 marks

Circle the correct underlined word.

1 The mourners <u>sauntered/filed/stamped</u> past the coffin.
2 The protesters <u>milled/ambled/streamed</u> through the city on their way to the parliament building.
3 Traffic has been <u>flowing/pouring/spilling</u> steadily all day.
4 Journalists were <u>sauntering/milling/trudging</u> around the hotel, waiting to interview the star.

**Manner: behaviour and body language**

**65.1**

10 marks

Cross out ten more spelling or vocabulary mistakes in this text and write the correct word above each mistake.

*etiquette*

Years ago, social ~~etickett~~ was more important than now. Men had to be gentlemannish and ladies had to be ladyish. Nowadays people do not stand at ceremony so much and cortesie is not so important. Minding your Qs and Ps is a thing of the past and people are more onhand with one another. I think young people no longer respect their betters and olders or observe the social grace, and don't care whether something is the doable thing or not. People might call me tight-laced, but I think good manners are important.

**65.2**

8 marks

Rewrite these sentences using the words in brackets. Change the form of the words if necessary.

1 I wish you'd get rid of that self-satisfied smile! (SMIRK)
2 Her remarks shocked a lot of people. (EYEBROWS)
3 I couldn't sit still with embarrassment. (SQUIRM)
4 He was constantly making small, nervous movements. (TWITCH)
5 He made a sudden movement as the doctor stuck the needle in his arm. (FLINCH)
6 The audience gave an embarrassed laugh when the actor forgot his lines. (TITTER)
7 He just disapproved of the idea and told us not to be so naïve. (SNIFF)
8 She gave a broad smile when we told her the good news. (BEAM)

**65.3**

16 marks

Write these 16 words in the correct columns in the table below.

| | | | | | |
|---|---|---|---|---|---|
| gawp | frown | whimper | scowl | glare | ogle |
| giggle | chortle | leer | grizzle | snigger | glower |
| sob | guffaw | scan | sniffle | | |

| 'crying' words | 'angry' words | 'laughing' words | 'looking' words |
|---|---|---|---|
| | | | |
| | | | |
| | | | |
| | | | |
| | | | |

**65.4**

6 marks

Circle the correct underlined word.

1 Laura and Joe couldn't stop guffawing/giggling/chortling during the lecture, and hoped no one could hear them.
2 Kevin longed for a girlfriend, and always stood glaring/glowering/leering at the pretty girls as they left work, but most of them found it embarrassing.
3 Mr Thumbow greeted the news with a loud titter/guffaw/snigger which echoed round the room.
4 Anne grizzled/whimpered/sobbed her heart out when her beloved old dog died.
5 Professor Borum glared/leered/ogled angrily at the two students and accused them of cheating in the exam.
6 Rebecca glowered/scanned/frowned as she tried to make sense of her bank statement.

Your score

/40

# Sound: from noise to silence

**66.1** Fill the gaps in these sentences. You are given the first letter.

10 marks

1  We love living in the country; it's so much q............................ than in a town, particularly at night.
2  It was so quiet in the classroom that you could have heard a p............................ drop.
3  The children were as quiet as m............................ all through the lesson.
4  There was an e............................ silence in the dark cave.
5  Let your father have some p............................ and quiet after his busy week at work.
6  The police tried to interrogate him but he insisted on remaining s............................ until his lawyer arrived.
7  The sound of chalk scratching across a blackboard is such a horrible g............................ noise.
8  The violin makes a very high-p............................ sound.
9  He opened the door n............................ and crept up the stairs so quietly that no one realised he was there.
10  Please turn your music down. I can't hear myself t............................ .

**66.2** Complete these sentences with a word from the box. Write the verb in the correct form.

20 marks

| | | | | |
|---|---|---|---|---|
| crash | creak | hammer | hoot | pound |
| ring out | sizzle | slam | squeak | wail |

1  Jack ................................ the door so violently that I thought it would fall off its hinges.
2  I could hear the sausages ................................ in the hot frying pan.
3  We didn't get much sleep because people ................................ their car horns all night.
4  We could hear police sirens ................................ throughout the night.
5  Why do stairs always seem ................................ at night?
6  I wish you'd oil your bedroom door. The way it ................................ is driving me mad.
7  A gunshot ................................ and suddenly everyone froze in fear.
8  We were quite a way from the nightclub but we could still hear the music ................................ away.
9  We couldn't understand who could be ................................ at our door at that time of night.
10  I could hear the waves ................................ against the rocks.

**66.3** Answer these questions.

10 marks

1  Name the small animal which is most likely to squeak.
2  What do you call the very first films which did not have any sound?
3  What rhyming verb could you use instead of *hoot* in the phrase *hoot your horn*?
4  Are the words *noiseless* and *soundless* used more in formal or informal English?
5  If you say that someone has a *grating* voice, do you like the sound of their voice?
6  If someone lets out a *piercing* scream, is it a quiet scream or a loud one?
7  What is the root of the word *deafening* and what does it mean?
8  What is more likely to make a deafening noise – machinery or wind in trees?
9  What is more likely to make a high-pitched noise – a mobile phone or a car alarm?
10  What does it mean if someone says they had a quiet day at work?

**Your score**

/ 40

# 67 Weight and density

### 67.1
**10 marks**

Complete these pairs of sentences using the same word. You are given the first letters.

1 a) We had to carry a lot of cu............................ equipment on the expedition.
  b) Everything goes so slowly because of the cu............................ bureaucracy.
2 a) Parents have many bur............................ responsibilities.
  b) It is a bur............................ duty, but I must carry it out nevertheless.
3 a) He walked like some lu............................ giant.
  b) A huge, lu............................ juggernaut was holding up the traffic and nobody could overtake.
4 a) It's quite a we............................ volume of over 800 pages; it will take a long time to read it.
  b) We discussed some rather we............................ philosophical issues but didn't really reach any conclusions.
5 a) This is such an unw............................ suitcase. Don't we have a smaller, lighter one?
  b) It was a very long and unw............................ application process. I almost gave up at one point.

### 67.2
**10 marks**

Match the words on the left with the correct set of typical collocations on the right.

| | | | | |
|---|---|---|---|---|
| 1 | impermeable | a) | mattress | glue | sauce |
| 2 | ponderous | b) | medicine | juice | chemicals |
| 3 | lumpy | c) | barrier | shield | rocks |
| 4 | impenetrable | d) | silence | deliberation | thesis |
| 5 | undiluted | e) | forest | darkness | plot |

### 67.3
**5 marks**

Complete the sentences with the correct preposition or particle.

1 She always weighs ..................... with an opinion whenever people are discussing anything.
2 Poor guy! He's so weighed ..................... with problems these days.
3 We should weigh ..................... all the alternatives before making a decision.
4 The traffic in the city usually thins ..................... after about 6.30 p.m.
5 If you want to help you can weigh ..................... a kilo of flour and 400 grams of butter for me.

### 67.4
**10 marks**

Circle the correct underlined word.

1 The plates were disgusting: there was thickened/congealed/lumpy food all round the edges.
2 Do you have to thin/sift/dilute this orange juice or can you drink it as it is?
3 The mist is beginning to thicken/solidify/congeal. We'd better sail back to the harbour immediately.
4 It was a very old bag of cement and it had thickened/solidified/congealed completely so we couldn't use it.
5 This white spirit is very good if you need to sift/thin/dilute the paint before you use it.

### 67.5
**5 marks**

Complete the table. Do not write in the shaded box.

| adjective | noun | verb |
|---|---|---|
| thick | thickness | |
| | lump | |
| | weight | weigh |
| | burden | burden |
| solid | solidity | |

**Your score**

/40

# 68 Colour: range and intensity

**68.1**

*10 marks*

**Answer these questions.**

1 Would you be pleased if someone said you had mousy hair? Why? / Why not?
2 If someone paints their walls magnolia, what colour are the walls?
3 If a friend asks you to buy them a burgundy scarf, what colour scarf do they want?
4 If a girl has forget-me-not eyes, what colour are her eyes?
5 If you are feeling blue, what sort of mood are you in?
6 If you say something is a red-letter day for you, what kind of day is it?
7 If someone tells you to use your grey cells, what do they want you to do?
8 What are the three primary colours?
9 What is special about fluorescent colours?
10 Which colours are stronger: pastels or vivid colours?

**68.2**

*16 marks*

**What are these colours? Describe them using ordinary colour words.**

*Example*: charcoal – **dark grey**

| | |
|---|---|
| 1 amber | 9 jade |
| 2 auburn | 10 mauve |
| 3 beige | 11 navy |
| 4 chestnut | 12 poppy |
| 5 cornflower | 13 ruby |
| 6 crimson | 14 sapphire |
| 7 emerald | 15 scarlet |
| 8 ginger | 16 turquoise |

**68.3**

*4 marks*

**Correct the vocabulary mistake in each of these sentences.**

1 Jean has beautiful navy eyes.
2 No one talks about our uncle; he's the grey sheep of the family.
3 I hate those red knuckle rides at theme parks and refuse to go on them.
4 Billy's turned a bit mauve; I hope he's not going to be sick.

**68.4**

*10 marks*

**Circle the correct underlined word.**

1 Take a torch. It's <u>jet/pitch</u> black outside.
2 Do you like her <u>shocking/electric</u> pink top?
3 Jill looks afraid; she's as white as a <u>sheet/snow</u>.
4 I'm <u>green/pink</u> with envy at Vanessa's new job.
5 I'd hate to work in an office. I'd much rather have a <u>white/blue</u>-collar job.
6 Fabiola has beautiful <u>jet/pitch</u> black hair and eyes.
7 Criticising Jim's driving always makes him see <u>black/red</u>.
8 It's not clearly right or clearly wrong; it's very much a <u>grey/pink</u> area.
9 Police are trying to clamp down on the <u>grey/black</u> market of DVDs.
10 They treated us like royalty! They really rolled out the <u>purple/red</u> carpet.

# 69 Speed

**69.1**

10 marks

Complete these sentences with verbs indicating fast movement. You are given some letters.

1 He just wh............................ past on his bicycle and didn't see me at all.
2 I'll just z............................ across to the canteen and get a cup of coffee.
3 Sorry, I must da............................ . I've got a train to catch.
4 The dog to............................ across the garden chasing a rat.
5 I think I'll n............................ into town during the lunch break. I need a few things.
6 The thieves bo............................ when they heard the police car siren.
7 Those jobs you gave us took no time at all. We just ra............................ through them.
8 Suddenly a cat dar............................ across the garden as if it had been frightened by something.
9 Can you p............................ into my office for a few minutes? There's something I want to show you.
10 The children car............................ down the slope on their sledge, the snow flying in their faces.

**69.2**

10 marks

Cross out the odd one out in each set of collocations.

1 You can plunge into <u>sadness/a swimming pool/your jacket</u>.
2 <u>Eyebrows/House prices/A bird</u> can soar.
3 <u>Hopes for peace/Profits/A picture on the wall</u> can plummet.
4 <u>A car/Your hopes/Economic growth</u> can accelerate.
5 <u>Exports/A cake/Share prices</u> can slump.

**69.3**

10 marks

Rewrite these sentences using the movement verbs from exercise 69.2. Use each verb once. Make any other necessary changes.

1 We suddenly felt much less hopeful when we heard the bad news.
2 The rocket made a rapid ascent into the stratosphere.
3 When we were told of her death, we immediately felt great despair.
4 After the recession, there was a rapid increase in economic growth.
5 There was a sharp decline in exports as a result of the revaluation of the currency.

**69.4**

10 marks

Answer these questions.

1 Complete the three verbs beginning with sc- which could be used for fast movement by small animals.     sc.................y     sca.................r     sc.................le
2 Complete the two verbs beginning with cr- which could be used of slow movement by an insect.     cr.................     cr.................
3 Fill the gaps with a suitable phrasal verb: 'I wish you'd sp................. ................. ! Why are you walking so slowly?'
4 If prices tumble, do they rise or fall?
5 Complete the verb beginning with tot- which could describe unsteady, slow movement by an elderly person.     tot.................
6 If you sidle up to someone, how are you moving?
7 If you dawdle, are you likely to arrive at your destination (a) in good time (b) late?

Your score

/40

# Cause and effect

**70.1**
10 marks

Choose the best verb from the box to complete each sentence. Write the verbs in the correct form.

| cause | generate | give | produce |
|-------|----------|------|---------|

1 Our business didn't ............................................. much income for the first couple of years.
2 The typhoid outbreak was ............................................. by contaminated water.
3 Jane's piano playing has ............................................. us a great deal of pleasure over the years.
4 Did the fire ............................................. much damage?
5 Will you be able to ............................................. much enthusiasm among the staff for the idea?
6 Can you please ............................................. the report by Friday at the latest?
7 They couldn't ............................................. me any reason as to why the computer had crashed.
8 Jack couldn't ............................................. any evidence to support his argument.
9 His radio interview should ............................................. a lot of good publicity.
10 What ............................................. you the motivation to go into politics?

**70.2**
10 marks

Circle the correct underlined word.

1 I don't think the speakers intended to precipitate/incite/cause the crowd to violence.
2 They say that familiarity breeds/prompts/gives contempt.
3 Whatever produced/sparked/prompted you to say something so foolish?
4 My computer is generating/giving/resulting me a lot of problems at the moment.
5 The dog looked very fierce and I didn't want to induce/breed/provoke it in any way.
6 What would you say was the main factor which sparked/brought/resulted off the rebellion?
7 Rather to everyone's surprise, the film didn't precipitate/generate/induce much interest.
8 Do you think the crisis will spark/give/bring about a change of government?
9 The computer crash resulted/produced/caused in my losing a lot of work.
10 Nothing would generate/induce/provoke me to make a speech in front of so many people.

**70.3**
20 marks

Rewrite these sentences using the words in brackets.

1 The power cut resulted in my getting stuck in the underground and missing my flight. (OWING)
2 The TV ad generated a lot of orders for our new product. (THANKS)
3 The new software has caused us a lot of problems. (CONSEQUENCE)
4 The use of the Internet has caused enormous changes in our lives. (BROUGHT)
5 The article generated a lot of readers' letters. (RESULTED)
6 The crash meant that the motorway was closed for most of the day. (DUE)
7 The President's visit precipitated a number of protests. (SPARKED)
8 Leo's poor eyesight meant that he was never any good at sport. (RESULT)
9 This magazine has provided us with a lot of useful information. (GIVEN)
10 The Prime Minister's speech gave rise to many questions. (PROMPTED)

**Your score**

/40

# 71 Comparison and contrast

## 71.1
5 marks

Fill in the missing prepositions. There may be more than one possible answer.

1 be akin .....................
2 feel an affinity .....................
3 be tantamount .....................
4 be indistinguishable .....................
5 correspond .....................

## 71.2
5 marks

Use the expressions from exercise 71.1 to fill the gaps in these sentences.

1 To give up the struggle now would be ............................................... a complete surrender.
2 His view of the situation simply did not ............................................. reality.
3 I always feel a strong .......................................... people who are searching for their natural parents. I too was an adopted child.
4 These days, one shopping centre is .......................................... another. They all have the same shops and layout.
5 The Mercury Guest House is more .......................................... a cheap motel than a proper hotel.

## 71.3
10 marks

Rewrite these sentences using the word in brackets. Make any other necessary changes.

1 The northern lakelands are not unlike parts of Finland. (DISSIMILAR)
2 The flora and fauna exist in great variety. (DIVERSE)
3 The dialect in the north is not at all like that found in the south. (DISTINCT)
4 The two regions were so different in every way that she found it difficult to settle. (DISPARATE)
5 Their views on immigration contrast sharply. (DIVERGENT)

## 71.4
10 marks

Answer these questions.

1 Which adjective from the verb *change* means 'so similar they could be exchanged for one another'?
2 Which is the correct spelling for the adjective meaning 'different and separate, not overlapping': (a) discreet (b) discrete?
3 Complete the missing word in this sentence: If I say 'Failure in business is like losing a penalty shoot-out', I am using a sporting an............................ .
4 How can you rewrite this sentence using the verb form of the adjective *equal*?
'To say that capitalism is *equal* to democracy is a mistake.'
5 Fill in the missing words: 'There is a strong artistic affinity ..................... European paintings of the fifteenth century ..................... those of the late nineteenth century.'

## 71.5
10 marks

Cross out the five vocabulary mistakes in this text and write the correct word above each mistake.

After walking for a few miles we saw a building that looked more akimbo to a castle than a guest house. In fact, it was not unsimilar to the old castle in my home town. As we got nearer, we realised there were also some wooden houses, which were almost undistinguishable from the surrounding forest. To use a gardening analogue, the houses seemed to be sprouting from the ground, just like trees. I felt a strong infinity for this lovely old group of buildings as it reminded me of my childhood home.

Your score

/ 40

# 72 Difficulties, dilemmas and hitches

**72.1** Write the words from the box in the appropriate category.

10 marks

| adversity | dilemma |
|---|---|
| pitfall | hitch |
| impediment | ordeal |
| glitch | setback |
| tribulation | snag |

| *minor problem* | *more serious problem* |
|---|---|
| | |
| | |
| | |

**72.2** Match an adjective from the left with the noun on the right it is most likely to describe.

8 marks  Use each noun only once.

1 wayward          theory
2 stiff             measure
3 traumatic         boredom
4 convoluted        competition
5 abstruse          journey
6 insufferable      child
7 arduous           sentences
8 obstructive       experience

**72.3** In each dialogue, Mark responds to Julie in two more or less similar ways. Complete the

10 marks  responses. You are given the first letters to help you.

1 JULIE:  I've got to get a very early train tomorrow morning!
  MARK:  Oh dear. What a p....................!
         Oh dear. What a d....................!
2 JULIE:  Dave looks a bit upset.
  MARK:  Yes, I wonder what's b.................... him.
         Yes, I wonder what's u.................... with him.
3 JULIE:  Have you sorted things out with your boss now?
  MARK:  Yes, I'm off the h.................... now, thank goodness.
         Yes, I'm in the c.................... now, thank goodness.
4 JULIE:  Have you had a hard week at work?
  MARK:  Yes, I've been s.................... my guts out.
         Yes, I've been f.................... myself to death.
5 JULIE:  Is everything OK with Melissa at work?
  MARK:  Not really. She's in a bit of a h.................... . She's lost some important papers.
         Not really. She's in a bit of a f.................... . She's lost some important papers.

**72.4** Circle the correct underlined word. Then explain why you rejected the other words.

12 marks
1 Changing jobs is always a bit of a hassle/stumbling block.
2 Sue had quite a convoluted/gruelling time giving birth to triplets.
3 The Minister has a slight speech impediment/obstacle.
4 I wonder if you could help me with a stiff/tricky situation that's come up at work.
5 An economic depression always means a lot of people suffering hardship/snags.
6 Jan has a lot of complex issues/decisions to make before the end of the year.

# 73 Modality: expressing facts, opinions, desires

**73.1**

10 marks

Use expressions from the box to complete B's responses in these conversations.

| I must confess | that'll be | you must be joking | you must have been frightened |
|---|---|---|---|

I must confess    that'll be    you must be joking    you must have been frightened
it might well never happen    what, may I ask    who should I see but
you still might    I should be so lucky    accidents will happen

1  A: It will be a disaster for us if they open a nightclub next door to our family restaurant.
   B: Oh, don't worry, ....................................................

2  A: Garry rang me at midnight last night!
   B: Did he? And ...................................................., did he want at that time of night?

3  A: Oh dear, I'm afraid I spilt coffee on your CD.
   B: Oh, never mind. ....................................................

4  A: It was such a loud bang. I thought something had exploded.
   B: Really? ....................................................

5  A: Sally said you'd had a big win on the lottery. Is that right?
   B: ....................................................! It was only ten pounds.

6  A: Max said you met an old friend of ours today.
   B: Yes, believe it or not, I was in town and .................................................... Joe Watts.

7  A: I bet you were glad to hear you didn't have to go into hospital.
   B: Yes, .................................................... I was very relieved.

8  A: Someone's at the door.
   B: Oh, .................................................... the plumber. He said he'd come at ten.

9  A: Steve was holding Debbie's hand at the party last night.
   B: Steve? ....................................................! He can't stand Debbie!

10 A: Well, I applied for two jobs and I've already been rejected for the first one.
   B: Oh, well, never mind. .................................................... get the other one.

**73.2**

10 marks

Complete the missing words in this text.

The boss decided it would be (1) pr............................t to warn people that the cost of the staff weekend conference could rise. She knew it was (2) in............................e that some people would be unhappy, but she believed it was (3) es............................l that everyone should know that the price could go up. There was every (4) li............................d that the accommodation cost would increase because it was high season. However, attendance was (5) op............................l, so if anyone didn't wish to go they didn't have to.

**73.3**

20 marks

Rewrite the underlined parts of these sentences using an expression based on the words in brackets. Make any other necessary changes.

1  My car engine <u>isn't working</u>. Can you help me? (START)
2  If I were <u>in your situation</u> I'd simply say no. (BOAT)
3  <u>It is likely that</u> they will postpone the decision till the economy improves. (PROBABILITY/ALL)
4  There <u>will be</u> some problems. There always are. (BOUND)
5  <u>It's not likely</u> that he'll get the job. He's not qualified. (ODDS/AGAINST)
6  I am sorry. I have no <u>alternative</u> but to terminate your contract. (OPTION)
7  He's always <u>dreamt of</u> becoming a super-rich business tycoon. (ASPIRATIONS)
8  <u>Do you have to</u> wear a seat belt in the rear passenger seat? (COMPULSORY)
9  The government <u>has made a firm decision</u> to clamp down on tax evasion. (RESOLVE)
10 <u>It's likely that</u> he'll forget all about it. (ODDS)

**Your score**

/40

**74.1** Complete these sentences using a word from the same root as the word in brackets.

10 marks

1 With this formula you can calculate the standard .......................................... from the norm. (DEVIATE)
2 When planning an experiment you have to take all the .......................................... into account. (VARY)
3 In planning your budget, you should .......................................... on the side of caution. (ERROR)
4 Do you keep a record of your monthly .......................................... ? (EXPEND)
5 Do the figures show a .......................................... between intelligence and gender? (RELATE)
6 Even at a .......................................... estimate, there were over a thousand people there. (CONSERVE)
7 These are our .......................................... sales and profit figures for next year. (PROJECT)
8 The argument in this article seems to me to be .......................................... . (FLAW)
9 Success in life sometimes seems to be in .......................................... proportion to real talent. (INVERT)
10 I've looked through the report and am afraid I've noted some .......................................... . (CONSIST)

**74.2** Choose a word from the box to fill the gaps in these sentences.

12 marks

| run | blip | round | consistent | discrepancy | erratic |
| fluctuate | fold | proportion | recorded | sustain | tot |

1 There's been a three-.......................................... increase in the number of .......................................... sightings of eagles in the area.
2 We decided to .......................................... our figures down just to be on the safe side.
3 Could you .......................................... up these figures for me? I can't get a .......................................... answer.
4 The price of gold has been very .......................................... over the last few weeks. It's very unusual for it to .......................................... so much.
5 I asked John to check the figures too and he found a .......................................... between our totals.
6 I was horrified to see that the bill for our meal had .......................................... into three figures, especially as the cost of the food seemed to be in inverse .......................................... to its quantity.
7 Do you think we can .......................................... these high sales figures or are last month's outstanding results just a .......................................... ?

**74.3** Answer these questions.

18 marks

1 What kind of figure is a ballpark figure?
2 If someone's salary in dollars runs into six figures, what is the lowest it could be?
3 If you round 6.6 up, what number do you get?
4 If exchange rates seesaw, what happens to them?
5 What would be a more formal word for 'seesaw' in question 4 above?
6 If a change is said to be a blip, what is being suggested about the change?
7 What kind of estimate is a conservative estimate?
8 If the cost of making something increases by a factor of three, how much does it rise by?
9 What do the letters IQ stand for, and is the average IQ 10 or 100?
10 Give two ways of replacing 'per' in the sentence 'Hotel rooms cost £80 per night.'
11 If you wanted to discover why an identical house plant did much better in one student's room than in another, name three variables you might take into consideration.
12 If you say that people are neither wholly good nor wholly bad but somewhere along the continuum, what do you mean?
13 What is a simpler way of saying aggregated in 'I've aggregated all the figures'?
14 If something quadruples, how much does it increase?

Your score

/40

# 75 Permission and prohibition

**75.1**
*5 marks*

Write down the prepositions which normally follow these verbs. If no preposition is required, write 'X'.

1 assent ......................
2 accede ......................
3 condone ......................
4 endorse ......................
5 acquiesce ......................

**75.2**
*5 marks*

Complete these sentences using verbs from exercise 75.1. Write the verbs in the correct form.

1 The committee concluded that the Defence Minister had ........................................ in the secret arms deal.
2 The employers finally ........................................ to the union's demand for representation on the board.
3 However bad the crime, we should never ........................................ the use of torture.
4 The City Council have ........................................ to a proposal to rebuild the main sports stadium.
5 As committee Chair, I fully ........................................ the new membership campaign.

**75.3**
*18 marks*

Circle the correct underlined word.

1 She was <u>baited/barred/bailed</u> from the sport for two years after a positive drug test.
2 The new legislation <u>outlawed/outbid/outdid</u> the use of mobile phones while driving.
3 Some countries always <u>vacate/veil/veto</u> resolutions at the United Nations which don't suit them.
4 I don't think the Prime Minister would ever <u>compromise/countenance/comprise</u> a referendum on the constitution. He doesn't believe in referendums.
5 The committee has <u>authorised/actuated/autographed</u> the use of quotations from web pages in student essays.
6 The United Nations has <u>lifted/quit/repelled</u> the trade <u>bargain/embrace/embargo</u> on the Republic of Hevania.
7 The police have <u>adapted/adopted/adhered</u> a policy of <u>nil-tolerance/zero-tolerance/none-tolerance</u> towards football hooligans.

**75.4**
*12 marks*

Cross out the six vocabulary or spelling mistakes in this text and write the correct word above each mistake.

In 2003, the government gave the go-along to a franshize system for city bus services.

Companies were more or less given blank-carte to establish routes and timetables.

However some firms thought they had been given the white light to increase fares and

close unprofitable routes, so the government had to introduce new rules to clamp down

at profiteering, and financial sanctities were imposed on firms that broke the rules.

# 76 Complaining and protesting

**76.1** Match the beginnings of these complaints to their endings.

*10 marks*

| | |
|---|---|
| 1 The teacher said he took exception | to pay more attention in class. |
| 2 Sue would be well advised | to play their music rather loudly at night. |
| 3 Something will have to be done | of their lack of consideration. |
| 4 My parents are always finding fault | from a little more attention. |
| 5 I've just about had enough | not his highest priority. |
| 6 The union leader remonstrated | with everything I do or say. |
| 7 I wish he wouldn't | to Ben's attitude. |
| 8 His appearance would benefit | with the new director. |
| 9 It's clear that personal hygiene is | whinge so much. |
| 10 Our neighbours tend | about the mess on your desk. |

**76.2** Fill in the missing word in each of these complaints and protests.

*9 marks*

1 It's a ............................................ stuffy in this room.
2 You ............................................ possibly expect him to believe that!
3 You'll have to ............................................ something about the situation.
4 I'm afraid you do have a ............................................ to make rather too many mistakes.
5 I'm ............................................ up with his constant fault-finding.
6 I wish people ............................................ refrain from smoking in restaurants.
7 She's not happy unless she's got something to grouse ............................................ .
8 I wish to complain in the ............................................ possible terms about your standards of service.
9 I take ............................................ to that remark and insist that you apologise at once.

**76.3** What are the noun forms of these verbs?

*8 marks*

| | | | | | | | |
|---|---|---|---|---|---|---|---|
| 1 advise | 3 complain | 5 gripe | 7 grumble |
| 2 object | 4 protest | 6 remonstrate | 8 tend |

**76.4** Complete each of these sentences with one of the nouns from exercise 76.3 in the correct form. You may use the nouns more than once. You may not need to use them all.

*8 marks*

1 I would like to make a(n) ............................................ to that remark.
2 Your brother should be able to offer you some helpful ............................................ .
3 Harriet does have a(n) ............................................ to exaggerate things.
4 Roger registered a formal ............................................ with the manager about the restaurant's food and service.
5 You'll do much better in your exam if you take your teacher's ............................................ .
6 Sociologists have observed some fascinating new ............................................ in young people's behaviour.
7 Anyone who does not like the council's new proposals has a month in which to register a(n) ............................................ .
8 Everyone enjoys having a(n) ............................................ from time to time.

**76.5** What would a polite British teacher really mean by these sentences?

*5 marks*

*Example*: It's a bit noisy in here. **You must be quieter.**

1 Your handwriting would benefit from a little more care.
2 You would be well advised to do plenty of revision before your next test.
3 You don't seem to check your work carefully enough.
4 This subject doesn't seem to be your highest priority.
5 Your essays tend to be a bit short.

**Your score**

/40

**77.1**
10 marks

Complete the adjectives which typically combine with these nouns. You are given some letters.

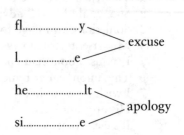

fa....................e ⟶ pretext
fl....................y ⟶

c............t- i............n ⟶
con....................g ⟶ alibi
per....................t ⟶
ph....................y ⟶

fl....................y ⟶ excuse
l....................e ⟶

he....................lt ⟶ apology
si....................e ⟶

**77.2**
10 marks

Use adjective–noun pairs from exercise 77.1 to complete these sentences.

1 Josh said the dog had eaten his homework. The teacher thought that was a pretty
   ........................................... .
2 He came to my office under the ........................................... that he needed someone's phone
   number. What he really wanted was to ask for a pay rise.
3 Carson could not have committed the murder. He had a ........................................... .
   He had witnesses to prove he was 100 miles away at the time.
4 I wish to offer my most ........................................... to all of you. I did not mean to
   offend you.
5 He tried to claim he had been in a restaurant with friends at the time of the robbery, but it was
   a ........................................... and he was found guilty.

**77.3**
10 marks

Cross out five vocabulary mistakes in this text and write the correct word above each mistake.

As he was sentenced to death for the murders, Jake Dagger showed no remonstrances. He knew

that it was likely he would get a last-minute reprise from the President, as other criminals

had before him. His co-defendant, Lucy Motion, was equipped, and walked free from the

courtroom. She is now seeking an apologisement from the police, but a senior officer said

he believed the force had been completely exhilarated and had nothing to apologise for.

**77.4**
10 marks

Answer these questions.

1 Complete this sentence with an expression that means 'an official forgiveness after someone's
   death for crimes they were wrongly convicted of'.
   The judge granted Hughes a pos........................... pa........................... .
2 Which verb means 'say one is sorry for a crime and ask for forgiveness'? r...........................t
3 Use the definitions to help you unjumble the jumbled words.
   a) agreement to stop war while peace discussions take place RAMCEISTI ...........................
   b) agreement not to fight, or to work together peacefully DROACC ...........................
   c) declaration that fighting will stop for a period ECTRU ...........................
   d) formal document agreeing not to fight or agreeing to end a war TRYATE ...........................
4 Which verb can be used before the answers to both (a) and (c) in number 3? de...........................
5 Which verb can be used before the answers to both (b) and (d) in number 3? s...........................
6 Which adjective can be used before the answers to both (b) and (d) in number 3?
   p...........................

Your score
/40

**78.1** Complete these sentences using a word from the same root as the word in brackets.

10 marks
1 People made some ........................................... remarks about my performance. (COMPLIMENT)
2 It is said that imitation is the sincerest form of ........................................... . (FLATTER)
3 The aims of the project are ........................................... , but will it actually succeed? (LAUD)
4 Do give your parents my ........................................... on their golden wedding anniversary. (CONGRATULATE)
5 Isabel never fails to behave in a ........................................... fashion. (PRAISE)
6 Daisy behaves in such a ........................................... way whenever the boss is around. (SMARM)
7 The Prime Minister paid tribute to the new Chancellor with some well-chosen, ........................................... remarks. (LAUD)
8 At the end of the performance, the orchestra received a ........................................... ovation. (STAND)
9 I wish Kerry wasn't such a ........................................... ! She can be quite fun when she isn't trying desperately to impress management. (CRAWL)
10 No one likes a waiter who is obsequious and ........................................... . (SERVE)

**78.2** Use your knowledge of word combinations or collocations to help you fill the gaps. You are given the first letter.

10 marks
1 He's the kind of man who likes to p........................... women compliments.
2 Flattery will get you n........................... .
3 The new opera w........................... plaudits from even the toughest of critics.
4 She got a p........................... on the back for finishing the report on time.
5 I've heard a lot about you. Nadia is always s........................... your praises.
6 Oliver Scott is now the t........................... of the town for his role in the latest Bond film.
7 References don't usually say anything negative, but they can d........................... with faint praise.
8 The boy will get a big head if everyone keeps h........................... praise on him.
9 At the memorial service there were a number of excellent speeches p........................... tribute to the deceased.
10 Ever since she started her new job, Sally has been extolling the v........................... of her boss.

**78.3** Put these words into five pairs with similar meanings.

10 marks

| | | | | | |
|---|---|---|---|---|---|
| back-handed | servile | slimy | suck up to | obsequious | praiseworthy |
| double-edged | laudable | smarmy | lick someone's boots | | |

**78.4** Explain the difference between the following expressions.

10 marks
1 *slimy* and *obsequious*
2 *to get a pat on the back* and *to win plaudits*
3 *a double-edged compliment* and *a back-handed compliment*
4 *to fish for compliments* and *to pay compliments*
5 *widely praised* and *praised to the skies*

# 79 Promises and bets

**79.1**

10 marks

Complete the missing words in these conversations. You are given some letters.

1 FRAN:      I could have s...........................n she said she'd be here at eight o'clock.
  BILL:      Well I think you're wrong. I'm absolutely certain she said nine o'clock.

2 ZAYNAB:    For such a young child, Jane shows great p...........................e on the piano.
  LUKE:      Yes, I think she'll be a really good musician one day.

3 PADDY:     Jane seems to have t...........................d over a new l...........................f.
  NINA:      Yes, she does seem to have changed for the better.

4 YOLANDA:   On our last day at school we all pl........................... eternal friendship, but since then
             we've lost touch with one another.
  JULIAN:    Yes, that's typical, isn't it?

5 KIM:       The weather pr........................... to be good this weekend, so let's go sailing.
  DANA:      Yeah, great idea. Let's do it.

6 PAULA:     Do you think dictionaries should include s...........................r w...........................?
  GUY:       Well, bad language is a part of everyday life, so I suppose the answer is yes.

7 WALTER:    I can't believe he denied being at the club whilst under o...........................h. People
             saw him there.
  STEVE:     He did. But I don't think the court believed him.

8 JOE:       I'm very disappointed in Lily. She b........................... her promise to sponsor our
             charity event.
  ORLA:      Yes. If someone makes a promise they should keep it.

9 DIANE:     What's the civil marriage ceremony like in your country?
  KRISTA:    Well, the couple exchange v...........................s and give each other a ring, then sign a
             register.

10 RUPERT:   Do you ever make N........................... Y........................... r...........................s?
   ULLA:     Oh yes, but I've always broken them by the end of January!

**79.2**

10 marks

Circle the two correct words in each group of three.

1 I think I'll have a <u>flutter/pledge/bet</u> on the Irish horse.
2 He <u>pledged/staked/vowed</u> never to leave me.
3 I <u>wager/swear/bet</u> you £10 he won't win.
4 She made a solemn <u>oath/promise/swear</u> never to betray him.
5 Most people don't <u>keep/make/put</u> resolutions.

**79.3**

20 marks

Rewrite the underlined parts of these sentences using expressions based on the words in brackets.
Make any other necessary changes.

1 He's the type who <u>makes big unrealistic promises</u> and then lets you down.  (MOON/PROMISE)
2 She's a young tennis player <u>who will do very well one day</u>.  (PROMISING)
3 I think she lives in Harrow Street, but I <u>couldn't be absolutely sure</u>.  (SWEAR)
4 Most of my classmates use *English Vocabulary in Use* and <u>think it's fantastic</u>.  (SWEAR)
5 <u>The best advice I can give you</u> is to try and e-mail him. He never answers the phone.
  (YOUR/BET)
6 I often <u>put a small bet</u> on big sports events.  (FLUTTER)
7 He might turn up to help you, but don't <u>consider it a certainty</u>!  (BET)
8 <u>I'm sure</u> they'll be divorced within a year, the way they're behaving.  (MONEY/PUT)
9 Mr Dew has generously <u>said he will give</u> £10,000 to the charity.  (PLEDGE)
10 My mother disapproves of films containing <u>bad language</u>.  (SWEAR)

Your score

/40

**80.1**

10 marks

Rewrite these sentences using the word in brackets.

1 If only we'd known each other twenty years ago! (WISH)
2 He was sad when the council closed the community centre. (LAMENTED)
3 The football hooligans' behaviour was appalling. (DISGRACE)
4 I wish I'd studied harder when I was your age. (REGRET)
5 I wonder what happened to James, the boy I sat next to at school. (BECAME)
6 Many people look back on the past in an over-sentimental way. (SPECTACLES)
7 The thing about Adam that is particularly prominent in my memory is his red hair. (STANDS)
8 I mourn my lost youth. (WISH)
9 I hope you'll write to us or ring us sometimes when you go back home. (TOUCH)
10 I rue the day I decided to emigrate. (REGRET)

**80.2**

20 marks

Put these words in order to make sentences expressing regrets and reminiscences.

1 what / be / aren't / Things / used / they / to
2 now / shame / have / you / It's / to / a / leave
3 happiest / life / the / are / Schooldays / of / days / your
4 remorse / their / showed / behaviour / They / of / no / for / sign
5 make / They / to / like / cars / don't / used / they
6 time / mourn / I / the / of / passing
7 next / what / I'll / forget / never / happened
8 were / In / things / different / old / the / days / good
9 turn / clock / If / we / the / back / only / could
10 wonder / ended / doing / I / up / often / Richard / what

**80.3**

10 marks

Complete the dialogue using words from the box.

| days | disappointed | disappointing | forget | good times |
| make | remember | pity | whatsisname | wonder |

NED: It's (1) ............................................ our team didn't win.
JOE: Yes, it's a (2) ............................................ .
NED: Do you (3) ............................................ how they brought the cup home in 1975?
JOE: How could I ever (4) ............................................ ?
NED: We certainly had some (5) ............................................ going to matches in the 70s, didn't we?
JOE: We sure did. Those were the (6) ............................................ .
NED: Yes, they don't seem to (7) ............................................ footballers like they used to.
JOE: No, I often (8) ............................................ what happened to all the good players, people like
(9) ............................................, you know? The one who scored the winning goal in 1975.
NED: You mean Jack Crosby? I heard he's completely left football and is running a nightclub in
Florida. I was so (10) ............................................ .

**81.1**

10 marks

Complete the missing words in these sentences. You are given some letters.

1 All these products must c...........................m to European Union standards or we cannot sell them.
2 These figures do not t...........................y with those produced by the accountant. Can you explain that?
3 I do not a...........................e of Internet chat rooms. They attract crazy and dangerous people.
4 His views on war co...........................e with mine completely.
5 Gropov's philosophy co...........................rs with Karinski's. They agree on all major points.

**81.2**

10 marks

Write the jumbled letters in the correct order.

1 Ms Long said that existing VIDNSIOSI ........................................... within the Conservative Party would only get worse.
2 The union boss said she had made every effort to heal the FIRT ........................................... between the union and management.
3 The events caused a PLIST ........................................... in the Labour Party, resulting in the formation of the breakaway New Democratic Party.
4 In his speech the minister called for an end to SNEDIST ........................................... within the party.
5 There has been considerable CODSIRD ........................................... in the university sector recently over plans to reduce funding.

**81.3**

5 marks

Complete this table with the missing word forms.

| noun | verb |
|------|------|
| compromise | |
| | settle |
| difference | |
| concession | |
| | divide |

**81.4**

5 marks

Circle the correct prepositions.

1 I'm prepared to compromise <u>in/at/on</u> some issues, but not all.
2 My opinion coincides <u>to/with/on</u> yours.
3 I am <u>in/on/at</u> accord with the government on foreign policy.
4 There have already been several concessions <u>for/to/in</u> the demands made by the union.
5 I don't approve <u>of/to/with</u> his behaviour in any way.

**81.5**

10 marks

Rewrite these sentences following the instructions in brackets.

1 I think we should be a little more discreet in this matter. (Use the noun form of DISCREET.)
2 I think we have to agree that there is a difference of opinion between us. (Use the verb form of DIFFERENCE.)
3 The boss conceded several times to the union leaders. (Use the noun form of CONCEDE.)
4 The two parties have compromised in their dispute. (Use the noun form of COMPROMISE.)
5 The employers and the unions have settled their dispute over staffing levels. (Use the noun form of SETTLE.)

# 82 Academic writing 1

## 82.1
10 marks

Replace the underlined parts of this text with more academic English equivalents from the box.

| advocates | authoritative | coherent | comprehensive | crucial |
|---|---|---|---|---|
| empirical | notwithstanding | perceives | somewhat | whereby |

Jackman <u>is in favour of</u> a <u>rather</u> different approach to the subject. He <u>sees</u> the main problem as being the lack of <u>practically observed</u> data and argues that more <u>thorough</u> surveys are <u>very important</u> before any <u>complete and accurate</u> conclusions can be drawn. <u>Despite this</u>, he praises one study done by Braithwaite in the 1990s, arguing that it suggests a <u>logically structured</u> method <u>by which</u> larger scale studies could be carried out.

## 82.2
10 marks

Circle the correct underlined word.

1 Sometimes politicians produce statistics which <u>distort/deviate</u> the real situation.
2 Look at the figures and see if you can <u>demonstrate/deduce</u> a formula that would help you to calculate the value of x.
3 The data suggests that exposure to cats' hairs is more likely to <u>reside/trigger</u> an allergic reaction in left-handed people.
4 You should read the book by Burke as well as the one by Hare because their approaches <u>overlap/complement</u> each other very well.
5 The <u>incidence/sequence</u> of left-handedness is greater among men.
6 Experts were puzzled by the <u>predominant/widespread</u> occurrence of a new computer virus.
7 The figures presented by Hall are <u>ambiguous/arbitrary</u> in that they can be interpreted in several different ways.
8 Potts advocates a conservative approach, whereas Gibb argues <u>likewise/the converse</u>.
9 The amount of algae is increasing, <u>whereby/thereby</u> reducing levels of oxygen in the water.
10 This symbol is used to <u>denote/infer</u> standard deviation.

## 82.3
10 marks

Choose one of the incorrect words from exercise 82.2 to complete these sentences.

1 Barnes maintains that economic factors determine a child's chances of success in life; Hughes argues ............................................. , supporting Barnes' theories with his own data.
2 He didn't say so directly, but we could ............................................. that he did not approve of the work.
3 I shall now outline the methods ............................................. we hope to achieve our desired results.
4 If you do not read the articles in ............................................., they will not make sense.
5 Light brown hair is ............................................. in Scotland, although red hair is also common.
6 The answer to the problem might seem to ............................................. in the animal's diet.
7 The results of the survey ............................................. an increasing tendency to mistrust politicians.
8 The school took the ............................................. decision to divide children into groups according to the letters their names began with.
9 To do well in an essay question you should not ............................................. from the question set.
10 Yates's work will ............................................. with Brown's, so don't read them both.

## 82.4
10 marks

What are the verb forms of these nouns?

| concept | contradiction | conversation | denotation | deviation |
|---|---|---|---|---|
| distortion | negation | perception | appendix | residence |

Your score

/40

# 83 Academic writing 2

**Choose the correct answer, (a), (b) or (c).**

1 If you posit something, you (a) suggest it is a fact (b) position it carefully in the text (c) argue against it.

2 If something epitomises something, it (a) is more important than it (b) is a perfect example of it (c) emphasises it.

3 If a point in an essay underscores another point, it (a) emphasises it (b) is less important than it (c) distorts or perverts it.

4 If someone expounds something, they (a) remove it from the text (b) reveal something no one else knows (c) propose and develop arguments for it.

5 If someone reiterates something, they (a) retract or withdraw it (b) repeat or restate it (c) reduce or simplify it.

**83.2**

12 marks

**Complete the crossword.**

Down

1 The economic issue is beyond the .......... of this essay

2 verb meaning 'to include' or 'to put one's arms around someone'

3 verb meaning 'to quote' or 'to refer to someone's work'

4 noun form of the verb 'to epitomise'

Across

5 noun form of the verb 'to preface'

6 verb form of the noun 'category'

**83.3**

18 marks

**Complete the missing words in these extracts from academic texts.**

In this chapter it has been impossible to (1) d........................... with the history of traditional music in every detail, and we have only touched (2) u........................... some aspects. We shall (3) r...........................n to the history of the music briefly in Chapter 6. The topics to be (4) a........................... in the next chapter include the types of instruments which are commonly used and the various song and dance forms.

We shall consider the factors influencing the process in (5) de........................... order, starting with the most important, namely the civil war of 1994–1996. The opposing sides in the war were (6) m........................... up of different, loosely allied factions, and we are (7) f........................... to conclude that the war might have ended sooner had there been a more united front. Looking at the protagonists in (8) as........................... order, we begin with the least significant military figures and end with General Ujima, the ruthless head of the regime. This paper will attempt to (9) a........................... for the climate which led to deep political divisions and, finally, war.

Your score

/40

# 84 Writing: style and format

**84.1**

10 marks

**Answer these questions.**

1 Which words on the front cover of this book are written entirely in upper case?
2 What do you call these different kinds of brackets?
   a ( )
   b [ ]
3 What word is used to refer to a style of lettering on a printed document or a word processing programme?
4 What do you call these different types of print?
   a *This is test number eighty-four.*
   b **This is test number eighty-four.**
5 Circle the correct underlined word to complete this instruction from an application form.
   *Please write your name in* black/block *capitals, i.e. JOHN SMITH.*
6 What do the lines below have in front of them?
   • Idioms
   • Phrasal Verbs
   • Collocations
7 How would you distinguish between these two sets of symbols?
   ' '   and   " "
8 What is this symbol * called?

**84.2**

20 marks

**Explain the difference between the following expressions.**

1 *to write something down* and *to write something up*
2 *to scribble* and *to doodle*
3 *to cut and paste* and *to copy and paste*
4 *a title* and *a subtitle*
5 *to jot something down* and *to make a note of something*
6 *to print a document* and *to format a document*
7 *to indent a line* and *to put a line in a shaded box*
8 *a manuscript* and *a first draft*
9 *upper case* and *lower case* letters
10 *a chapter heading* and *a sub-heading*

**84.3**

10 marks

**Match the beginnings of these sentences with their endings.**

| | |
|---|---|
| 1 Jane scribbled a note | out my lecture notes for Sam. |
| 2 You should put all the headings | and paste these sections of the document. |
| 3 I copied | in bold. |
| 4 I'm hoping to submit | of your reference number. |
| 5 Ben is writing | every paragraph. |
| 6 Let's all just jot | round direct speech. |
| 7 It'll save time if you copy | the final draft soon. |
| 8 It's a good idea to indent | to her mum. |
| 9 Don't forget to put single quotes | down our first thoughts and then discuss them. |
| 10 Make a note | up his thesis at the moment. |

**Your score**
/40

# 85 Lexical strategies for speaking

**85.1**

10 marks

Use the words from the box to rewrite these sentences without using the word *thing*.
Use each word once only and make any other necessary changes.

| | | | | |
|---|---|---|---|---|
| dislike | situation | fuss | action | firstly |
| problem | subjects | secondly | matter | tool |

1 We'd love to retire early, but the thing is we simply don't have the money.
2 I know it's a nuisance, but I wish she wouldn't make such a big thing about it.
3 One of the things he touched on in his lecture was globalisation.
4 Those kids frighten old people and the police can't do a thing about it.
5 As things are at present, I cannot see the government funding such a project.
6 My belt is too tight. Where's that thing for making holes in leather?
7 He has a thing about cats. He hates them coming into his garden.
8 For one thing, I don't think it will work, and for another thing it will be very costly. (*2 marks*)
9 I think we should get things sorted out as soon as possible.

**85.2**

8 marks

Use expressions with the verb *get* to rewrite the underlined words in the second speakers'
responses. Use the words in brackets, where they are given.

1 ZAYNAB:  I thought Tom was going to start his own company.
  MANDY:  Well, he was, but he never <u>took action and organised himself</u>. (TOGETHER)
2 BRIAN:  Have you discussed it with Bernard yet?
  LUKE:  No, but if I can <u>be alone with him</u> for an hour or so tomorrow, I will. (HIS OWN)
3 MAHMUD:  You have to save the file in a different format.
  KEN:  Sorry, I don't <u>understand</u>.
4 JENNY:  Right, what other jobs are left to do?
  FRAN:  Well, we need to <u>post these letters</u>.

**85.3**

10 marks

Put these words in the correct order to make logical sentences.

1 you / told / not / times / I've / umpteen / that / do / to
2 work / of / done / She / scrap / hasn't / a / day / all
3 flu / of / week / touch / last / a / had / I
4 took / of / paperwork / to / permission / get / bureaucracy / It / and / masses
5 teachers / hate / company / I / excepted / present / course / of

**85.4**

12 marks

Cross out six mistakes in this conversation and write the correct words above each mistake.

PAULA:  I was talking to whosisname yesterday, oh, you know, Bill Knight. I've never met
anyone so childlike, and I mean that in the possible nice way.

ERIK:  Yes, I know what you mean. But a lot of people have a slightly childish side, except
for you, of course.

PAULA:  Well, no intended offence, but you can be very silly yourself at times, and you know it.

ERIK:  Mm. I accept that up to the point, but I wouldn't say I was childish.

PAULA:  Well, I think we all are occasionally, me including. And if you don't care me saying,
so are most of your friends.

Your score

/40

ERIK:  Hm. Well, we're all silly and immature then.

# Speech: style and articulation

**86.1**    **Answer these questions.**

10 marks

1 If someone is winding you up, are they trying to please or to tease you?
2 If someone lisps, how would they say the name Suzie?
3 If someone's speech is slurred, are they more likely to be old or drunk?
4 Is someone more likely to shriek if they see a snake or a fly in the house?
5 If someone slags off their colleagues, are they saying nice or nasty things about them?
6 If you wanted to butter someone up, would you be more likely to praise them or give them some money?
7 If someone is mumbling, what would you probably ask them to do?
8 Is someone who is angry more likely to murmer, mumble or mutter?
9 Do you like it if someone nags you? Why or why not?
10 How would you describe someone who sp-sp-speaks l-l-like th-this?

**86.2**    **Which word is the odd one out in each of these groups and why?**

10 marks

1 murmur, shout, yell
2 mumble, roar, mutter
3 stammer, scream, lisp
4 whinge, nag, wind up
5 chatter away, slag off, bicker

**86.3**    **Fill the gaps in these sentences.**

10 marks

1 I was surprised that he agreed to lend me his car ........................................... a murmur.
2 She's so clever and witty that she always makes me feel ...........................................-tied when she's around.
3 What are you muttering about ........................................... your breath?
4 I hate the way Tom is always whining ........................................... something or other.
5 You'll have to ........................................... your voice – I can't hear you.
6 A lot of small children speak ........................................... a lisp.
7 We spent all evening gossiping ........................................... old school friends.
8 If I butter my mum ........................................... , she might lend me the car at the weekend.
9 Don't you dare yell ........................................... me!
10 I can't hear you ........................................... the noise of the traffic.

**86.4**    **Look at the words in the box and answer the questions below.**

10 marks

| bicker | butter up | slag off | gossip | murmur | mutter | nag | roar |
| scream | shriek | stammer | stutter | whinge | wind up | yell | |

1 Write down three words from the box that are informal.
2 Write down two words from the box that suggest loud noises.
3 Write down two words that suggest talking about other people.
4 Write down two words that suggest being unhappy about something or someone.
5 Write down one word that suggests the way a lover might speak to his or her beloved.

Your score

/40

**87.1** Fill the gaps to complete the vague expressions.

10 marks

1 There were quite a f............................ people who couldn't get tickets for the concert.
2 There was a sm............................ of French names on the list of prize winners, but most were German.
3 The new building will cost somewhere i............................ the r............................n of 50 million euros.
4 The wedding was very expensive and cost i............................ excess o............................ 20 thousand pounds.
5 Bed and breakfast in a private house usually costs 30 pounds, g............................ or t............................ a couple of pounds.
6 There were fifty or s............................ people at the meeting.
7 We need a big cardboard or wooden box, or something along those l............................ .

**87.2** Use vague language expressions based on the words in the box to rewrite the underlined parts of

16 marks these sentences.

| dollop | lashings | a bit on the ... side | to that effect |
|---|---|---|---|
| a bit of | stuff | or whatever | dash |

1 It's always <u>quite</u> an effort explaining things to her.
2 I think you should just add a <u>very small amount</u> of olive oil to the spinach.
3 I put a <u>large spoonful</u> of cream onto each bowl of strawberries.
4 If you want more information, send me an e-mail, <u>or a letter, or a fax, or phone me</u>.
5 The apartment was nice, but it was <u>rather</u> small.
6 These buns are delicious served with <u>large quantities</u> of jam on them.
7 He said, "I'll never resign," or words <u>of similar meaning</u>.
8 This <u>substance</u> is excellent for removing stains caused by fruit juices.

**87.3** Answer these questions. You are given some clues.

14 marks

1 What other word means the same as *lashings*?  o............................s
2 What two words can normally be used instead of *around* in sentences such as 'There were *around* 50 people there'? (a) in formal and informal contexts: a............................t
(b) in more formal contexts: ap............................y
3 What suffix can be added to 'thirty' to replace *around* in the sentence 'She's around thirty.'?
4 Is the expression 'more or less' typically used with (a) numbers (e.g. *more or less 50 people*) or (b) with other types of expressions (e.g. *more or less finished*)?
5 Is this sentence likely to be heard in (a) a formal or (b) an informal context?
When we're there, we usually go to sports events and that.
6 What two expressions involving the word *like* could be used in this sentence?
I've had some tests and interviews **and similar things**.
7 What suffix could be added to the word *plastic* in this sentence to make it more vague?
It was made of a plastic material.

Your score
/40

**88.1**

10 marks

Write one word to complete the idioms in these sentences.

1  I wish he wouldn't ram his ideas down our .......................................... so much.
2  My new digital camera is really state-of-the-.......................................... .
3  The soldiers rounded all the villagers up and shot them in .......................................... blood.
4  Hi, Mike. Long time no .......................................... .
5  We've come up against a bit of a stumbling .......................................... , I'm afraid.
6  Are you having second .......................................... about getting married?
7  We seem to be talking at cross .......................................... .
8  I was amazed when Kirsten turned up out of the .......................................... last night.
9  Liz often says that every time she opens her mouth, she puts her .......................................... in it.
10  When teachers have a new class, they sometimes play a game to break the
   .......................................... .

**88.2**

18 marks

Rewrite the underlined parts of these sentences using expressions based on the words in brackets.
Make any other necessary changes.

1  I'm afraid we're going to have to start again <u>from the very beginning</u>. (SCRATCH)
2  I like to be fashionable but <u>there's no way I would wear</u> a mini skirt. (LINE)
3  She turned up <u>completely unexpectedly</u>. (BLUE)
4  Make sure you <u>watch</u> the children – they can be quite naughty. (EYE)
5  Diane always behaves in a very <u>arrogant</u> way. (MIGHTY)
6  There's a great restaurant <u>very close to our house</u>. (DOORSTEP)
7  Tony <u>never tells his parents</u> about his girlfriends. (DARK)
8  I <u>can't see a thing</u> without my contact lenses. (BAT)
9  Ron says he's feeling a bit <u>ill</u> today. (WEATHER)

**88.3**

6 marks

Put the words from the box into pairs to make six idiomatic expressions.

| | | | | | |
|---|---|---|---|---|---|
| believe | block | ended | gritty | half- | hearted |
| long- | make- | nitty- | open- | stumbling | winded |

**88.4**

6 marks

Use an expression from exercise 88.3 to complete each of these sentences.

1  Don't ask Jack to make the speech. He's far too .......................................... .
2  Everything has been agreed in general terms, but now we need to start discussing the
   .......................................... .
3  We were making good progress with the project until we came up against the
   .......................................... of building regulations.
4  I sometimes think that Suzie doesn't know the difference between ..........................................
   and reality.
5  You should make more of an effort and not be so .......................................... about your
   homework.
6  The report is quite .......................................... and doesn't come to any clear-cut conclusions.

# 89 Idioms for situations

## 89.1
10 marks

Complete the idioms in these sentences using the picture clues.

1   2   3   4   5

1 After a bad year, fortunately, things are now ........................................................ up.
2 It was a great success. Everything ran like ........................................................ .
3 The government intervened to solve the problem at the ........................................................ .
4 Good news! Our plan worked like ........................................................ !
5 We took six months to plan our website and now I'm pleased to say it's up
........................................................ .

## 89.2
6 marks

Decide whether these idioms describe positive (+) or negative (–) situations. Write + or – in the brackets after each one.

1 It threw me completely. ( )
2 Everything fell into place. ( )
3 It's a complete shambles. ( )
4 It's as clear as mud. ( )
5 It went according to plan. ( )
6 We got our wires crossed. ( )

## 89.3
6 marks

Use idioms from exercise 89.2 to complete these sentences.

1 You asked if I understand. No, sorry, I'm afraid ........................................................
2 Just when I thought we would never succeed, ........................................................
3 Sorry about the mix-up last night. ........................................................
4 It was all set up to make him admit his guilt. Luckily, ........................................................
5 I wasn't expecting her to say that. ........................................................
6 That company is totally disorganised. ........................................................

## 89.4
10 marks

Complete these sentences with words from the box.

| | | | | |
|---|---|---|---|---|
| trees | brush | dream | teacup | under |
| bad | wood | carpet | storm | muddy |

1 Oh no! I've lost my credit card as well as my ticket! This is like a ................ ................ !
2 Let's try and keep it clear and simple. Let's not ................ the waters.
3 It's all a bit confusing and sometimes you can't see the ................ for the ................ .
4 I think people will soon forget all these arguments. It's just a ................ in a ................ .
5 Let's discuss the problem openly and not just ................ it ................ the ................ .

## 89.5
8 marks

Complete these idiomatic expressions.

1 Oh no! Now the switch has broken! That's all we ................ !
2 He said he couldn't pay me. That was the l................ t................ I wanted to hear.
3 I know it's all quiet now, but it's just the c................ before the s................ .
4 It would m................ life e................ if you would cooperate and stop being so difficult.
5 I have no idea where your coat disappeared to. It's a m................y to me.
6 Could you explain that again? You've l................ me there.
7 Phew! That was a c................ call! I got my job application in just before the deadline.
8 Oh no! Jim's gone off with the key and I don't know how to contact him. What a p................ !

Your score
/40

# Idioms that comment on people 1

**90.1** Match the beginnings of these sentences with their endings.

10 marks

| | |
|---|---|
| 1 Paula only has eyes | of her dreams. |
| 2 Matthew is the man | of the gab. |
| 3 Pat could talk the hind legs | over heels in love. |
| 4 Kay is one sandwich short | on my wick. |
| 5 Gary certainly has the gift | on the uptake. |
| 6 Jack and Fay fell head | between the ears. |
| 7 Sam's arrogance really gets | of a load. |
| 8 Gordon has got nothing | for Johnny. |
| 9 Tony can be a bit slow | of a picnic. |
| 10 Helen is several bricks short | off a donkey. |

**90.2** Complete the idioms in this paragraph with one word.

10 marks

I don't care much for his sisters, but I have a (1) ............................................. spot for Wayne.
He's (2) ............................................. fool and he's a mine of (3) ............................................. on all sorts
of interesting subjects. He certainly (4) ............................................. his stuff as far as finance is
concerned and he's undoubtedly the (5) ............................................. behind the family business.
He's also devoted to his mother and thinks the (6) ............................................. of her. I've never
(7) ............................................. it off with his two sisters, though. I think Meg's as thick as two
short (8) ............................................. . She never seems to have the (9) ............................................. idea
what's going on. As for Gina, her silly comments always get my (10) ............................................. up.

**90.3** Write the idioms from the box in the correct category.

10 marks

| | | | |
|---|---|---|---|
| walking on air | on cloud nine | down in the mouth | in seventh heaven |
| in your element | down in the dumps | over the moon | on top of the world |
| as miserable as sin | look like the cat that's got the cream | | |

| *sad* | *happy* |
|---|---|
| | |
| | |
| | |

**90.4** One word is wrong in each of these sentences. Correct the mistakes.

10 marks

1 I'm getting a bit fed up with the way Myra raves on and on for her new job.
2 Charles is certainly bright but he upsets others by being such a sharp aleck.
3 The way Roger talks down to other people really goes on my nerves.
4 You really need to use your brown matter to solve cryptic crosswords.
5 Sue and Larry are the perfect couple; they're done for each other.
6 Mark's been in the business for years and he certainly knows what's that.
7 I'm sorry I told Emma your plans. I didn't mean to let the cat out of the house.
8 If you come and see me after the meeting I'll make you in the picture.
9 Tina's very bright – you'll never be able to pull the hat over her eyes.
10 Your dad wasn't born today – he'll guess what you're up to.

**91.1** Use idioms based on the words in brackets to complete these sentences.

10 marks

1 Suzanne surprised everyone by joining the army, but she's always been a bit of
......................................................... (HORSE)
2 That film was horrible. All the blood and violence just ........................................................... (STOMACH)
3 He never lets me finish what I'm saying. It .......................................................... (NUTS)
4 I was so shocked by what she said that I found myself completely at
......................................................... (WORDS)
5 Jess is such a dreamer. He always seems to be in .......................................................... (OWN)
6 My mother doesn't want me to have a motorbike but I know I can persuade my father.
He's a real .......................................................... (TOUCH)
7 She could solve her career problems but she seems to lack the will. She's her
......................................................... (ENEMY)
8 Lucy is such a refined woman, but her new boyfriend is the complete opposite. He seems a
bit of a .......................................................... (DIAMOND)
9 Oh I'm not surprised Aysha spoke so directly. She never .......................................................... (MINCES)
10 I've tried everything. I simply don't know what to do. I'm at ..........................................................
(TETHER)

**91.2** Complete the crossword.

10 marks

Across
1 He was so angry he hit the .......................................... .
3 Jeff is so energetic and full of ........................................... .
4 He's a ........................................... in the grass.

Down
2 She got very angry and blew a ........................................... .
3 She just drives me round the ........................................... .

**91.3** Match the beginnings of the idioms with their endings.

6 marks

| | |
|---|---|
| 1 give someone | up the wrong way |
| 2 be | the measure of someone |
| 3 be | a brave face on it |
| 4 rub someone | the benefit of the doubt |
| 5 get | your own person |
| 6 put | at loggerheads |

**91.4** Answer these questions.

14 marks

1 If you feel that you 'want to curl up and die', how exactly do you feel?
2 If you are 'dead on your feet' you are still alive, but what are you?
3 If someone is 'eating out of the palm of your hand', what are they actually doing?
4 If you are 'all at sea', but nowhere near the sea, what are you?
5 If there is 'bad blood' between two people, how is their relationship?
6 If someone 'goes ballistic', what emotion are they experiencing?
7 Which two verbs can fill the gap in this sentence: 'She can ............................. him round her little
finger'?

Your score

/40

# Idioms that comment on stories and reports

**92.1**

Complete these sentences.

1  A:  I'm sure it won't rain!
   B:  Famous last ............................................ .
2  We were sitting there twiddling our ............................................ waiting for the teacher to arrive.
3  Everything went wrong that day and, to ............................................ it all, the car broke down.
4  A:  I should never have agreed to help mend her car!
   B:  Well, you live and ............................................ .
5  A:  I bumped into an old schoolfriend while backpacking in Asia.
   B:  It's a small ............................................ .
6  Such a lot has happened today, but, to cut a long ............................................ short, I've resigned!
7  When I walked into the room I suddenly had the weirdest feeling of déjà ............................................ .
8  I was ............................................ my own business when a man started shouting at me.
9  I never thought I'd pass the exam – it just goes to ............................................ that anyone can do it.
10 A:  She thought she'd lost her keys but then she found them at the bottom of her handbag.
   B:  So, all's well that ............................................ well.

**92.2**

Which of the idioms from exercise 92.1 could you use to ...

1  express relief that everything turned out all right in the end?
2  express surprise at meeting someone you know in an unexpected place?
3  comment on the fact that you are not doing anything special?  (2 answers)
4  describe a feeling that you have experienced something before?
5  suggest that bad experiences can make you wiser?
6  mention that you are giving a relatively brief account of an event?
7  emphasise that what someone said is likely to be wrong?
8  suggest that something is the worst in a series of bad events?
9  suggest that something is the logical or moral conclusion of a situation?

**92.3**

Put the words in the correct order to make sentences and idioms.

1  all / You / win / can't / them
2  beat / you / them / If / join / them / can't
3  those / was / things / just / of / It / one
4  another / thing / led / to / One
5  up / Jane / blue / of / turned / the / out
6  petrol / cap / out / Then / all / I / of / to / it / ran
7  bad / could / my / something / about / was / I / to / it / in / bones / happen / that / feel
8  without / a / Kyle / reorganising / all / as / my / by-your-leave / CDs / so / started / much
9  far / good / So / so
10 have / coming / the / would / it / I / my / As / restaurant / met / of / luck / boss / out

# 93 Phrasal verbs 1

**93.1**

10 marks

One verb in each sentence can be replaced by the phrasal verb *take off*. Rewrite the sentences using *take off* and make any other necessary changes.

1 George left the room and departed without saying goodbye to anybody.
2 The waiter removed the bad bottle of wine and said he would deduct 20% from the bill.
3 The plane taxied along the runway then soared into the sky.
4 She removed her jacket and helped us remove the table to give us room to dance.
5 When I got home, I removed the sweater from the bag, removed the label and tried it on.

**93.2**

8 marks

Fill in the missing prepositions or particles in these phrases.

| | |
|---|---|
| keep .............. the grass | stand .............. election as President |
| keep .............. your English | stand .............. your friends when they need you |
| keep the truth .............. somebody | stand somebody .............. on a date |
| keep .............. .............. somebody walking fast | stand .............. .............. a sick colleague |

**93.3**

6 marks

Put the words in the correct order to make logical sentences containing phrasal verbs.

1 off / flight / on / time / The / took
2 over / scandal / weeks / of / a / couple / blew / The / after
3 took / police / heard / car / a / robbers / off / The / they / when / arriving
4 computer / up / photo / my / on / I / blew / the
5 station / taxi / The / up / outside / pulled / the
6 Her / late / home / she / told / father / her / off / because / came

**93.4**

10 marks

Replace the underlined phrasal verbs in these sentences with a verb from the box. Write the verbs in the correct form and make any other necessary changes.

| | | | | |
|---|---|---|---|---|
| stop | recover | conceal | extract | enlarge |
| distinguish | extinguish | resign | betray | scold |

1 It was a major operation, and she was seriously ill, but she <u>pulled through</u>.
2 I find it difficult to <u>tell</u> crows and blackbirds <u>apart</u>.
3 When the truth came out, the Chairperson <u>stood down</u>.
4 I promised I wouldn't <u>tell on</u> him if he cheated in the test.
5 The dentist had to <u>take</u> three of her teeth <u>out</u> after the accident.
6 His mother <u>told</u> him <u>off</u> for not phoning to say where he was.
7 The train <u>pulled up</u> at a small country station.
8 The storm <u>blew out</u> our lamp and we were in complete darkness.
9 I'll take that photo of my mother and get it <u>blown up</u>; it's such a nice one.
10 I'm convinced she's <u>keeping</u> something <u>from us</u>.

**93.5**

6 marks

Circle the correct underlined verb.

1 The stress finally <u>hit/told/set</u> on him and he had to take early retirement.
2 You should <u>hold/talk/stand</u> up for what you believe in, and be prepared to fight for it.
3 He's going to try to break the world record for eating hamburgers but I don't think he'll <u>make/hand/pull</u> it off.
4 The minister said his party <u>held/stood/believed</u> for the basic rights of all citizens.
5 A row has <u>burst/split/blown</u> up between the union and the employers.
6 Please <u>stand/be/walk</u> back from the platform edge when the train is approaching.

Your score

/40

**94.1** Match the phrasal verbs on the left with their meanings on the right.

10 marks

| | | |
|---|---|---|
| 1 | catch on | persevere |
| 2 | doze off | become less extreme |
| 3 | dumb down | make something seem less important |
| 4 | ease up | fall asleep |
| 5 | lay on | become popular |
| 6 | play it down | gradually reduce or destroy |
| 7 | slog away | make something less intellectually demanding |
| 8 | stick it out | pass on secret information |
| 9 | tip off | work hard |
| 10 | whittle away | provide |

**94.2** Choose phrasal verbs from exercise 94.1 to fill the gaps in this e-mail. Write the verbs in the
10 marks    correct form.

Hi, Jean

How are things with you? It's been raining heavily here all day though it seems to be
(1) ............................................. a bit now. We're both busy. Larry is (2) ............................................. at
his thesis. He keeps threatening to give up but I hope he'll (3) ............................................. . I'm
designing a new kids' toy. I just hope it (4) ............................................. as our savings are being rapidly
(5) ............................................. at the moment. I try to (6) ............................................. for Larry as I don't
want him to be worried about anything else but his thesis. He's been (7) .............................................
that his external examiner is likely to be Prof Carr, who has a reputation for toughness. In the
evenings I do what I can to (8) ............................................. nice meals to keep him going. We're both
so tired after dinner that we just (9) ............................................. in front of the TV. They say the
programmes are being (10) ............................................. but we never watch long enough to know
whether that's true or not!

Nell

**94.3** Fill the gaps with the correct preposition or particle.

10 marks

1 The rain was pelting ..................... this morning but it's easing ..................... now.
2 A big problem has cropped ..................... but I'm trying to sort it ..................... so Jo doesn't worry.
3 They're laying ..................... an extra bus to the station. We'll catch it if we step ..................... it.
4 Jane's advice initially made me determined not to bottle ..................... my feelings any longer, but
    that determination has now worn ..................... .
5 The boys were intending to stow ..................... but bottled ..................... at the last moment.

**94.4** Rewrite these sentences using the words in brackets.

10 marks

1 Whenever I sit in that armchair beside the fire, I fall asleep. (DOZE)
2 I'd have got home at 6 p.m. if a problem hadn't suddenly occurred at work. (CROPPED)
3 It's raining heavily in London at the moment. (PELTING)
4 The boy got to this country by hiding in the hold of a plane. (STOWING)
5 Psychologists say it's better not to hide your feelings. (BOTTLE)
6 I never expected DVDs to become popular. (CATCH)
7 It always takes a few hours for a dental anaesthetic to lose its effect. (WEAR)
8 Please hurry up or we'll be late. (STEP)
9 I was planning to sing in the competition but I lost my courage. (BOTTLED)
10 We can organise the final details later. (SORT)

**Your score**

/40

# 95 Phrasal verbs 3

**95.1**

10 marks

Complete the phrasal verbs in these sentences by filling the gaps with the correct particle and a preposition. You are given the first letter of the particle.

*Example*: The thieves got a.way.... ..with.. dozens of valuable works of art.

1 It was nice to meet Sally again after so long and to catch u..................... ..................... all the news.
2 I sometimes think the boss has it i................... ................... me. She's always criticising my work.
3 Young athletes often miss o.................. ................. normal teenage life because they train so hard.
4 I really think it's time to do a.................. ................... that old printer and get a new one.
5 I should redecorate my bedroom but I'm so busy; I can't seem to get r.................. .................. it.

**95.2**

8 marks

Read these remarks and then answer the questions.

ROB:     I'm sorry the report's late. I just had an impossible amount of work to do last week.
HARRY:   Philip was so angry the other day, but he seemed calmer yesterday.
PENNY:   We're starting to sell a new, different range of products and services.
JASON:   They just told me they didn't need me any more, so I'm unemployed now.
LORNA:   Profits were bad last year but they're increasing now.
OLIVIA:  I couldn't help it. I just got so excited.
BEN:     I was just so shocked by what she told me.
MILLIE:  I'm so annoyed. I can't stop thinking about it. In fact I'm furious.

1 Who was taken aback?            5 Who was snowed under?
2 Who was laid off?               6 Whose business is branching out?
3 Who got carried away?           7 Who simmered down?
4 Who has got worked up?          8 Whose business is picking up?

**95.3**

14 marks

Cross out seven mistakes with phrasal verbs and write the correct word above each mistake.

I had a bad week last week. First I fell down with Carol – it was a stupid argument, then I came below with a cold and had to stay in bed for two days. I felt very grumpy and took it off on my sister, as if it was her fault. I decided I needed something to happy me up so I invited another friend round and opened out to her and told her my troubles. We just cooled out listening to some new CDs she'd bought. She was bubbling out with excitement; she'd just met a new man who she'd fallen madly in love with.

**95.4**

8 marks

Write these phrasal verbs in the correct metaphorical category.

| go down with   fall out with   simmer down   chill out   pick up |
| bottom out   be snowed under   bubble over   come down with |

| 'weather' metaphor | 'high and low' metaphor | 'cooking' metaphor |
|---|---|---|
|  | go down with |  |

Your score
/40

# 96 Divided by a common language: American and British English

**96.1** Complete the word puzzle by giving the American English equivalent for each of the underlined words.

10 marks

1 Go straight on at the <u>road junction</u>.
2 We travelled along the <u>long-distance motorway</u>.
3 We walked along a lovely little <u>footpath</u> through the woods.
4 Don't forget to turn the <u>tap</u> off.
5 That brown wire in the plug is the <u>earth</u>.
6 Cross the street at the <u>pedestrian crossing</u>.
7 The <u>flyover</u> takes the road across the river.
8 I'm going to try to <u>reverse</u> into this parking space.  (2 words: _ _ _ _  _ _ )
9 We live <u>diagonally opposite</u> to the school.
10 We bought a new <u>cooker</u> last week.

**96.2** Decide whether these sentences are more likely to be said by a British person or by an American person. Underline the words in each sentence that tell you the answer.

20 marks

1 We rented a house by the creek and spent the weekends exploring little trails nearby.
2 I'll wait in the parking lot while you load up the shopping cart.
3 We stopped at a petrol station just before joining the motorway.
4 There's a frying pan next to the cooker.
5 The flight will deplane momentarily.
6 Coach class passengers are only allowed one piece of carry-on baggage.
7 It's very expensive to rent a skip.

**96.3** Complete this table of British English and American English equivalents.

10 marks

| | British English | American English | | British English | American English |
|---|---|---|---|---|---|
| 1 | path | | 6 | | dumpster |
| 2 | | skillet | 7 | trolley | |
| 3 | | take a left | 8 | disembark | |
| 4 | hand luggage | | 9 | shortly | |
| 5 | | stove | 10 | | creek |

**97.1** Match the underlined words, which you might hear in Ireland, with their correct meaning
10 marks   (a) or (b).

1   The <u>gardai</u> arrived immediately after the accident.
    (a) soldiers  (b) police
2   Our <u>Taoiseach</u> announced his retirement yesterday.
    (a) Bishop  (b) Prime Minister
3   The <u>craic</u> was amazing at Zeno's last night.
    (a) food  (b) fun
4   This <u>boreen</u> will take you to the village of Castlecroe.
    (a) lane  (b) bus
5   There's a big <u>fleadh</u> on in the town this week.
    (a) trade fair  (b) music festival

**97.2** Match these sentences with the person who is most likely to say them.
10 marks

| | |
|---|---|
| 1  The washroom's over there. | someone from Malaysia |
| 2  She has two lovely bairns. | someone from Hong Kong |
| 3  We shifted last week to a bigger house. | an Australian |
| 4  I don't believe it, mate! | a Canadian |
| 5  It's okay. We pay at the shroff. | a Scot |

**97.3** Answer these questions.
20 marks

1   In which country are you most likely to hear someone say 'Struth!', Canada, Hong Kong or Australia?
2   Which of these two words is from the Caribbean and means a godmother?
    (a) didgeridoo  (b) macommere
3   What is an informal word for 'man' which is used in Britain and in Australia?
    b............................
4   Is a dingo  (a) a musical instrument  (b) a type of vehicle  (c) a wild dog? In which country are you most likely to find a dingo?
5   Australians often abbreviate words. How do they abbreviate the words
    (a) Australia and  (b) beautiful?
6   Which word is used in Australia to describe wild, uncultivated land, especially the desert?
7   Which word might you hear in South Africa to describe the natural, uncultivated land away from towns?
8   The word 'eejit' is used in Ireland and means in British English
    (a) Egypt  (b) idiot  (c) exit.
9   If a Scottish person says they live in a 'wee' house, is their house  (a) big or  (b) small?
10  In Australian English, to call someone a 'stupid ocker' is to call them crude and ignorant. True or false?

**Your score**

/40

# 98 Language and gender

**98.1**
10 marks
What is now the preferred, non-sexist form of these words or expressions?

| | |
|---|---|
| 1 cleaning lady | 6 manpower |
| 2 Miss or Mrs | 7 air hostess |
| 3 foreman | 8 spokesman |
| 4 to man an office | 9 male nurse |
| 5 chairman | 10 man-hours |

**98.2**
12 marks
Put the words from the box into the correct category.

| | | | | | |
|---|---|---|---|---|---|
| butch | effeminate | female | feminine | male | manly |
| mannish | masculine | sissy | tomboy | virile | womanly |

| negative | neutral | positive |
|---|---|---|
| | | |
| | | |
| | | |
| | | |

**98.3**
12 marks
Choose the best word from the box in exercise 98.2 to fill each gap. Use each word once only.

1 She's such a ............................................ – she'd far rather climb trees than play with dolls.
2 A stag is a ............................................ deer.
3 Come on, John, jump! Don't be such a ............................................ !
4 In some languages some nouns are ............................................ and others are ............................................ .
5 The hero of an adventure film is usually going to be handsome and ............................................ .
6 Usually ............................................ mammals feed their young with their own milk.
7 Little boys used to be taught that it isn't ............................................ to cry.
8 Nancy is very big and ............................................; she often gets mistaken for a man.
9 I don't know why Zoë has her hair in such a ............................................ style. She'd look much nicer if she let it grow longer.
10 In the past the ............................................ virtues were said to include motherliness, cleanliness and modesty.
11 He's got a very ............................................ voice – I thought he was a woman when he answered the phone.

**98.4**
6 marks
Answer these questions.

1 Why do most English people now use the word firefighter rather than fireman?
2 Does the word mankind only refer to men?
3 What is another word that means the same as mankind?
4 Is Ms Lucy Jones married or single?
5 If someone calls someone's use of language sexist, do they approve or disapprove?
6 What might someone who is extremely concerned about using non-sexist language say instead of 'manhandle'?

Your score

/40

**99.1**

5 marks

Which words refer to higher social classes or people with more money and which refer to lower social classes or more ordinary people? Tick (✓) the appropriate box.

|  | hoi-polloi | plebby | posh | toff | oik |
|---|---|---|---|---|---|
| *higher* |  |  |  |  |  |
| *lower* |  |  |  |  |  |

**99.2**

5 marks

Use the words from exercise 99.1 to fill the gaps in these sentences.

1 She married a real .......................................... and now she goes round looking like a duchess.
2 Since he won the lottery he doesn't want to mix with the .......................................... any more.
3 Being so upper class, she couldn't cope with his .......................................... attitude to everything.
4 They live in a very .......................................... part of town where the houses cost a fortune.
5 They're just a bunch of stupid .......................................... . All they do is get drunk and cause trouble.

**99.3**

18 marks

Answer these questions.

1 Which expression involving the word 'crust' refers to people with money and influence?
2 What expression can be used to refer to educated middle-class people always ready to offer an opinion on everything? the c.......................... c..........................
3 What type of people are described as 'new money'?
4 What adjective based on the verb 'stick' refers to people who behave in a snobbish way?
5 What adjective beginning with sn...................... also means 'snobbish'?
6 What might an upper-class person say instead of 'lunch'?
7 What expression consists of two words beginning with 'r' and means 'uncultured lower-class people'?
8 Which social class does the word 'bourgeois' refer to?
9 What two words beginning with 'l' mean 'toilet'?

**99.4**

6 marks

Use some of the answers from exercise 99.3 to fill the gaps in these sentences.

1 She's very .......................................... . She think she's of a higher class than everyone else.
2 (A servant is speaking to her employer) Lady Winter telephoned, Madam. She said she will meet you for .......................................... tomorrow in Pierre's restaurant at 12.30.
3 I don't like this pub. It's full of rough, lower-class people who cause trouble. Let's go somewhere away from the .......................................... .
4 Wilfred is a real member of the .......................................... . He loves giving his opinion on political or cultural matters.
5 He was a hippy, but he's become very .......................................... ; he's joined the golf club and has bought a big house in the suburbs.
6 Most of the people who buy big country houses are .......................................... . The old aristocrats can't afford them any more.

**99.5**

6 marks

Decide whether these sentences are more likely to be said by a person of the younger generation or the older generation and write 'young' or 'old' after each sentence.

1 What time is the news on the wireless?
2 That camera of yours is wicked.
3 I need to buy a new pair of slacks.
4 Is that your new bike? Cool.
5 What a chump you are, David!
6 What would you like to drink, old sport?

Your score

/ 40

**100.1**

*10 marks*

Answer the questions about these headlines.

# PALACE BLAST SENSATION

1 Where has something happened?
2 What probably happened there?

## Crackdown on litter louts

3 What are litter louts?
4 What is being done about them?

## TYPHOON RIPS THROUGH HOLIDAY SUNSPOT

5 Where has something happened?
6 What has happened there?

## MP besieged by press

7 Who is in the news?
8 What is happening to him or her?

## Cops target city thugs

9 Who is in the news?
10 What are the 'cops' doing?

**100.2**

*10 marks*

Look at these typical headlines and answer the questions below.

**Car company cuts costs**          **MP TO VISIT STATES**

**TV star's lone terror**          **Teenage thug charged**

1 Which headline uses alliteration?
2 Which two abbreviations are used?
3 Which two words suggest violence?
4 Which headline is about something in the future?
5 Write out each headline in a complete sentence.

**100.3**

*20 marks*

Newspapers are prepared so quickly that sometimes the journalists do not see double meanings in the headlines they write. Explain what the story was probably about and how the headline could also be interpreted.

1 **Kids make nutritious snacks**
2 **Local high school dropouts cut in half**
3 **Stolen painting found by tree**
4 **New study of obesity seeks larger test group**
5 **Pop star appeals to Pope**
6 Milk drinkers turning to powder
7 British left waffles on public transport
8 Police begin campaign to run down illegal workers
9 **Drunks get nine months in violin case**
10 *Police head seeks arms*

**Your score**

/40

# Key

## Test 1

**1.1**
1 as soon as possible
2 for example (from the Latin *exempli gratia*)
3 note (from the Latin *nota bene*)
4 that is (from the Latin *id est*)
5 European Union
6 unidentified flying object
7 before Christ
8 value added tax
9 identity
10 personal computer

`10 marks`

**1.2**
1 I'd prefer to watch a good documentary rather than a **sitcom** any day.
2 I've loved **sci-fi** ever since I was a kid.
3 The city was founded in about 500 **AD**.
4 Accommodation is expensive. Even a **bedsit** will cost you 600 pounds a month.
5 The information leaflet had a useful list of **FAQ**s.

`10 marks: 2 marks per sentence`

**1.3**
To let: 2-bedroom **self-contained** flat near city centre. **Central heating** and all **modern conveniences**. Rent £800 **per calendar month exclusive** (of bills). (5 marks)

Room to let in shared **fully furnished** flat. Suit **non-smoking professional** female. £100 **per week inclusive** (of bills). (5 marks)

For Sale: Large family house in pretty village 8 **miles** from Cambridge. Garden. **Double garage**. Tel: 0132 56374 for details. (2 marks)

`12 marks`

**1.4**
1 AIDS (acquired immune deficiency syndrome)
2 NATO (North Atlantic Treaty Organisation)
3 RSVP (reply please – from the French *Répondez s'il vous plaît*)
4 PTO (please turn over)
5 ONO (or nearest offer)

`5 marks`

**1.5**
1 HI JOEL! See you AT THE MATCH TOMORROW?
2 NO WAY. For your information I'M BROKE. BUY ME A TICKET?
3 You are JOKING!

`3 marks`

## Test 2

**2.1**
1 The speaker thinks that the prices are too high.
2 The hospital does not have enough staff.
3 An exchange which allows young people to experience other cultures, e.g. they spend time attending a school in another country.
4 He got a better seat, e.g. he was moved from economy to first class.
5 They are coming home the following day.
6 The speaker suggests that it was secretive and possibly dishonest.
7 It has improved.
8 Underlying or deeper causes of crime could be some of the following: poverty, unemployment, drugs, or alienation from society. In other words, anything that you think might be a deeper social reason suggesting why people might turn to crime.
9 That it's too low, that Helen is capable of more than the other person thinks.
10 The people are on opposite sides of a border between two countries.

`10 marks`

**2.2**   1 e   2 c   3 a   4 f   5 d   6 g   7 h   8 b   9 j   10 i   `10 marks`

**2.3**  
1 abdicated  
2 condolences  
3 intravenously  
4 promoted  
5 ejects  

6 adjoining *or* adjacent  
7 interrelated  
8 emitting *or* to emit  
9 afloat  
10 extraterrestrial  

20 marks: I mark for choosing the correct word, I mark for putting it in the correct form

# Test 3

**3.1**  
soundproof    additive-free    fibre-rich    like-minded  
crime-ridden    newsworthy    washable    stress-related  
student-led    health-conscious  
Some other words are also possible, e.g. crime-free, health-related, likeable. 20 marks: 2 marks per item

**3.2**  
1 career-minded  
2 waterproof  
3 guilt-ridden  
4 trustworthy  
5 class-conscious  

6 staff-led  
7 Sugar-free  
8 protein-rich  
9 work-related  
10 workable  

10 marks

**3.3**

| | noun | verb | adjective | adverb |
|---|---|---|---|---|
| occupant | ✓ | | | |
| moisten | | ✓ | | |
| costly | | | ✓ | |
| golden | | | ✓ | |
| heavily | | | | ✓ |
| relevant | | | ✓ | |
| sweeten | | ✓ | | |
| lively | | | ✓ | |
| claimant | ✓ | | | |
| warmly | | | | ✓ |

10 marks

# Test 4

**4.1**  
1 autosuggestive  
2 telepathic  
3 destabilised  
4 premeditated  
5 biodegradable  
6 retroactive  

7 criminology  
8 biography  
9 Linguistics  
10 cybercafé  
11 monograph  
12 postgraduate  

12 marks

**4.2**  
1 heliport   from helicopter + airport *or* helipad   from helicopter + launching pad  
2 breathalyser   from breath + analyse  
3 vegeburger   from vegetarian + burger *or* vegetable + burger  
4 motel   from motor + hotel  
5 smog   from smoke + fog  
6 brunch   from breakfast + lunch  

18 marks: I mark for each blend, I mark for each of the two words that make up each blend

**4.3**  
1 personal signature   auto = self; graph = writing  
2 phone calls paid for in advance of making them   pre = before; paid = bought  
3 the study of the climate   ology = study of  
4 after having an operation   post = after  
5 moving things away from the centre   de = opposite action

6 the range or variety of living organisms   bio = life; diversity = variety
7 looking back   retro = back; spect = look (as in inspect, aspect, prospect, etc.)
8 crimes based on the Internet   cyber = relating to the Internet and robots
9 expert in technical things   techno = relating to advanced machines; wizard = magician, expert
10 movement forward   pro = forward; gress = go (as in congress, transgress, digress)   `10 marks`

## Test 5

**5.1**  1 stock; borrowings    2 sources    3 lexicon    4 enriched
5 classical    6 loan    7 linguistic    `16 marks: 2 marks per word`

**5.2**

| language | word |
|---|---|
| German | rucksack |
| Russian | intelligentsia |
| Spanish | hammock |
| German | gimmick |
| Greek | tonic |
| Portuguese | palaver |
| Arabic | amber |
| Japanese | hara-kiri |
| Hindi | cot |
| Icelandic | mumps |
| Farsi | tabby |
| Dutch | roster |
| Turkish | turban |

`12 marks`

**5.3**  1 amber       5 tonic       9 intelligentsia
2 gimmick     6 roster      10 cot
3 hara-kiri    7 tabby       11 hammock
4 palaver      8 mumps      12 turban    `12 marks`

## Test 6

**6.1**  1 stationary          6 interfering
2 shade             7 shadows
3 continually        8 complement
4 intervene         9 stationery
5 complimented     10 continuously    `10 marks`

**6.2**  1 moist             8 outlook
2 topic             9 theme
3 upend            10 aroused
4 evade            11 altered
5 damp             12 avoid
6 rouse            13 change
7 serial;   ends up (2 marks)    14 lookout    `15 marks`

**6.3**  1 a) safety  b) security  (2 marks)
   2 You would rehearse a play or a concert and you would revise for an exam or test.  (4 marks)
   3 flu, rioting, i.e. an outbreak of flu/rioting  (2 marks)
   4 A train might be held up because of snow. If a decision is upheld, then it stays as it was.  (2 marks)
   5 You might pick flowers or strawberries and you might pick up a friend from the airport or a pen that's fallen on the ground.  (4 marks)
   6 A breakout is more likely to happen from a prison.  (1 mark)       `15 marks`

# Test 7

**7.1**  1 b    2 a    3 a    4 b    5 a    6 b       `6 marks`

**7.2**  1 workmates
   2 monotonous
   3 nine-to-five
   4 workload
   5 freelance
   6 self-employed       `12 marks: 2 marks per word`

**7.3**  1 a job-share
   2 flexi-time
   3 a shift worker
   4 a dead-end job
   5 paperwork       `10 marks: 2 marks per item`

**7.4**  1 shift    2 repetitive    3 irregular    4 antisocial    5 behind    6 levels
       `12 marks: 2 marks per word`

# Test 8

**8.1**  1 paternity      6 overworked
   2 glass          7 career
   3 snowed         8 experience
   4 shortlisted    9 turned
   5 entitlement   10 passed       `10 marks`

**8.2**  I would certainly recommend John Geddes for a job in your company. He is a very **dynamic** and **ambitious** young man and I am sure he could be a high **achiever** in any **career** he chooses. The job description you sent me is a little **ambiguous** but it looks as if you are **seeking** someone with very **diverse** abilities. John has many of these and I am sure he would be willing and **eager** to acquire any other skills that the position requires.       `8 marks`

**8.3**  1 ambiguous     5 eager
   2 dynamic        6 seeking
   3 career         7 achiever
   4 ambitious      8 diverse       `8 marks`

**8.4**  1 For me, **job satisfaction** (*or* **job security**) is more important than a large salary. As I'm not particularly money **motivated** (*or* **minded**), I'm looking for a **career** that I will find **rewarding** in itself. I would certainly far rather work in a close-**knit** team than have a very prestigious and **lucrative** position in a company where I felt isolated.
   2 When Don was **demoted** to being just a middle manager, he lost a lot of the **perks** (*or* **privileges**) he had previously enjoyed as a top manager and he also no longer received a large salary **increment** (*or* **increase**) each year.
   3 Are you **resourceful**? We need people who can find imaginative ways of doing things. And are you self-**reliant**? We need people who can do things independently. Do you think you might **fit** this description? If you also have an **adventurous** spirit and enjoy challenges, then call or write today!       `14 marks`

# Test 9

**9.1**  a) hard sell    b) niche market    c) confusion marketing    d) inertia selling
e) loss leader

1 niche market    2 loss leader    3 hard sell    4 confusion marketing
5 inertia selling

10 marks

**9.2**  1 Business leaders are always complaining about too much **red tape**.
2 **Cold calling** is extremely annoying.
3 It's always a good idea to **shop around** before buying household goods.
4 The country estate of Lord Blethercomb **came** (*or* **went**) **under the hammer** in 1998.
5 The estate will be sold to the **highest bidder**.
6 Unfortunately our local bookshop has been **swallowed up** by a big high street chain.
7 Car manufacturers often rely on **brand loyalty** in order to make further sales.
8 Gerald is selling his computer and he said he would let me **have first refusal** (**on it**).
9 The two companies **hammered out a deal** after 18 hours of negotiations.
10 We bought the bicycle **on approval**.

20 marks: 2 marks per item

**9.3**  1 niche market  (2 marks)
2 a bid, a bidder  (2 marks)
3 capital assets  (2 marks)
4 entrepreneurship  (1 mark)
5 lucrative  (1 mark)
6 to merge  (1 mark)
7 reached *or* arrived at *or* achieved  (1 mark)

10 marks

# Test 10

**10.1**  

| | |
|---|---|
| a lack of resources | to acknowledge receipt |
| a penalty clause | to amass a fortune |
| an outstanding account | to default on a payment |
| low morale | to miss a deadline |
| the survival of the fittest | to submit a tender |

10 marks

Note that *to acknowledge payment* is also possible as a collocation.
*An outstanding tender* would also be possible although *outstanding* would then have the meaning of 'exceptionally good' rather than 'not yet delivered'.

**10.2**  1 Henry had already **amassed** a (large) **fortune** by the time he was 30.
2 Please **acknowledge receipt** (of the parcel).
3 Unfortunately, you have **missed the deadline** (for completing your report).
4 The staff are suffering from **low morale**.
5 In business just as in the natural world, it is a case of **the survival of the fittest**.
6 Please note **a penalty clause** (in the contract).
7 The firm's problem is (that it has) **a lack of resources**.
8 If you are interested in doing the work, you should **submit a tender** by 1 June.
9 We no longer do business with that company because they have **defaulted on a payment**.
10 The company still has **an outstanding account** (with us).

20 marks: 1 mark for choosing the correct collocation for each sentence; 1 mark for rewriting the sentence in an accurate and appropriate way

**10.3**

10 marks

# Test 11

**11.1**  1 **Rote learning** is a strong tradition in some cultures. *or* **Learning by rote** is ...
2 I had several (little) **mnemonics** when I was preparing for my exams. *or* I used several ...
3 After studying geography for ten years, I feel I know the subject **inside out**.
4 Some things just have to be **learnt by heart** when you study for exams. *or* ... learned by heart ...
5 I have an exam next week. I'll just have to **bury myself in** my books.

10 marks: 2 marks per sentence

**11.2**

| | | |
|---|---|---|
| 1 | He's only nine but he's already writing little stories at school. | composition |
| 2 | It's 100,000 words long and breaks new ground in genetics. | thesis |
| 3 | It's 5,000 words long and I have to hand it in at the end of term. | assignment |
| 4 | It's 10,000 words long and it was part of her Master's degree. | dissertation |
| 5 | I submitted a selection of my work for assessment. | portfolio |
| 6 | It was on local history; I did interviews and made videos. | project |
| 7 | It was published in the *Journal of Zoological Sciences* in 1994. | paper, article |

8 marks:
1 mark per word

**11.3**  I have a lot of essays to ~~make~~ **do** this term. I usually make a first ~~draught~~ **draft** and then I write it ~~under~~ **up (or out)**
in its final form a day or two before I have to ~~remit~~ **submit** it to my tutor. I'm always nervous when I'm
waiting for ~~backwash~~ **feedback** from him, but he always ~~asserts~~ **assesses** our work very fairly and I've had some
quite high ~~notes~~ **marks (or grades)** so far this term.

12 marks: 1 mark for finding each
mistake, 1 mark for correcting it

**11.4**  1 past papers
2 drop out
3 carry out
4 the inter-library loan system *or* inter-library loans
5 (academic) journals or periodicals
6 revise
7 finals
8 plagiarise
9 mind maps
10 deadline

10 marks

# Test 12

**12.1**　1　False. A comprehensive school is one that all children can enter without taking any special exam. *or* A selective school is one that chooses pupils on the basis of their ability.
　　　2　True
　　　3　False. The three Rs are reading, writing and arithmetic.
　　　4　True
　　　5　True
　　　6　False. A co-educational or mixed system of education is one in which boys and girls are educated together. *or* A two-tier educational system is one with two distinct parallel levels of education, one of which is much better than the other.
　　　7　True
　　　8　False. Special needs education is for children who are unable to learn in the normal way.
　　　9　True
　　10　False. Literacy means the ability to read and write. *or* Illiteracy means an inability to read and write.

> 10 marks: $\frac{1}{2}$ mark for correctly deciding true/false; 1 mark for an appropriate correction

**12.2**　1　continuing education
　　　2　league tables
　　　3　lifelong education
　　　4　mature students
　　　5　one-to-one class
　　　6　Parent–Teacher Association
　　　7　peripatetic teacher
　　　8　school governor
　　　9　selective school
　　10　supply teacher

*School teacher* and *selective education* would also be possible collocations.

> 10 marks

**12.3**　1　lifelong education, continuing education  (2 marks)
　　　2　in a number of different schools
　　　3　two: one pupil and one teacher
　　　4　pass an entrance exam
　　　5　League tables usually publish schools' examination results.
　　　6　They are older than most other students.
　　　7　A supply teacher is needed when a regular teacher is ill or away on a course.
　　　8　Their role is to support and monitor the work of a school.
　　　9　one school

> 10 marks

**12.4**　1　comprehensive
　　　2　depresses
　　　3　perceive
　　　4　better-off
　　　5　perpetuated
　　　6　literacy
　　　7　numeracy
　　　8　bullying
　　　9　inherent
　　10　well-off

> 10 marks

# Test 13

**13.1**　1　diligent
　　　2　obliging
　　　3　altruistic
　　　4　placid
　　　5　sagacious
　　　6　opportunistic
　　　7　procrastinate
　　　8　tactless
　　　9　chauvinistic
　　10　flashy

> 10 marks

**13.2**　sharp-tongued – terse
　　　astute – shrewd
　　　cunning – sly
　　　morose – sullen
　　　generous – unstinting
　　　dogged – resolute
　　　frugal – thrifty
　　　extravagant – immoderate
　　　tolerant – broad-minded
　　　diligent – industrious

> 10 marks

**13.3**  1  Edward is an old-fashioned, **gallant** gentleman.
2  Don't take any notice of Jack; he gets carried **away** sometimes.
3  A lot of politicians are basically **unscrupulous** and obsessed with power.
4  Arthur is very **industrious** and hard-working.
5  Kim is very self-**seeking**, always trying to gain every advantage for himself.

10 marks: 1 mark for finding each mistake, 1 mark for correcting it

**13.4**  1  Why am I so **naïve**? Some people seem to be much more **intuitive** and can see when trouble is coming.
2  My parents are so **stingy**! I like spending money on clothes and going out, but my parents say I **am superficial**.
3  I don't think I have a **magnetic** personality, and I think people find me too **sober**.
4  My colleagues at work are all so **witty** and always seem able to come out with **pithy** comments that are just right for the situation.
5  I think I'm **work-obsessed/a workaholic**. (2 marks)

10 marks

# Test 14

**14.1**
| | | |
|---|---|---|
| 1 passionate | 6 | loyalty |
| 2 inseparable | 7 | supportive |
| 3 faithful | 8 | fondness |
| 4 trustworthy | 9 | respectful |
| 5 platonic | 10 | considerate |

10 marks

**14.2**
| | | |
|---|---|---|
| 1 heels | 6 | fire |
| 2 with | 7 | hit |
| 3 got | 8 | heart |
| 4 of | 9 | spirits |
| 5 with | 10 | sight |

10 marks

**14.3**  Hi, Georgia,
The blind date was OK, though I wouldn't say he was a man ~~for~~ **after** my own heart. He was quite amiable but I'm not sure that ~~amiableness~~ **amiability** is what I'm really looking for in a man. He talked a lot about his family – he's obviously devoted ~~with~~ **to** them and he talked in a very ~~affectionful~~ **affectionate** way about his sisters, which I liked. But I really don't think we were very ~~good~~ **well**-matched. Oh well, better luck next time.
Anna

10 marks: 1 mark for finding each mistake, 1 mark for correcting it

**14.4**  1  strong connection – close bond
2  close friends – bosom buddies
3  a person who has been with you all your life – lifelong companion
4  connections because of a blood relationship – family ties
5  to share the same attitude to life – to be soulmates

10 marks: 2 marks per item

# Test 15

**15.1**  1 unswerving    2 scrupulously    3 true    4 casual    5 bitter    10 marks: 2 marks per item

**15.2**  1 honest; dishonest
2 content *or* contented; discontented
3 welcome *or* welcoming; unwelcome *or* unwelcoming
4 supportive; unsupportive
5 critical
6 ally

**15.3**  Friends don't always see eye ~~at~~ *to* eye. I hate it when people talk ~~under~~ *behind* my back. I've always been loyal ~~at~~ *to* my friends, but some of them have been critical ~~in~~ *of* me and said things to other people which are not true. I've always tried to be honest ~~for~~ *with* them, and I've never been disloyal ~~on~~ *to (or towards)* them.

**15.4**  1 No, there is a rift between them and a rift means a division or disagreement.
2 Gemma
3 Wednesday
4 b
5 Edna's side of the family and Bob's side.
6 False. Hilda thinks that discord or disagreements are normal, but not physical fights.
7 Harry and Gemma
8 False. They hate his guts, so they dislike him very strongly.
9 c
10 True

# Test 16

**16.1**  
1 defusing
2 hankering
3 blissfully
4 exultant
5 appeasement
6 placated
7 covetous
8 jubilation
9 raptures
10 conciliatory

**16.2**  1 thrilled    2 over    3 air    4 for    5 for

**16.3**  1 Angelica Pretty is very happy and excited.
2 The captain of Liverpool United is extremely pleased.
3 Anita Howley is extremely happy.
4 Julia wants her father's approval very much. (*Yearn* suggests a certain sadness and it is usually used about things that you may not be able to have.)
5 Nora Parker has a strong desire to experience adventure.

**16.4**  1 Jim looks miserable but Rosa looks full of the joys of spring.
2 Ever since we moved to the country I've felt on top of the world.
3 I've lived abroad for years now but I still hanker after my mum's cooking.
4 I stick to my diet but I still have occasional cravings for chocolate.
5 Biddy did her best to defuse the tense situation.
6 They have appointed an officer to conciliate between the two sides.
7 I feel great pity for sick children.
8 Josh's parents were blissfully ignorant of his poor marks.
9 Alicia has an implacable hatred for injustice.
10 Since I got the job, I feel as if I've been walking on air.

**16.5**  appease the enemy
covet a prize
defuse tension
exultant mood
implacable hatred

10 marks

# Test 17

**17.1**
1 She was scornful of (*or* towards) my attempts at writing poetry.
2 The sight of so much rotting food and filth everywhere revolted me. *or* I was revolted by the sight of ...
3 Her comments were very unsympathetic.
4 I am not averse to the idea of renting a flat in the city centre.
5 He loathed people who lacked moral courage.
6 Some modern buildings are repulsive.
7 Violence is abhorrent. *or* I find violence abhorrent.
8 His table manners are revolting.
9 I don't understand why he is so hostile towards the plans.
10 War fills me with abhorrence. *or* I have an abhorrence for war.

20 marks: 2 marks per sentence

**17.2**
1 Mr Peabody acted in a very **officious** manner.
2 Everyone commented on his rather **puerile** behaviour.
3 People tend to become rather **fuddy-duddy** as they grow older.
4 Eric has a **nit-picking** attitude to detail when he reads our reports.
5 She responded to our complaint in a rather **off-hand** way.
6 I suppose you could say Rory has a somewhat **brash** personality.
7 Lara is a bit **fickle**; she'll think one thing one day and the opposite the next.
8 The apartment was absolutely **squalid** when we took it over.
9 Why does she always wear such **dowdy/drab** clothes?
10 He had a very **sloppy/slovenly** attitude to the job.

10 marks

**17.3**

| | | | |
|---|---|---|---|
| 1 | obnoxious | 6 | grasping |
| 2 | aversion | 7 | bland |
| 3 | ostentatious | 8 | pretentious |
| 4 | trite | 9 | pompous |
| 5 | instant | 10 | obsequious |

10 marks

# Test 18

**18.1**
1 double; sallow
2 skinny *or* scrawny (scrawny is more strongly negative than skinny)
3 place
4 scowling
5 taps; clenches
6 biting; picks
7 leering

10 marks

**18.2**

| | | | | | |
|---|---|---|---|---|---|
| 1 | Sean | 5 | Glyn | 9 | Robbie |
| 2 | Bill | 6 | Tony | 10 | Nick |
| 3 | Harry | 7 | Dick | | |
| 4 | Mark | 8 | Tom | | |

10 marks

**18.3**

| words relating to skin | words relating to tidiness of appearance |
|---|---|
| complexion | unkempt |
| sallow | scruffy |
| swarthy | not have a hair out of place |

| words relating to build | gestures and facial expressions |
|---|---|
| portly | tap your fingers |
| corpulent | clench your fist |
| gangling | scowl |
| lanky | grimace |
| overweight | leer |
| stout | pout |
| | raise your eyebrows |
| | shrug |

20 marks

# Test 19

**19.1**
1 He's (very) impetuous and makes a lot of mistakes.
2 She is (always very) pushy.
3 He is garrulous.
4 He is impulsive and can't help spending money on other people.
5 She is (rather/very) taciturn.

10 marks: 2 marks per item

**19.2**
1 reserved
2 unapproachable
3 introvert *or* intravert
4 extrovert *or* extravert
5 effusive
6 gullible
7 haughty
8 aloof
9 diffident

18 marks: 2 marks per item

**19.3**
1 I've always found Georgina (to be) quite approachable.
2 She's an excitable child.
3 Liam is such a flirt!
4 If he hadn't been pushy, he would never have got his promotion.
5 Iris always looks at you disdainfully if you say something mildly funny.

5 marks

**19.4**
1 obstinate
2 unscrupulous
3 (a) conceited (1 mark)
  (b) modest (1 mark)
4 self-important
5 naïve
6 conscientious

7 marks

# Test 20

**20.1**
1 I'm afraid his grandfather passed away last night. *or* I'm afraid his grandfather passed on last night.
2 She may be ninety but she (still) has all her wits about her.
3 This flu is awful – I feel (as if I'm) at death's door.
4 Rob received a large inheritance from his late grandmother.
5 My uncle bequeathed me a small house in the country. *or* I was bequeathed a small house in the country by my uncle.
6 The accident looked very serious but fortunately there were no fatalities.
7 There were legal problems because the old man died without making a will. *or* … without having made a will. *or* … without leaving a will.
8 Funeral services can help people who have been bereaved to deal with their grief. *or* Funeral services can help the bereaved to …
9 My old aunt quite enjoys living in sheltered accommodation.
10 Dan lives in his late father's house.                                                    `10 marks`

**20.2**
1 foetus; uterus; placenta
2 deliver; caesarean; section
3 cremation; scatter; ashes
4 pregnancy; fallopian; tube(s); womb
5 conceive; fertility; drugs
6 made; history
7 went; labour                                                                                `20 marks`

**20.3**
1 die
2 'Perish' sounds more dramatic and is more eye-catching for a headline.
3 killed
4 'Slaughtered' suggests that they were killed violently.
5 The story will be about the fact that smoking may increase a pregnant woman's risk of losing her baby during pregnancy.
6 A miscarriage is not intended, whereas an abortion is the intentional ending of a pregnancy, usually by a medical operation.
7 termination
8 It suggests that it will not survive much longer.
9 The driver died.
10 You will read an article about the life of a famous singer who has recently died.        `10 marks`

# Test 21

**21.1**
1 B: Yes, it's very time-consuming.
2 B: Yes, it seems to be very lucrative.
3 B: Yes, it's been very fruitful.
4 B: Yes, it sounds very rewarding.
5 B: Yes, it's very relaxing.                                                    `10 marks: 2 marks per item`

**21.2**
1 Jane's a **shopaholic**. Her wardrobe is full of new clothes she's never worn.
2 Martin's a real **dabbler**. He took up the guitar, then basketball, then joined a poetry club, but none of them lasted longer than a couple of weeks.
3 Barbara's a real culture **vulture**. She's always going to the opera and art exhibitions.
4 After a hard week in the office, Carla always finds gardening at the weekends very **therapeutic**.
5 Pam is quite lazy, but her sister Roxanne is such a **doer**; she just never stops!          `5 marks`

**21.3**    1  I'm (heavily/really) **into** scuba diving these days.
2  What do you normally **get up to** on Saturday mornings, anything special?
3  I value my **time off** very much.
4  A lot of people get **hooked on** the Internet and spend hours online.
5  I have a (very) **full diary** next week, so we'd better meet the week after.
6  She divides her time **fifty/fifty** (or **fifty-fifty**) between London and Frankfurt.
7  I **went off** football because of all the violence and hooliganism.
8  **Automation** has transformed factory work.
9  Since I retired I've become **a** (real) **couch potato**.
10  Jack **locks himself away** for days on end when he's writing
poetry.                                                          20 marks: 2 marks per sentence

**21.4**    1  free time, leisure time, spare time *or* time off  (2 marks)
2  mass production
3  labour-saving
4  A vulture is a ferocious consumer of any meat it can find and waits for every
opportunity to find it.                                              5 marks

# Test 22

**22.1**    dress codes              ahead of your time
casual clothes           up to the minute
a slave to fashion       on the high street
to set a trend           to be dressed to kill
off the peg              all the rage                                10 marks

**22.2**    1  feather      3  cuff      5  hem      7  frill      9  straitjacket
2  glove        4  seams     6  cloak    8  dagger    10  shoestring    10 marks

**22.3**    1  The bus was extremely crowded.
2  Was it really necessary to keep everything so secret?
3  It's not fair to ask Tim to speak without allowing him time to prepare.
4  The book tells you how to cook delicious meals without spending much money.
5  It was a wonderful achievement for Hanna to win the essay competition.
6  The service on the train is very basic but it is perfectly adequate.
7  Vincent refused to let his bosses restrict his freedom.
8  They've been having a lot of secret meetings at work.
9  Lisa will leave Ben if she starts to feel that she is trapped.
10  Mel and Victor have a very close working relationship.           10 marks

**22.4**    1  They're loose.
2  Not much at all.
3  They should wear less formal clothes than usual.
4  No, because frumpy means old-fashioned and boring.
5  It becomes more popular.
6  You'd wear clean and tidy but informal clothes, for example, a smart pair of trousers,
perhaps with a shirt but no tie for a man, and for a woman trousers and an attractive top.
7  It is more likely to be the wife.
8  They want to know if they have to dress in a formal way.
9  You'd probably feel pleased because 'snazzy' suggests modern and stylish.
10  She's probably wearing a tailored suit with smart high-heeled shoes.   10 marks

# Test 23

**23.1**    1  a) council housing *or* council houses  b) high-rise flats *or* tower blocks
2  c) squat
3  d) penthouse  e) pied à terre                              10 marks: 2 marks per item

**23.2** 1 Iris    2 Tanya    3 James    4 David    5 Lara    6 Lucas

12 marks: 2 marks per item

**23.3** 1 Barry was fed up with **the rat race** and went off to live in the country.
2 When I told the waiter I had worked in the restaurant five years ago he brought me a **drink on the house.**
3 I know Glenda got upset, but it's about time someone told her a few **home truths.**
4 **Subsistence farming** is the typical pattern in the northern part of the country.
5 The hotel was OK, but it was **nothing to write home about.**
6 That lovely old building on the corner has **got a new lease of life** since it was converted into an art gallery.
7 She led **a dog's life** for twenty years as a servant to Lady Trollop.
8 Within two years of its launch, the new product had become a **household name/word.**
9 Whenever I meet a handsome man it turns out he's already married – **it's the story of my life!**

18 marks: 2 marks per sentence

# Test 24

**24.1** 1 Joe was supposed to be taking me out last night but he **stood me up.**
2 As she works in PR, Sally is used to **rubbing shoulders** with the rich and famous.
3 I hope I haven't **outstayed my welcome.**
4 Who does Amal **hang out with** these days?
5 Dave decided to **drop** Pam when he heard she'd been dating another man.
6 Is the wedding going to be a **white/black tie** occasion?
7 Tristram got his job through **the old boy / old school tie network.**
8 My sister says she has much more fun when she **goes on** (*or* has) **a girls' night out.**
9 Hugh is not particularly interested in **climbing the career ladder.**
10 Do you fancy having a night **on the town** this evening?

20 marks

**24.2** 1 a launch party
2 a fancy dress party
3 a hen night *or* a hen party *or* a hen do
4 a housewarming party
5 a stag night *or* a stag party *or* a stag do

5 marks

**24.3** 1 A *party animal* is someone who loves going to parties, whereas a *party pooper* is someone who spoils parties by being miserable or complaining all the time.
2 *To be pally with* means simply to be friendly with someone (no sexual connotations), whereas *to be an item* is to be in a relationship with someone (e.g. boyfriend and girlfriend).
3 *To hobnob* is to socialise with people who are important and famous, and *to knock around with* people is to spend time with people in a casual and friendly way.
4 *Socialising* is spending leisure time with other people, and *networking* is spending time with other people with the aim of helping your career.
5 A wedding *reception* is a party after a wedding ceremony, and a wedding *party* is the group of key people at a wedding (i.e. the bride and groom and their immediate families and close friends).

10 marks

**24.4** I went to a great **bash** (*or* **get-together**) last night. I enjoyed it because it gave me a chance to mix with my new colleagues. They're nice – much less **cliquey** than I thought at first. Hope we can do **lunch** some time soon. Or do you fancy going **clubbing** one night? Shall I see you at that **get-together** (*or* **bash**) that Julie's organising for her cousin from Australia?
Shelley

5 marks

## Test 25

**25.1** *Fields of Darkness* was a **gripping** and **memorable** film, even though the plot was in some ways **far-fetched**. Some critics have said it's **overrated** and **hackneyed**, but I disagree. I found it **moving** and even **harrowing** at times.

On the other hand, another film I saw recently, *Three Delicate Balances*, had **an impenetrable** and **disjointed** plot (or ... a plot which was **impenetrable** and **disjointed**.) I also feel that the director thought that if he threw in a few **risqué** scenes it would make a good movie, but it just didn't work.

10 marks

**25.2** 1 memorable    2 understated    3 lauded    4 bombed
5 a standing ovation

10 marks: 2 marks per item

**25.3** 1 version    2 interpretation    3 portrayal    4 rendition

4 marks

**25.4** 1 b    2 a    3 c    4 a    5 b    6 b    7 a    8 c

16 marks: 2 marks per item

## Test 26

**26.1**
1 True
2 False. If you pull the wool over someone's eyes, you trick or deceive them.
3 True
4 False. A philistine is someone who is unable to appreciate art.
5 False. If people vote with their feet, they show they do not like something by walking out or not going to see it.
6 True
7 False. If someone is visually literate, they understand the visual arts.
8 True
9 False. 'Fad' does mean fashion, but it suggests that the speaker disapproves of it and thinks it will not last long.
10 True

10 marks: $\frac{1}{2}$ mark for true/false,<br>1 mark for each correction

**26.2**
evocative – uninspiring
colourful – drab
highbrow – lowbrow
peerless – run-of-the-mill
impenetrable – transparent
pedestrian – dazzling
tongue-in-cheek – earnest
sophisticated – primitive
undemanding – challenging
dreary – intriguing

Note that pedestrian – intriguing and dreary – dazzling are also possible opposites.

10 marks

**26.3**
1 a broadsheet A tabloid newspaper caters for people's lowbrow tastes, whereas a broadsheet mostly deals with more highbrow issues.
2 an opera An opera is more sophisticated, as nursery rhymes are aimed at young children who are unlikely to have sophisticated tastes.
3 a detective story The aim of a detective story is to intrigue, whereas the aim of a computer manual is to explain and instruct in straightforward terms.
4 a piece of jewellery Jewellery is more likely to be exquisite as exquisite suggests extremely detailed and beautiful.
5 a painting A painting is more likely to be evocative because it is more likely to create images or memories in your mind, whereas a carpet is more likely to be simply functional.
6 a comedy sketch A comedy sketch is more likely to be tongue-in-cheek as a TV ad is aiming to sell a product and so must give the impression that it believes in that product.
7 a watercolour A watercolour is much more likely to be described as run-of-the-mill, as there are far more of them than there are ancient Greek vases.

8 a book on philosophy  A book on philosophy is more likely to be challenging because it will make readers think, whereas a comic aims to amuse readers.

9 a clown  A clown is more likely to behave in a clumsy way, whereas an athlete is much more graceful.

10 a ballerina  A ballerina's performance is more likely to be dazzling, though certainly a drummer may be dazzling too at times, though usually the drummer is not the centre of attention in the way that the ballerina is.

10 marks: ½ mark for each correct answer, ½ mark for a suitable explanation

**26.4**

1 Carla <u>paints</u> her ex-husband <u>in a very bad light</u>.
Carla describes her ex-husband in a very negative way. *Or* Carla is very negative about her ex-husband.

2 The characters in the novel are rather <u>black-and-white</u>.
The characters in the novel are rather lacking in complexity. *Or* The characters in the novel lack complexity.

3 I would certainly recommend this article – I found it very <u>illuminating</u>.
I would certainly recommend this article – I found it gave me a lot of insights.

4 We are all <u>moulded</u> by the things that happen to us in our youth.
We are all influenced by the things that happen to us in our youth.

5 Although Paul Hart usually plays quite <u>colourful</u> people, his character in this play is a rather ordinary person.
Although Paul Hart usually plays people with a strong personality, his character in this play is a rather ordinary person.

10 marks: 1 mark for correctly underlining the metaphorical language in each sentence, 1 mark for rewriting the sentence as suggested

# Test 27

**27.1**

1 macabre
2 compelling
3 lugubrious
4 enigmatic
5 poignant

10 marks: 2 marks per item

**27.2**

1 wry (2 marks)
2 It was a brilliant book, a real page-turner. (2 marks)
3 It was a brilliant book. I just couldn't put it down.  (2 marks)
4 compulsive (2 marks)
5 bedtime reading (2 marks)
6 tale (1 mark)
7 memoirs (1 mark)
8 setting (1 mark)
9 log *or* logbook (1 mark)
10 manual (1 mark)

15 marks

**27.3**

1 Her first novel was **heavy going**.
2 I tried his latest novel but just couldn't **get into it** *or* **get on with it**.
3 It was an absolutely **chilling** narrative.
4 His new novel is a **breathtaking** achievement.
5 I have to say I think his poetry was **lightweight**.

10 marks: 2 marks per item

**27.4**

1 chronicle – account of a sequence of events
2 journal – written record of what someone has done each day
3 blurb – short text on the back cover of a book saying what it is about
4 anthology – collection of poems or stories by different authors
5 compendium – collection of detailed information about a subject

5 marks

## Test 28

**28.1** *Possible answers*

1  flour, bread, pasta, cereal, biscuits
2  vegetables, meat, fruit, produce
3  eggs, chicken(s), turkey(s)
4  milk, cheese, yogurt, meal(s), diet
5  recipe, restaurant, cooking, meal, menu, pizza, burger, dish
6  food(s), products, crops, fruit, vegetables
7  orange squash, a drink, cordial, acid, medicine
8  drink, yogurt, cereal bar, ice cream, tea
9  meal, food, cooking
10 steak, gossip, bone, fruit (e.g. orange, plum, lemon)

> 10 marks: ½ mark for each correct answer

**28.2** ... wanted to <u>spice up</u> our social life [wanted to make our social life more interesting and lively]
It had <u>all the ingredients for</u> success [It had all the necessary characteristics for success]
... things began <u>to turn a bit sour</u> [things became less pleasant or went wrong]
... some rather <u>unsavoury</u> characters [suspicious, unpleasant people]
... some <u>half-baked</u> scheme [a scheme that was not thought through properly, unrealistic]
... started <u>grilling them</u> about it [interrogating them, asking them lots of probing questions]
... feel like <u>a recipe for disaster</u> [likely to lead to disaster]
... the really <u>juicy</u> bits [interesting and exciting parts]
... let Ray <u>stew</u> [let Ray worry or suffer]

> 18 marks: 1 mark for underlining each metaphor, 1 mark for explaining it

**28.3**  1 heavy  2 starch  3 light  4 cereal  5 fat  6 oil

> 12 marks: 2 marks per item

## Test 29

**29.1**
1 out of their way       6 pot luck
2 tooth                  7 get-together
3 off-putting            8 get
4 parties                9 teetotal
5 grab                   10 brusque

> 10 marks

**29.2**
1 Put your credit card away. This meal is on me.
2 I was wined and dined every night when I visited our headquarters in Seville.
3 Shall we split the bill?
4 Do you mind if Maria joins us for dinner tonight?
5 Mark, I'd like you to be my guest for dinner tonight.

> 10 marks: 2 marks per sentence

**29.3**
1 Sea View
2 Pittsburgh
3 Lobster House
4 Golden Bengal
5 Green Bough
6 Panorama

> 6 marks

**29.4**
1 Would anyone like **seconds**? *or* Would anyone like **second helpings / a second helping**?
2 I've put on a bit of weight so I've started to **count the calories**.
3 Does anyone in your group have any special (*or* particular) **dietary requirements**?
4 I won't have any dessert, thanks. I don't want to **overdo** it.
5 Sally **is a** (rather) **fussy eater**; she won't eat this, she won't eat that.
6 Would you like some **nibbles** before we eat?
7 I don't feel like cooking tonight. Shall we get a **takeaway** (meal)?
   *Or* Shall we get a **takeout**?

> 14 marks: 2 marks per sentence

# Test 30

**30.1**
1 reckless
2 on-the-spot
3 tailbacks
4 roadworthy
5 pile-up
6 gridlock
7 head-on
8 give-way
9 towaway
10 hit-and-run

10 marks

**30.2**
road rage
back-seat driver
air bags
penalty points
exhaust emissions

5 marks

**30.3**
1 penalty points
2 back-seat driver
3 road rage
4 exhaust emissions
5 air bags

5 marks

**30.4**
1 sounding
2 skidded
3 jumped
4 towed
5 clamped
6 diverted
7 banned
8 conked out
9 pull over
10 collided

20 marks: 1 mark for selecting the correct verb, 1 mark for putting it in the correct form

# Test 31

**31.1**
1 non-refundable
2 stopover
3 scheduled
4 cancellation fee
5 transfers
6 self-catering
7 unlimited mileage
8 half board
9 all in *or* all inclusive
10 economy

10 marks

**31.2**
upper deck
guest house
charter flight
full board
fare type

10 marks: 2 marks per item

**31.3**
1 I don't want to go with an organised group. I want to be my own boss.
2 I like to keep on the move (or keep moving) when I'm on holiday.
3 It really was the holiday of a lifetime.
4 I don't mind roughing it.
5 It was a trekking holiday where you slept under the stars every night.
6 Low-cost airlines offer value for money.
7 We spent a fortune on our trip to Japan. *or* Our trip to Japan cost us a fortune.
8 We spent a week out in the wilds; it was wonderful.

16 marks: 2 marks per sentence

**31.4**
1 chalet
2 B and B
3 cruise
4 inn

4 marks

## Test 32

**32.1**

| | |
|---|---|
| 1 beaten | 6 subject |
| 2 flora | 7 tour |
| 3 supplement | 8 available |
| 4 ordinary | 9 value |
| 5 nature | 10 drive |

10 marks

**32.2**

1 The view of the mountains from our hotel balcony was **awe-inspiring**.
2 **Eco-tourism** is becoming increasingly popular.
3 You will find a great deal of **wildlife** in the forest.
4 Waterfront, **self-catering** villas are very popular at all times of the year.
5 The region offers **unrivalled** opportunities for water and other sports.
6 The **heartland** of the country is a wild and spectacular bush area.
7 The church is built on the **site** of a Roman temple.
8 If you would like us to arrange a customised tour for you, tell us what you want and we will give you a **quotation** (*or* **quote**).
9 There is no need to have a **four-by-four** vehicle for driving in town.
10 Flora refers to plants and **fauna** refers to animals.

10 marks

**32.3**

| | |
|---|---|
| 1 rainforest | 6 unwind |
| 2 sector | 7 boasts |
| 3 discerning | 8 a hike |
| 4 ramble | 9 virgin |
| 5 hordes | 10 Recharge |

10 marks

**32.4**

1 bush = an area of land, especially in Africa and Australia, covered with natural bushes and trees, which has never been farmed and where there are very few people
2 tract = a large area of land
3 stunning = extremely beautiful or attractive
4 trek = a long walk, usually over land such as hills, mountains and forests
5 wealth = a large amount of something good, e.g. experience, information. We usually talk about a wealth of things, not people.
6 savour = to enjoy food or an experience slowly in order to appreciate it as much as possible
7 seeks = searches for or tries to find
8 itinerary = a detailed plan or route of a journey
9 promising = showing signs that it is likely to be successful or enjoyable
10 escape = get free from or avoid

10 marks: 1 mark per definition. You do not need to define the words in exactly the same way but can give yourself a mark if you have conveyed the basic idea of each word.

## Test 33

**33.1**

1 drought
2 vegetation
3 arid
4 prone
5 coniferous

10 marks: 2 marks per item

**33.2** 1 Lucinda  2 Ciaran  3 Paco  4 Thomas  5 Jeesha

10 marks: 2 marks per item

**33.3** The farmers in the north grow ~~serials~~ *cereals* such as maize and wheat, and ~~trend~~ *tend* their sheep and cattle in small fields. In the south, ~~padded~~ *paddy* fields can be seen where the farmers grow rice. The central area is dominated by ~~prayers~~ *prairies* where cattle graze on the rich grasslands. The north is a cold area of frozen ~~tandra~~ *tundra*.

10 marks: 1 mark for finding each mistake, 1 mark for correcting it

**33.4** 1 manufacturing    2 forefront    3 settled    4 generates
5 descendant

10 marks: 2 marks per item

# Test 34

**34.1**

| hot | cold | wet or damp |
|---|---|---|
| clammy | chilly | clammy |
| stifling | freezing | deluge |
| sweltering | nippy | muggy |
| muggy | | |
| roasting | | |

10 marks: 1 mark for each word you wrote in the correct column

**34.2**  1 misty-eyed
2 current political climate
3 thunderous applause
4 whirlwind romance
5 has a very sunny disposition
6 winds of change
7 met with a frosty reception
8 a hail of bullets
9 under a cloud of suspicion
10 in a haze

10 marks

**34.3**  1 arid                    6 sultry
2 precipitation        7 latitude
3 moderate *or* maritime    8 solar
4 mean                  9 continental
5 oppressive           10 elevation

10 marks

**34.4**  1 It's raining very heavily!
2 What a hot/heavy day!
3 It's cold today, isn't it!
4 Economic prospects look good. *Sunny* is used here in a metaphorical way.
5 The train went quickly and noisily down the track. *Thundered* is used here in a metaphorical way.
6 The most common or frequent winds are westerly.
7 Katie is very busy or has a lot of work. *Snowed under* is used here in a metaphorical way.
8 She looked at me in a cold, unfriendly way. *Icily* is used here in a metaphorical way.
9 I don't have a clear idea of his plans. *Hazy* is used here in a metaphorical way.
10 Karl's political views sometimes affect his judgement so that he doesn't see things as they really are. *Cloud* is used metaphorically here.

10 marks

# Test 35

**35.1**  1 tower    2 glass ceiling    3 brick wall    4 hit; roof
5 cement *or* consolidate

16 marks: 2 marks per word

**35.2**  1 to    2 through    3 in    4 in *or* into

4 marks

**35.3**  1 tower
2 roof
3 locked
4 back

8 marks: 2 marks per item

1 wall, a wall of silence
2 A college degree is the gateway to a better-paid job. *Or* A college degree offers a gateway to …
3 provide, hold, offer, are
4 an ivory tower
5 c
6 limit

*12 marks: 2 marks per item*

# Test 36

**36.1**
1 It's time to **weed out** some of our less efficient employees.
2 It's a journalist's job **to dig up** interesting facts about celebrities' lives.
3 At his age, it's time to think about **putting down roots**.
4 John's been **living in clover** for some years.
5 At last Paul **is reaping the rewards of** all his hard work.
6 Pat seems to be getting a bit snobbish; we'd better **nip that in the bud**.
7 The idea had been around for many years before it really **took root**.
8 Her problems **stem from** her childhood.
9 Becky was always **the apple of the** (*or* **her**) **teacher's eye**.
10 She **shed a lot of weight** when she started walking to work.

*10 marks*

**36.2**
| 1 seeds | 2 budding | 3 withering | 4 shed | 5 flourishing |
| 6 potato | 7 shrivelling | 8 grass | 9 mushrooming | 10 fading |

*10 marks*

**36.3**
Daisy's idea for opening a clothes shop <u>was germinating</u> while we were on holiday in Spain one year ago and she had some very <u>fruitful</u> discussions with some Spanish businessmen she happened to meet there. So you could say that <u>the seeds of her success</u> <u>were planted</u> on a Spanish beach. Her first shop <u>flourished</u> and soon she was <u>branching out</u> into interior furnishings as well. Shops with the Daisy name <u>sprouted up</u> all over the country. Last year when the economy was generally <u>wilting</u>, she had to <u>prune back</u> a bit. She had to <u>shed</u> some employees but now things seem to be looking up again.

Plants germinate when the seed begins to sprout or grow. Here Daisy had a small idea which grew and developed while she was on holiday.

A tree that is fruitful bears a lot of fruit. The discussions which Daisy had with Spanish businessmen gave her a lot more ideas. (Note that fruitful is usually used in a metaphorical way.)

Seeds are the small things from which something big grows. The 'seeds of her success' refers to the initial small idea from which the successful business was to grow.

Seeds are planted or sown when they are put in the ground with the hope of their growing into something big. The initial idea for Daisy's business came to her in Spain and would later develop into something very successful.

Flourishing literally means flowering. Daisy's business flourished, which means that it did very well like a healthy, flowering tree or plant. (Note that flourish is usually used in a metaphorical way.)

Branch out means to grow in different directions as a tree does when it gets larger. Here Daisy's business was expanding and starting to sell different things.

A seed sprouts when it begins to grow small shoots. Daisy's business expanded as she opened new shops in the same way that a plant spreads. (Note that we often say 'sprout up' rather than just 'sprout', especially when we are referring to new buildings.)

A plant wilts if it does not get enough water; it begins to lose its firmness and die. If the economy is wilting then it is not doing very well.

If you prune back a bush or tree, you cut it back. Here Daisy had to make some cuts in her business because times were difficult.

A tree sheds or loses its leaves in autumn. Here Daisy's company had to lose some employees, i.e. make them redundant.

*20 marks: 1 mark for underlining each metaphor, 1 mark for explaining it*

# Test 37

**37.1**　1　carnivore　　2　mammal　　3　predator　　4　reptile　　5　herbivore

10 marks: 2 marks per item

**37.2**　1　herbivores (noun) *or* herbivorous (adjective)
　　　　2　mammal
　　　　3　carnivores
　　　　4　reptiles
　　　　5　predators
　　　　6　tame
　　　　7　rodents
　　　　8　Poachers
　　　　9　domesticated
　　　10　Wild

10 marks

**37.3**　1　Large carnivorous animals (*or* creatures) roamed the earth millions of years ago.
　　　　2　The elephant was so docile when his keeper approached him.
　　　　3　These animals prey on small mammals.
　　　　4　He's an animal rights activist.
　　　　5　The dog was incredibly fierce when cornered.

10 marks: 2 marks per item

**37.4**　1　her<u>bi</u>vorous　　2　<u>rep</u>tile　　3　<u>pre</u>dator　　4　<u>car</u>nivore　　5　do<u>mes</u>ticated　5 marks

**37.5**　1　sanctuary　　2　Blood　　3　ivory　　4　habitat　　5　shelter *or* sanctuary　5 marks

# Test 38

**38.1**　1　case　　　4　Global; levels　　7　dioxide
　　　　2　effect　　5　species　　　　8　pressure
　　　　3　doom　　6　fuels　　　　　9　sustainable

10 marks: 1 mark per word

**38.2**

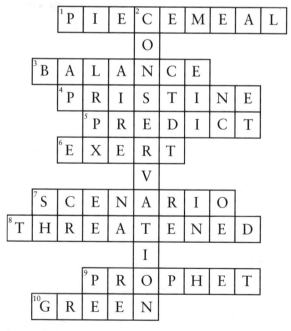

10 marks

**38.3**　1　a pristine **environment**　　　6　finite **resources**
　　　　2　exhaust **emissions**　　　　7　project **sustainability**
　　　　3　**prophets** of doom　　　　8　shrinking **habitats**
　　　　4　uncontrolled **deforestation**　9　in a **piecemeal** fashion
　　　　5　**climatic** changes　　　　10　**demographic** projections

20 marks: 1 mark for finding each mistake, 1 mark for correcting it

## Test 39

**39.1**  1 Q-Mark   2 Panther   3 Q-Mark   4 Zigma
5 Panther

**39.2**  1 shoddy   2 backlog   3 incompetent   4 substandard
5 guarantee

**39.3**  I hate the ~~unpersonal~~ *impersonal* service you get when you phone a big company. You usually get an automated voice, but even if you get a human, they are often ~~incooperative~~ *uncooperative* and just put you on ~~waiting~~ *hold* for hours. They have no sense of ~~urgentness~~ *urgency*.

It's often easier to deal with things online, but if it's not a secure ~~sight~~ *site* it can be dangerous to give personal information.

**39.4**  1 privacy policy   2 browse   3 nationwide   4 online auction
5 killer

## Test 40

**40.1**  1 dogs
2 cameras
3 asylum; migrants  (2 marks)
4 statement
5 officials *or* officers; checks  (2 marks)
6 warrant
7 offence; fine *or* penalty

**40.2**  1 plain clothes   2 drug squad   3 traffic wardens
4 anti-corruption squad   5 paramilitary police

**40.3**  1 photofit picture
2 surveillance operations
3 random checks
4 entry restrictions
5 undercover police

Note that 'undercover operations' is also possible.

**40.4**  1 random checks
2 undercover police
3 photofit picture
4 Surveillance operations
5 entry restrictions

**40.5**  1 stop                    6 entry
2 roadblocks          7 clear
3 security             8 tapping
4 vaccination        9 test
5 card; customs  (2 marks)

## Test 41

**41.1**  1 convert   2 fanatics   3 Adherents   4 eradicate   5 bigots

**41.2**  1 **I'm not a bigot,** but I do have strong principles.
2 I'm not **an adherent of** communism, but I do believe in workers' rights.
3 I believe in animal rights, but I'm not a **fanatic.**

*Test Your English Vocabulary in Use (Advanced)*

4 Every politician promises to **eradicate** poverty, but no one ever succeeds.
5 He became a **convert to** Buddhism in 1994. 10 marks: 2 marks per item

**41.3**
1 credible, credulous  (2 marks: 1 mark per word)
2 implausible  (1 mark)
3 attribute  (1 mark)
4 postulate  (1 mark)
5 ingenuous  (2 marks)
6 ushered  (1 mark)
7 tenet  (1 mark)
8 b  (1 mark)
9 Give someone the **benefit** of the **doubt**.  (2 marks)
10 b  (1 mark)
11 Pull the **other one**!  (2 marks)  (This is connected with the expression 'to pull someone's leg' and is a short form of 'Pull the other leg, it's got bells on!')
12 I wasn't born **yesterday**!  (1 mark)
13 gullible  (1 mark)
14 credence  (1 mark)
15 radical  (1 mark)
16 bigotry  (1 mark) 20 marks

## Test 42

**42.1**
| | |
|---|---|
| 1 commemorates | 6 spectacular |
| 2 superstitious | 7 ceremonial |
| 3 celebratory | 8 celebrations |
| 4 atmospheric | 9 commemorative |
| 5 festivities | 10 renewal |

10 marks

**42.2**
| | |
|---|---|
| 1 sombre | 6 symbolise |
| 2 lantern | 7 harvest |
| 3 fast | 8 bi-centenary |
| 4 flamboyant | 9 penance |
| 5 raucous | 10 pagan |

10 marks

**42.3**
1 They are not eating.
2 They do penance if they have done something wrong.
3 A peacock is more flamboyant because it has brightly coloured feathers.
4 They celebrate because harvest time is when the crops have ripened and are picked. Therefore the community has successfully grown the food it needs to survive and has a reason to celebrate.
5 His bi-centenary will be in 2012.
6 It provides light.
7 A white dove symbolises peace.
8 People are more likely to wear sombre clothes at a funeral.
9 No, they aren't. Pagan beliefs usually refer to the primitive beliefs people had before the major religions were established.
10 No, you don't. Raucous suggests something loud and, often, unpleasant. 10 marks

**42.4**
| | |
|---|---|
| 1 traced | 5 associate; fasting |
| 2 sombre; celebration | 6 spectacle |
| 3 superstitions | 7 focus |
| 4 commemorates | 8 superstitious |

10 marks: 1 mark per word

## Test 43

**43.1**  1 Russian   2 Italian   3 Chinese   4 Malay   5 clumsy
6 English   7 Greek   8 Japanese   9 Dutch   10 Turkish   `10 marks`

**43.2**  1 isolating
2 Graeco-Latin
3 inflected
4 Semitic
5 Germanic   `5 marks`

**43.3**  1 lexicon   2 syntax   3 phonology   4 orthography   5 morphology   `5 marks`

**43.4**  1 modal verb – might, could
2 umlaut – naïve, Noël
3 character – g, w, z
4 acute accent – passé, café
5 diphthong – boil, now   (bɔɪl/, /naʊ/)
6 compound noun – keyboard, windscreen
7 morpheme – impolite, helpful
8 tilde – España, puño   `16 marks: 2 marks per item`

**43.5**

| noun | lexicon | modality | orthography | pictogram |
|------|---------|----------|-------------|-----------|
| adjective | lexical | modal | orthographic | pictographic |

`4 marks`

## Test 44

**44.1**  1 regent   2 succession   3 proclaimed   4 lays   5 depose   6 abuse
7 absolute   8 succeed   9 line   10 heir   `10 marks`

**44.2**  1 throne   2 crown   3 presidency; monarchy   4 reign; govern
5 stagecoach   6 politics   7 power   8 History   `10 marks`

**44.3**  1 serf – a person rather than a means of transport
2 armour – protective clothing rather than a group of soldiers
3 chariot – not a historical period
4 legion – not a period of history
5 stagecoach – not relating to medieval times
6 galleon – does not have wheels and move on land
7 highwayman – not connected to ruling a country   `14 marks: 1 mark for choosing the correct odd one out, 1 mark for an appropriate explanation`

**44.4**  1 armour   2 galleon   3 cart   4 highwayman   5 jester
6 chariot   `6 marks`

## Test 45

**45.1**  1 human poverty   includes other factors, e.g. life expectancy
2 absolute poverty   below a universally accepted, objective standard
3 relative poverty   poor only in connection to other people around you
4 income poverty   less money than the defined minimum in your country   `8 marks: 2 marks per item`

**45.2**  1 Gross National Product   2 Gross Domestic Product   `4 marks: 2 marks per item`

**45.3**  1 sanitation   2 destitute   3 illiteracy   4 malnutrition   `8 marks: 2 marks per item`

**45.4** trade deals    debt servicing    overseas aid    poverty line    life expectancy    `5 marks`

**45.5** 1 overseas aid    2 Life expectancy    3 trade deals    4 poverty line
5 Debt servicing    `5 marks`

**45.6** When I first tried to make my living as a sculptor I spent several years living in ~~perjury~~ [penury]. I did earn some money as time passed, but I was still living ~~by hand and mouth~~ [from hand to mouth] and money was ~~pressed~~ [tight]. I kept reminding myself that life for many people living in ~~depravated~~ [deprived] areas was worse than mine and that whole families were living ~~beyond~~ [below] the bread line. Then I sold a major work and my life was transformed.    `10 marks: 1 mark for finding each mistake, 1 mark for correcting it`

# Test 46

**46.1** 1 petition    2 constituents    3 centralised    4 lobbyists *or* lobbies
5 deputation *or* delegation    6 legislation    7 grievance; appeal
8 producers; consumers    `10 marks`

**46.2** tax concession
civil servant
paid-up member
Chancellor of the Exchequer
mass-produced
close-knit
well-funded
Friends of the Earth
annual budget
Child Poverty Action Group    `10 marks`

**46.3** 1 Friends of the Earth, Child Poverty Action Group
2 mass-produced
3 Chancellor of the Exchequer, annual budget, tax concession, well-funded, paid-up member
4 civil servant
5 close-knit    `10 marks`

**46.4**

```
  1C  O  2R  P  O  R  A  T  I  O  N
         E
         3P  R  E  S  S  U  R  I  S  E
  4C  O  U  N  T  E  R
            5E  X  C  H  E  Q  U  E  R
  6L  O  B  B  I  E  S
            E
         7C  O  N  S  T  I  T  U  E  N  C  Y
            T
  8L  E  G  I  S  L  A  T  E
            T
     9P  E  T  I  T  I  O  N
            V
      10G  R  I  E  V  A  N  C  E
```

`10 marks`

## Test 47

**47.1**
1 lodge an appeal
2 quash a conviction
3 contravene a law
4 impeach a president
5 abrogate a treaty
6 overturn a verdict
7 set a precedent
8 infringe on someone's rights
9 grant custody
10 annul a marriage
`10 marks`

**47.2**
1 impeach  2 contravened  3 infringe  4 granted  5 set
6 abrogated  7 lodge  8 overturned  9 annulled  10 quashed
`10 marks`

**47.3**
1 The **impeachment** of the President took place (*or* happened *or* occurred) in 1993.
2 There are **statutes** which protect children's rights.
3 The **infringement** of human rights is unacceptable in a civilised society.
4 Ms Carter said she had suffered (*or* been the victim of *or* been subjected to *or* experienced) sexual **harassment** at work.
5 The court ruled that Jones was guilty of **perverting** the course of justice.
6 The company was found guilty of **embezzling** large sums of money. `12 marks: 2 marks per sentence`

**47.4**
1 award  2 uphold  3 insider  4 bend  5 joyriding
6 trespass *or* trespassing  7 perjury  8 money laundering
`8 marks`

## Test 48

**48.1**
1 The government is trying to **wage war** on drug trafficking in this country.
2 It's regrettable if politicians resort to warfare **to gain** (*or* **achieve**) **their ends**.
3 If only we could **outlaw war**.
4 The guerrillas threw **an incendiary device** at the building.
5 Why not **rally the troops** (*or* **rally everyone together**) and explain the situation to them?
6 A nuclear war could result in **the annihilation of** (all) **mankind**.
7 **Biological warfare** is internationally banned.
8 England **was routed** by Australia in the final match. Note that *routed* includes the idea of *heavily* already, so it should not be included in your sentence.
9 Hostilities often **break out** for some petty reason.
10 There are international **peacekeeping** troops there.
`10 marks`

**48.2**
1 *A truce* is temporary, whereas there is a chance that *a ceasefire* may be permanent.
2 *A siege* is when a place is surrounded in order to attack it and *an ambush* is when people are unexpectedly attacked by hidden forces.
3 *Hostilities* are specific acts of warfare, whereas *warfare* is a general term for the activity of fighting a war, used in general expressions like 'modern warfare' or 'trench warfare'.
4 If hostilities *break out*, they start, whereas when they *cease*, they stop.
5 *To place an incendiary device* is simply to put it in position, whereas to *set it off* is to make it explode.
`10 marks`

**48.3**
1 deterrent  2 revulsion  3 besieged  4 nucleus  5 warring
6 empowers  7 causal  8 warfare; war  (1 mark for each answer)
9 operations
`10 marks`

**48.4**
1 explode  2 outbreak  3 resort  4 launch  5 aerial  6 powers
7 cause  8 means  9 set off  10 wage
`10 marks`

# Test 49

**49.1** 1 grants    2 burden    3 projects    4 sustainable    5 alleviated
6 lasting *or* long-term    7 encouraging    8 recovering    9 decline
10 achieve

**49.2** 1 trade
2 poverty
3 debt  Note that debt is usually singular in this context, but the plural form is also possible.
4 imposed

**49.3** 1 Many **debtor countries** are trapped in an impossible situation.
2 **Monetary union** is a controversial issue in the EU.
3 **Restrictive practices** have a negative impact on poorer countries.
4 The economies of **war-torn** countries take years to recover.
5 The currency was **devalued** last week; before, one Fadal was worth 50 US cents, now it is worth only 35.
6 The Kingdom of Gwatana **has emerged from a recession** lasting three years (*or* from a three-year recession). *or* The Kingdom of Gwatana is emerging from ...
7 The Lubanian economy **has gone into recession**.
8 Trade sanctions on Pergania **have been lifted**.

**49.4** 1 single currency    2 slump    3 Fiscal    4 boost    5 ailing    6 ease

# Test 50

**50.1** 1 They have none or very little. It means the same as 'I'm broke'. Both expressions are very colloquial.
2 You feel angry or upset because it means that the cheque is not accepted by the bank.
3 It shows when the card expires or stops being valid.
4 Who do/should/shall I make it/the cheque out to? *or* ... make out the cheque to?
5 You'd probably feel worried because fraud means using other people's cards illegally.
6 An insurance company might try to sell you health cover.

**50.2** 
1 store card
2 lump sum
3 golden handshake
4 life savings
5 share portfolio
6 loan shark
7 pension plan
8 insurance claim

**50.3** 
1 lump sum
2 loan shark
3 store card
4 golden handshake
5 insurance claim
6 life savings
7 pension plan
8 share portfolio

**50.4** 
1 ends
2 strapped *or* stuck
3 charging
4 tight
5 endowment
6 lump sum  (2 marks)
7 share portfolio  (2 marks)
8 premium(s)
9 claim
10 excess

# Test 51

**51.1** 1 obituary    2 feature    3 classified    4 editorial    5 agony

**51.2** 1 quarterly    2 facsimile    3 spine    4 supplement
5 possible answers: to advertise an event, to advertise a new restaurant, club, etc.
6 A booklet has fewer pages than a book , always has a soft cover, and usually gives information about something.

**51.3**  
1 manual      6 ghost  
2 brochures      7 agony  
3 leaflets      8 subscription  
4 prospectus      9 jacket  
5 pamphlet      10 lowdown

**51.4**  1 ghosts    2 agony    3 jacket    4 manual

## Test 52

**52.1**  
1 True  
2 False. When you buy new software, you first have to install it. You uninstall software that you want to get rid of from your computer.  
3 False. If you upload data, you put it onto a website from your computer. Taking something from a website to your own computer is downloading it.  
4 True  
5 True  
6 False. If you visit a chat room, you can't see the people you meet there.  
7 False. If you are working offline, you are not connected to the Internet. If you were connected to the Internet, you would be working online.  
8 True  
9 False. If you change your ISP, you find a new company to handle your Internet connection.  
10 True

**52.2**  
1 garbled  
2 instant messaging  
3 subscribed; newsgroup  
4 graphic images  
5 browsing

**52.3**  Someone ~~packed~~ *hacked* into our computer at work yesterday and managed to disrupt the whole system. We thought the ~~ante~~-*anti*-virus software would have prevented this from happening but it didn't. When we logged on to our e-mail this morning we were all bombarded with ~~ham~~ *spam* and had to spend ages deleting a lot of offensive and unwanted messages. Moreover, a lot of the messages we had sent ~~jumped~~ *bounced* back to us, which was extremely annoying. They called someone in to sort it out but that meant the system was ~~up~~ *down* for ages and we couldn't get any work done. I was supposed to be ~~swimming~~ *surfing* the Web all day to get information for a report I'm writing on trends in ~~e-commercial~~ *e-commerce* and what's happening these days to dotcoms. I couldn't do it of course so I'm going to have to go in and do some work at the weekend, I'm afraid.

## Test 53

**53.1**  1 b    2 innovative    3 a    4 b    5 alliteration

**53.2**  
1 eye-catching      5 proven  
2 rock-bottom      6 state-of-the-art  
3 sumptuous      7 tantalising  
4 opulent      8 alluring

**53.3**
1 appeal – appeal means 'attraction'; the other two words refer to lower prices for goods
2 fetch – to fetch means 'to bring', fetching (adjective) means 'attractive'; pamper and indulge can both be used as reflexive verbs (pamper yourself, indulge yourself) meaning to give yourself some special treat or pleasurable experience
3 whiteboard – a whiteboard is used for writing on; sandwich boards and billboards are used to advertise things
4 grasping – grasping means 'greedy'; fetching and alluring both mean 'attractive'
5 discount – a discount means a reduced price; trailers and sky-writing are both ways of advertising things
6 prove – prove means to show evidence; plug and advertise both mean to talk about or draw attention to something in order to sell or promote it

`12 marks: 1 mark per word, 1 mark per correct reason`

**53.4**
1 Lapford's   2 Gifford's   3 Doran's   4 Threadgold's   5 Kaplan's   `5 marks`

**53.5**
1 Zapemall **leaves other weedkillers standing.**
2 The hotel was fabulous – we were living **in the lap of luxury** for two weeks.
3 She gave several TV and radio interviews **to plug** her new novel.
4 With Ekta sunglasses you'll really **stand out in/among the crowd.**
5 I think these shoes are **outstanding** value at 35 euros.

`5 marks`

# Test 54

**54.1**
1 release (Note that 'statement' is usually used without the word 'press'.)
2 press
3 inches
4 copy
5 bite
6 headlines *or* front pages
7 stop
8 character
9 press; muck

`10 marks`

**54.2**
| | |
|---|---|
| 1 a glossy | 6 a rag |
| 2 libel | 7 a back copy |
| 3 the deadline | 8 a pressure group |
| 4 an exclusive | 9 a sound bite |
| 5 copy | 10 defamation of character |

`10 marks`

**54.3**   1 making   2 air   3 put   4 monitor   5 silly   `10 marks: 2 marks per item`

**54.4**
1 A press conference was held at the end of the summit meeting.
2 Inevitably the story received a lot of coverage.
3 The newspaper has to go to press by 9 p.m.
4 The actor collected all the press cuttings where he was mentioned.
5 All politicians want to put their gloss on events.
6 The Managing Director will issue a statement this afternoon.
7 I know some useful sources that you could tap for your story.
8 The actor was out of the country when the story broke.
9 The charity is seeking publicity for its fund-raising events.
10 I think the scandal will become public knowledge soon.

`10 marks`

## Test 55

**55.1**
   1  Mike
   2  Sarah, Anne
   3  Jim
   4  Rob
   5  Anne, Sarah
   6  Jason
   7  Rose
   8  Jackie
   9  Sue
  10  Danny, Rob

`10 marks`

**55.2**
  1  National Health Service
  2  General Practitioner
  3  tuberculosis

`6 marks: 2 marks per item`

**55.3**
  1  a) disease  b) attacks  c) failure
  2  a) lung *or* liver  b) breast *or* bowel  c) skin *or* stomach

`6 marks`

**55.4**
  1  hepatitis – inflammation of the liver
  2  tuberculosis – highly infectious disease in the lungs
  3  typhoid – fever, with red spots on the chest and abdomen
  4  bronchitis – inflammation of the breathing system; causes coughing
  5  diabetes – the body does not properly absorb sugar and starch
  6  cholera – intestinal disease; can be caused by bad drinking water

`6 marks`

**55.5**
family doctor
prescription charge
sore throat
blood transfusion
national insurance
hay fever

`12 marks: 2 marks per pair`

## Test 56

**56.1**
  1  I feel a bit **feverish**. Take an aspirin to reduce your temperature.
  2  My head is **throbbing/thumping**. You should lie down in a darkened room.
  3  I'm **allergic** to nuts. Don't eat that cake then.
  4  I feel **nauseous** in a car. Take these travel sickness pills.
  5  My nose is **bunged/blocked** up. Try inhaling steam.

`10 marks: I mark for completing the missing words, I mark for matching the symptoms to the response`

**56.2**
aches and pains – minor physical discomfort
donate blood – give blood for use in an emergency
contact lenses – things people wear in their eyes to correct their vision
cuts and bruises – minor physical injuries
herbal medicine – treatment based on using plants as remedies
off-colour* – not very well
out of sorts* – not very well
sick note – a doctor's letter explaining that you're ill and can't go to work
stiff neck – difficulty moving your head
under the weather* – not very well
*Note that these expressions are informal.*

`20 marks: I mark for each expression, I mark for an appropriate definition`

**56.3**

```
¹M E D I C A² T I O N
        R
        O
    ³S Y M P T O M S
        ⁴V A C C I N A T I O N
        ⁵S T I N G
        H
    ⁶T R E M B L E
⁷P R E S C R I P T I O N
    ⁸D O S A G E
    ⁹A C U P U N C T U R E
¹⁰D I Z Z Y
```

## Test 57

**57.1**
1 She is five months pregnant. *or* She became pregnant five months ago. *or* She has been pregnant for five months.
2 Babies who have been breastfed *or* Breastfed babies have more immunity to certain diseases.
3 I was suffering from extreme dehydration.
4 This is a symptom of a deeper problem.
5 The doctor diagnosed bronchitis.

10 marks: 2 marks per item

**57.2**
1 clotting *or* clots; side; effects
2 prognosis
3 fever; pitch

6 marks

**57.3**
| | |
|---|---|
| 1 sensitive | 6 fatal |
| 2 rash | 7 paralysed |
| 3 scarred | 8 ailing |
| 4 symptoms | 9 contagious |
| 5 jaundiced | 10 prognosis |

20 marks: 2 marks per item

**57.4**
1 a) stool(s)   b) excrement   c) pooh
2 an ulcer

4 marks

## Test 58

**58.1**
1 You'd feel embarrassed, because it means that you hit a goal into your own goalposts and so scored a goal for the other side.
2 It goes very well and you have no problems.
3 You may be promoted because you are one of the people who is being considered for promotion.
4 You feel annoyed because they are changing the rules in the middle of a game or changing the requirements when you have already started a job.
5 They are trying to avoid giving a direct answer or comment on a subject.
6 Neither person is winning. They are level with each other.
7 horse-racing

*Test Your English Vocabulary in Use (Advanced)*     **137**

8 a level playing field
9 You will be benefitting your heart and blood circulation.
10 burn

10 marks

**58.2**
| | | | |
|---|---|---|---|
| 1 | offal | 6 | cholesterol |
| 2 | diabetic | 7 | excrete |
| 3 | plaque | 8 | mood enhancer |
| 4 | fibre | 9 | pound |
| 5 | gut | 10 | insulin |

20 marks: I mark for spelling the word correctly, I mark for matching it to the definition

**58.3**
1 vessel – they can all be seen as containers of different kinds
2 convert – they all involve a change of state of some kind
3 depression – they all involve something (or someone) being down or low
4 tolerance – they all involve the ability to tolerate or live with something without problems
5 resistance – they all involve the ability to stand up to or fight against what is attacking you

10 marks: I mark for the correct word, I mark for explaining the connection between the different meanings

## Test 59

**59.1**
1 Low-tech     2 subsidies     3 Privatisation     4 sweeteners     5 Service
6 piecework     7 inward     8 relocate     9 Reskilling     10 Manufacturing

10 marks

**59.2**
| | | | |
|---|---|---|---|
| 1 | heavy industry | 6 | child labour |
| 2 | public-private | 7 | red tape |
| 3 | industrial espionage | 8 | cost-cutting |
| 4 | money laundering | 9 | union representation |
| 5 | infringe laws | 10 | lame duck |

10 marks

**59.3**
| | | | |
|---|---|---|---|
| 1 | Lame duck | 6 | union representation |
| 2 | child labour | 7 | public-private |
| 3 | money laundering | 8 | infinging (the copyright) laws |
| 4 | red tape | 9 | industrial espionage |
| 5 | heavy industry | 10 | Cost-cutting |

20 marks: 2 marks per item

## Test 60

**60.1**
| | | | |
|---|---|---|---|
| 1 | laptop | 6 | trackpad |
| 2 | hands-free | 7 | personal |
| 3 | pager | 8 | analogue |
| 4 | nerd | 9 | palmtop |
| 5 | techie | 10 | icons |

20 marks

**60.2**
| | | | |
|---|---|---|---|
| 1 | Ergonomics | 6 | digital camera  (2 marks) |
| 2 | Artificial Intelligence  (2 marks) | 7 | screensaver |
| 3 | Global Positioning System  (3 marks) | 8 | earpiece; microphone  (2 marks) |
| 4 | Biotechnologists | 9 | satellite |
| 5 | smart | 10 | thumbnail |

15 marks

**60.3**
1 a smart ID card
2 a pager
3 a laptop (computer)
4 the trackpad (on a laptop computer)
5 palmtop *or* handheld computer

5 marks

# Test 61

**61.1**  1 interplanetary  2 virtual  3 interactive  4 E-commerce
5 smart
`10 marks: 2 marks per item`

**61.2**  1 human genome         4 genetically modified
2 doomsday scenario     5 nuclear family
3 smart card            6 gridlocked
`12 marks: 2 marks per item`

**61.3**

| noun | verb | adjective |
|------|------|-----------|
| globe | globalise | global |
| gene |  | genetic |
| modification | modify | modified |
|  | widen | wide |
| therapy |  | therapeutic |
| designer | design |  |

`8 marks`

**61.4**  1 widen   2 designer   3 Global   4 modified   5 globalise
`10 marks: 2 marks per item`

# Test 62

**62.1**  1 agoraphobia   Claustrophobia is a fear of being in confined spaces like lifts or small rooms.
2 congested   Cramped is used about rooms or other enclosed spaces where there is not enough room.
3 compact   Poky is used about rooms or houses and has negative associations and so it does not fit in this context.
4 excessive   Extensive is used to mean covering a large area or having a great range. It doesn't, therefore, collocate with the word *drinking*.
5 scattered   Crammed is used about things that fit tightly in a restricted space, so is not appropriate for the sky.
`10 marks: 1 mark for choosing the correct word, 1 mark for the explanation`

**62.2**

| Positive associations | Negative associations |
|-----------------------|-----------------------|
| bustling | poky |
| roomy | incarcerated |
| extensive | congested |
| spacious | cramped |

compact (Although compact is used to point out that something is very small and does not have or take up much space, it does give a positive feel, suggesting that the room, house or piece of equipment that is described as compact is well-designed.)

rambling (Although rambling is used to suggest that something, usually a house or city, has a lot of different parts and covers a large area, it has positive associations because it is considered interesting. However if a speech or piece of writing is rambling, it is considered to be long and confusing.)
`10 marks`

**62.3**  1 sardines                          6 wide
2 stuffed *or* shoved (more informal)   7 bustling
3 incarcerated                      8 cramped
4 poky                              9 squeeze
5 spread/spreads *or* stretched/stretches  10 swing
`10 marks`

**62.4**

| noun | adjective | verb |
|------|-----------|------|
| congestion | congested |  |
| cramp* | cramped | cramp |
| space, spaciousness | spacious | space |
| extent, extension* | extensive | extend |
| claustrophobia | claustrophobic |  |
| width | wide | widen |

*Cramp as a noun means muscle spasms or pain in your muscles, often after a lot of exercise.

*Extent is used in phrases like 'to a certain extent', 'the extent of the problem', while extension is used in expressions like 'to have an extension built on your house', 'to get an extension on a coursework deadline'.

10 marks: 1 mark for a correct word in each of the empty boxes

## Test 63

**63.1**
1 donkey's
2 knots
3 blue moon
4 year dot
5 cows; home
6 less; time

10 marks: 1 mark for each word

**63.2**
1 once in a blue moon.
2 for donkey's years. *or* since the year dot.
3 since the year dot. *or* for donkey's years.
4 at a rate of knots.
5 in less than no time.
6 till the cows come home

6 marks

**63.3**
1 I'm on the phone at the moment. I'll be with you **in a sec**.
2 Just because I'm in my 50s, it doesn't mean I'm **over the hill**.
3 Mary Swann spent **all her born days** in the tiny village of Hickenbower.
4 He was a famous rock star in the 1980s, but now he's just **a has-been**.
5 I will keep protesting **till hell freezes over**. I will never give up.
6 I managed to contact him (just) **in the nick of time**.

12 marks: 2 marks per sentence

**63.4**
fleeting glimpse
pristine environment
inexorable decline
protracted negotiations
persistent cough
transient population

6 marks

**63.5**
1 (a) in a tick  (b) in a jiffy  ($\frac{1}{2}$ mark per expression)
2 for yonks
3 You can have this CD *for keeps*. (or ... this CD *for good*.)
4 in a flash
5 incipient
6 lingering

6 marks

## Test 64

**64.1**
1 Meandering suggests not moving in a straight line or route, but in a relaxed and indirect fashion.
2 Staggered suggests unsteady movement either because Bill is ill, exhausted or drunk.

3　Chased tells us that the children are running after each other, trying to catch each other.

4　Trickle suggests that the people are coming in ones and twos and that there are not very many of them.

5　Sidled suggests that Sadie is moving in a slightly sneaky way as if she is trying not to be noticed.

6　Trampled suggests that the action was done repeatedly and deliberately.

7　Staggeringly suggests amazingly well and in a way that surprises you.

8　Flooded suggests that people moved to the towns in large numbers.

9　Strode suggests walking in a confident and purposeful way.

10　Spilled suggests the idea of a lot of people moving quickly and automatically.

`20 marks: 2 marks per item`

**64.2**
| | | | |
|---|---|---|---|
| 1 struts | | 6 stumbles *or* lurches | |
| 2 limps | | 7 glides | |
| 3 tiptoes | | 8 ambles | |
| 4 lurches *or* stumbles | | 9 hobbles | |
| 5 trudges | | 10 stamps | |

`10 marks`

**64.3**
| | |
|---|---|
| 1 backward | 4 first |
| 2 giant | 5 significant |
| 3 unprecedented | 6 decisive |

`6 marks`

**64.4**　1 filed　2 streamed　3 flowing　4 milling

`4 marks`

# Test 65

**65.1**　Years ago, social ~~etickett~~ *etiquette* was more important than now. Men had to be ~~gentlemannish~~ *gentlemanly* and ladies had to be ~~ladyish~~ *ladylike*. Nowadays people do not stand ~~at~~ *on* ceremony so much and ~~cortesie~~ *courtesy* is not so important. Minding your ~~Qs and Ps~~ *Ps and Qs* is a thing of the past and people are more ~~on hand~~ *offhand* with one another. I think young people no longer respect their ~~betters and olders~~ *elders and betters* or observe the social ~~grace~~ *graces*, and don't care whether something is the ~~doable~~ *done* thing or not. People might call me ~~tight-laced~~ *strait-laced*, but I think good manners are important.

`10 marks`

**65.2**
1　I wish you'd stop smirking! *or* I wish you'd get rid of that smirk!
2　Her remarks raised a lot of eyebrows.
3　I squirmed with embarrassment. *or* I was squirming …
4　He was constantly twitching. *or* He was twitching constantly. *or* He had a nervous twitch.
5　He flinched as the doctor stuck the needle in his arm.
6　The audience tittered when the actor forgot his lines.
7　He just sniffed at the idea and told us not to be so naïve.
8　She beamed when we told her the good news.

`8 marks`

**65.3**
| 'crying' words | 'angry' words | 'laughing' words | 'looking' words |
|---|---|---|---|
| whimper | frown | giggle | gawp |
| grizzle | scowl | chortle | ogle |
| sob | glare | snigger | leer |
| sniffle | glower | guffaw | scan |

`16 marks`

**65.4**　1 giggling　2 leering　3 guffaw　4 sobbed　5 glared　6 frowned

`6 marks`

# Test 66

**66.1**  1 quieter    2 pin    3 mice    4 eerie    5 peace    6 silent    7 grating
8 pitched    9 noiselessly    10 think

10 marks

**66.2**
| | |
|---|---|
| 1 slammed | 6 squeaks |
| 2 sizzling | 7 rang out |
| 3 were hooting | 8 pounding |
| 4 wailing | 9 hammering |
| 5 to creak | 10 crashing |

20 marks: 1 mark for choosing the correct word, 1 mark for writing it in the correct form

**66.3**
1 a mouse
2 silent films/movies
3 toot
4 formal English, e.g. in a novel
5 No, you don't like it. You find it very unpleasant and irritating.
6 It is a very loud one. The word suggests that the scream might burst your eardrums.
7 deaf    It means unable to hear properly.
8 machinery
9 a car alarm
10 It means that they had a day without too much extra activity.

10 marks

# Test 67

**67.1**  1 cumbersome    2 burdensome    3 lumbering
4 weighty    5 unwieldy

10 marks: 2 marks per item

**67.2**
1 impermeable   c) barrier   shield   rocks
2 ponderous   d) silence   deliberation   thesis
3 lumpy   a) mattress   glue   sauce
4 impenetrable   e) forest   darkness   plot
5 undiluted   medicine   b) juice   chemicals

10 marks: 2 marks per item

**67.3**  1 in    2 down    3 up    4 out    5 out

5 marks

**67.4**  1 congealed    2 dilute    3 thicken    4 solidified    5 thin

10 marks: 2 marks per item

**67.5**

| adjective | noun | verb |
|---|---|---|
| thick | thickness | thicken |
| lumpy | lump | |
| weighty | weight | weigh |
| burdensome | burden | burden |
| solid | solidity | solidify |

5 marks

# Test 68

**68.1**
1 You would probably not be pleased because mousy is a negative word suggesting the hair is an uninteresting light brown colour.
2 The walls are a creamy white (with a tinge of pink).
3 They want a deep red one, the colour of red wine. (Burgundy is a region of France famous for its red wine.)
4 They are a bright blue, like that of the forget-me-not flower.
5 You are in a depressed or miserable mood.
6 It is a specially important day.
7 They want you to use your brain and think hard.
8 red, blue and yellow

    9  They shine bright in the dark.

   10  Vivid colours are stronger.
`10 marks`

**68.2**
| | | | |
|---|---|---|---|
| 1 | amber – orangy yellow | 9 | jade – deep green |
| 2 | auburn – reddish brown | 10 | mauve – pale purple |
| 3 | beige – light creamy brown | 11 | navy – dark blue |
| 4 | chestnut – deep reddish brown | 12 | poppy – bright red |
| 5 | cornflower – blue | 13 | ruby – deep red |
| 6 | crimson – deep red | 14 | sapphire – dark blue |
| 7 | emerald – bright green | 15 | scarlet – bright red |
| 8 | ginger – orangy red | 16 | turquoise – greenish blue |

`16 marks`

**68.3**
  1  Jean has beautiful **dark blue** eyes.

  2  No one talks about our uncle; he's the **black** sheep of the family.

  3  I hate those **white** knuckle rides at theme parks and refuse to go on them.

  4  Billy's turned a bit **green**; I hope he's not going to be sick.
`4 marks`

**68.4**
  1  pitch    2  shocking    3  sheet    4  green    5  blue    6  jet    7  red

  8  grey    9  black    10  red
`10 marks`

# Test 69

**69.1**
| | | | |
|---|---|---|---|
| 1 | whizzed | 6 | bolted |
| 2 | zip *or* zap *or* zoom | 7 | raced *or* rattled *or* ran |
| 3 | dash | 8 | darted |
| 4 | tore | 9 | pop |
| 5 | nip | 10 | careered |

`10 marks`

**69.2**
  1  your jacket    2  Eyebrows    3  A picture on the wall

  4  Your hopes    5  A cake
`10 marks: 2 marks per item`

**69.3**
  1  Our hopes (suddenly) plummeted when we heard the bad news. *or* When we heard the bad news, our hopes (suddenly) plummeted.

  2  The rocket soared into the stratosphere.

  3  When we were told of her death, we were (immediately) plunged into despair. *or* We were (immediately) plunged into despair when we told of her death.

  4  After the recession, economic growth accelerated (rapidly).

  5  Exports slumped as a result of the revaluation of the currency.
`10 marks: 2 marks per sentence`

**69.4**
  1  scurry, scamper, scuttle  (3 marks: 1 mark per verb)

  2  creep, crawl  (2 marks: 1 mark per verb)

  3  speed up  (1 mark)

  4  They fall.  (1 mark)

  5  totter  (1 mark)

  6  You are moving in a nervous or timid way, as if you don't want the person to notice you.

  7  b  (1 mark)
`10 marks`

# Test 70

**70.1**
| | | | |
|---|---|---|---|
| 1 | generate *or* produce | 6 | produce |
| 2 | caused | 7 | give |
| 3 | given | 8 | produce *or* give |
| 4 | cause | 9 | generate |
| 5 | generate | 10 | gave |

`10 marks`

**70.2**
| | | | |
|---|---|---|---|
| 1 | incite | 6 | sparked |
| 2 | breeds | 7 | generate |
| 3 | prompted | 8 | bring |
| 4 | giving | 9 | resulted |
| 5 | provoke | 10 | induce |

`10 marks`

**70.3**
1 Owing to the power cut, I got stuck in the underground and missed my flight.
2 Thanks to the TV ad we received a lot of orders for our new product. *or* We received a lot of orders for our new product thanks to the TV ad.
3 We have had a lot of problems as a consequence of the new software. *or* As a consequence of the new software, we have had a lot of problems.
4 The use of the Internet has brought about enormous changes in our lives.
5 The article resulted in a lot of readers' letters.
6 Due to the crash, the motorway was closed for most of the day.
7 The President's visit sparked off a number of protests.
8 As a result of his poor eyesight, Leo was never any good at sport.
9 This magazine has given us a lot of useful information.
10 The Prime Minister's speech prompted many questions.

`20 marks: 2 marks per sentence`

# Test 71

**71.1**
1 to
2 with *or* for (*with* is more frequently used)
3 to
4 from
5 to *or* with (*to* is more frequently used)

`5 marks`

**71.2**
1 tantamount to
2 correspond to/with
3 affinity with/for
4 indistinguishable from
5 akin to

`5 marks`

**71.3**
1 The northern lakelands are not dissimilar to parts of Finland.
2 The flora and fauna are very diverse.
3 The dialect in the north is (completely/totally) distinct from that found in the south.
4 The two regions were so disparate that she found it difficult to settle.
5 They have widely divergent views on immigration. *or* Their views on immigration are widely divergent.

`10 marks: 2 marks per item`

**71.4**
1 interchangeable
2 b
3 analogy
4 To equate capitalism with/to democracy is a mistake.
5 between; and

`10 marks: 2 marks per item`

**71.5** After walking for a few miles we saw a building that looked more ~~akimbo~~ *akin* to a castle than a guest house. In fact, it was not ~~unsimilar~~ *dissimilar* to the old castle in my home town. As we got nearer, we realised there were also some wooden houses, which were almost ~~undistinguishable~~ *indistinguishable* from the surrounding forest. To use a gardening ~~analogue~~ *analogy*, the houses seemed to be sprouting from the ground, just like trees. I felt a strong ~~infinity~~ *affinity* for this lovely old group of buildings as it reminded me of my childhood home.

`10 marks: 1 mark for finding each mistake, 1 mark for correcting it`

# Test 72

**72.1**

| minor problem | more serious problem |
|---|---|
| glitch | adversity |
| hitch | pitfall |
| setback | dilemma |
| snag | ordeal |
|  | impediment |
|  | tribulation |

10 marks

**72.2** Note that although it is also possible to make other pairings as indicated below, the suggested pairs make particularly strong combinations and allow you to use each noun once only.

1 wayward      child (of the words given, only child is likely to follow wayward)
2 stiff      competition
3 traumatic      experience (a decision or journey could also be traumatic)
4 convoluted      sentences (a theory could perhaps also be convoluted)
5 abstruse      theory
6 insufferable      boredom (a child could also be called insufferable)
7 arduous      journey (an experience could also be called arduous)
8 obstructive      measure (a child could perhaps also be called obstructive)

8 marks

**72.3** 1 MARK: Oh dear. What a pain! *or* Oh dear. What a pity!
           Oh dear. What a drag!
2 MARK: Yes, I wonder what's bugging him. *or* … what's bothering him.
           Yes, I wonder what's up with him.
3 MARK: Yes, I'm off the hook now, thank goodness.
           Yes, I'm in the clear now, thank goodness.
4 MARK: Yes, I've been slogging my guts out.
           Yes, I've been flogging myself to death.
5 MARK: Not really. She's in a bit of a hole. She's lost some important papers.
           Not really. She's in a bit of a fix. She's lost some important papers.

10 marks

**72.4** 1 Changing jobs is always a bit of a **hassle**. A stumbling block is an obstacle in the way of doing something else and so does not fit in this context.
2 Sue had quite a **gruelling** time giving birth to triplets. Convoluted means complex and indirect and is used about sentences and explanations, not physical things like giving birth.
3 The Minister has a slight speech **impediment**. The word impediment collocates very strongly or goes naturally with speech, whereas obstacle does not.
4 I wonder if you could help me with a **tricky** situation that's come up at work.
Tricky collocates strongly or goes naturally with situation, whereas stiff collocates better with nouns like opposition or competition.
5 An economic depression always means a lot of people suffering **hardship**. Snags are far too small and trivial to be appropriate for a serious context like this.
6 Jan has a lot of complex **decisions** to make before the end of the year. Decisions collocates or goes naturally with complex and make, whereas issue collocates with complex but not with make. You might have a lot of complex issues to consider.

12 marks: 1 mark for choosing the correct word, 1 mark for giving an appropriate reason why the other word was rejected

# Test 73

**73.1** 1 B: Oh, don't worry, **it might well never happen.**
2 B: Did he? And **what, may I ask**, did he want at that time of night?
3 B: Oh, never mind. **Accidents will happen.**
4 B: Really? **You must have been frightened.**
5 B: **I should be so lucky!** It was only ten pounds.

6 B: Yes, believe it or not, I was in town and **who should I see but** Joe Watts.

7 B: Yes, **I must confess** I was very relieved.

8 B: Oh, **that'll be** the plumber. He said he'd come at ten.

9 B: Steve? **You must be joking!** He can't stand Debbie!

10 B: Oh, well, never mind. **You still might** get the other one.

10 marks

**73.2**    1 prudent     2 inevitable     3 essential     4 likelihood
           5 optional

10 marks: 2 marks per word

**73.3**    1 My car (engine) **won't start**. Can you help me?

2 If I were **in the same boat** I'd simply say no.

3 **In all probability** they will postpone the decision till the economy improves.

4 There **are bound to be** some problems. There always are.

5 **The odds are against him getting** the job. *or* **The odds are against his getting** the job. He's not qualified.

6 I am sorry. I have no **option** but to terminate your contract.

7 He's always **had aspirations to become** a super-rich business tycoon.

8 **Is it compulsory to** wear a seat belt in the rear passenger seat? *or* Is wearing a seat belt in the rear passenger seat compulsory?

9 The government **is/has resolved** to clamp down on tax evasion. *or* The government **is firm in its resolve** to clamp down on tax evasion.

10 **The odds are** (that) he'll forget all about it.

20 marks: 2 marks per sentence

# Test 74

**74.1**   
1 deviation        6 conservative
2 variables        7 projected
3 err              8 flawed
4 expenditure      9 inverse
5 correlation     10 inconsistencies

10 marks

**74.2**   
1 (three) fold; recorded

2 round

3 tot; consistent

4 erratic; fluctuate

5 discrepancy

6 run; proportion

7 sustain; blip

12 marks: 1 mark per word

**74.3**   
1 It is an approximate figure or a guess.

2 $100,000

3 7

4 They go up and down.

5 fluctuate

6 The suggestion is that the change is temporary and likely to be short-lived.

7 It is a cautious one.

8 It increases to three times the original cost.

9 The letters stand for Intelligence Quotient and the average is 100. (2 marks)

10 Hotel rooms cost £80 a night.
    Hotel rooms cost £80 (for) each/every night *or* for one night. (2 marks)

11 amount of sunlight, amount/frequency of watering, temperature of room (3 marks)

12 You mean that people have different proportions of good and bad in their characters.

13 added (up)

14 It increases to four times the original amount.

18 marks: 1 mark per answer except where indicated

# Test 75

**75.1** 
1 assent to
2 accede to
3 condone X
4 endorse X
5 acquiesce in *or* to

5 marks

**75.2** 
1 acquiesced
2 acceded
3 condone *or* have condoned
4 assented
5 endorse

5 marks

**75.3** 
1 barred          5 authorised
2 outlawed        6 lifted; embargo
3 veto            7 adopted; zero-tolerance
4 countenance

18 marks: 2 marks per word

**75.4** In 2003, the government gave the go-~~along~~ *ahead* to a ~~franshize~~ *franchise* system for city bus services.

Companies were more or less given ~~blank carte~~ *carte blanche* to establish routes and timetables.

However some firms thought they had been given the ~~white~~ *green* light to increase fares and close

unprofitable routes, so the government had to introduce new rules to clamp down ~~at~~ *on* profiteering,

and financial ~~sancities~~ *sanctions* were imposed on firms that broke

the rules.

12 marks: 1 mark for finding each mistake, 1 mark for correcting it

# Test 76

**76.1** 
1 The teacher said he took exception to Ben's attitude.
2 Sue would be well advised to pay more attention in class.
3 Something will have to be done about the mess on your desk.
4 My parents are always finding fault with everything I do or say.
5 I've just about had enough of their lack of consideration.
6 The union leader remonstrated with the new director.
7 I wish he wouldn't whinge so much.
8 His appearance would benefit from a little more attention.
9 It's clear that personal hygiene is not his highest priority.
10 Our neighbours tend to play their music rather loudly at night.

10 marks

**76.2** 
1 bit *or* little     2 can't     3 do     4 tendency     5 fed
6 would     7 about     8 strongest     9 exception

9 marks

**76.3** 
1 advice
2 objection ('Object' is also a noun form but not in the sense of complaining.)
3 complaint
4 protest (Note that the stress is on the first syllable of the noun whereas it is on the second syllable of the verb.)
5 gripe
6 remonstrance *or* remonstration (both formal)
7 grumble
8 tendency

8 marks

**76.4** 
1 objection     2 advice     3 tendency     4 complaint     5 advice
6 tendencies     7 objection *or* protest     8 grumble *or* gripe

8 marks

**76.5**  1  Your handwriting is bad or untidy.
2  You don't know the work well enough, so you need to revise to pass the test.
3  Your work is full of mistakes.
4  You are not doing enough work in this subject.
5  Your essays are not long enough.

## Test 77

**77.1**

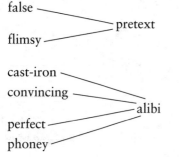

**77.2**  1  lame excuse *or* flimsy excuse
2  false pretext *or* flimsy pretext
3  perfect alibi *or* cast-iron alibi *or* convincing alibi
4  sincere apology/ies *or* heartfelt apology/ies
5  phoney alibi

**77.3**  As he was sentenced to death for the murders, Jake Dagger showed no ~~remonstrances~~ *remorse*. He knew that it was likely he would get a last-minute ~~reprise~~ *reprieve* from the President, as other criminals had before him. His co-defendant, Lucy Motion, was ~~equipped~~ *acquitted*, and walked free from the courtroom. She is now seeking an ~~apologisement~~ *apology* from the police, but a senior officer said he believed the force had been completely ~~exhilarated~~ *exonerated* and had nothing to apologise for.

**77.4**  1  posthumous pardon  (2 marks)
2  repent  (1 mark)
3  a) armistice   b) accord   c) truce   d) treaty  (4 marks)
4  declare  (1 mark)
5  sign  (1 mark)
6  peace  (1 mark)

## Test 78

**78.1**  1  complimentary     6  smarmy
2  flattery          7  laudatory
3  laudable          8  standing
4  congratulations   9  crawler
5  praiseworthy     10  servile

Note that 'laudable' means deserving praise and 'laudatory' means expressing praise.

**78.2**  1  pay         6  toast *or* talk
2  nowhere     7  damn
3  won         8  heaping
4  pat         9  paying
5  singing    10  virtues

**78.3**  back-handed – double-edged
servile – obsequious (both formal)
slimy – smarmy (both informal)
praiseworthy – laudable
suck up to – lick someone's boots          10 marks: 2 marks per pair

**78.4**  1 Both words are similar in meaning, but slimy is informal, whereas obsequious is formal.
2 Both expressions mean to do something that is praised, but to get a pat on the back is informal and is often used about children, whereas to win plaudits is a formal expression.
3 Both expressions can be understood in either a positive or a negative way, but a back-handed compliment seems to be deliberately critical or unkind, whereas a double-edged one is not always intentionally unkind.
4 To fish for compliments is to say something that tries to prompt another person to compliment you, whereas to pay compliments means to compliment someone else.
5 Widely praised and praised to the skies both mean highly praised, but praised to the skies is more informal and perhaps suggests more exaggerated praise than widely praised does.          10 marks: 2 marks per item

# Test 79

**79.1**
| | |
|---|---|
| 1 sworn | 6 swear words |
| 2 promise | 7 oath |
| 3 turned; leaf | 8 broke |
| 4 pledged | 9 vows |
| 5 promises | 10 New Year's resolutions |

10 marks

**79.2**
| | |
|---|---|
| 1 flutter, bet | 4 oath, promise |
| 2 pledged, vowed | 5 keep, make |
| 3 wager, bet | |

10 marks

**79.3**  1 He's the type who promises (you) the moon and then lets you down.
2 She's a promising young tennis player.
3 I think she lives in Harrow Street, but I couldn't swear to it.
4 Most of my classmates swear by *English Vocabulary in Use*.
5 Your best bet is to try and e-mail him. He never answers the phone.
6 I often have a (small) flutter on big sports events.
7 He might turn up to help you, but don't bet on it!
8 I'd put money on them being/getting divorced within a year, the way they're behaving.
9 Mr Dew has generously pledged £10,000 to the charity. *or* Mr Dew has made a generous pledge of £10,000 to the charity.
10 My mother disapproves of films containing swear words.          20 marks: 2 marks per sentence

# Test 80

**80.1**  1 I wish we'd known each other twenty years ago!
2 He lamented the closing/closure of the community centre. *or* He lamented the fact that the council closed the community centre.
3 The football hooligans' behaviour was a disgrace.
4 I regret not studying harder when I was your age. *or* I regret that I didn't study harder when I was your age.
5 I wonder what became of James, the boy I sat next to at school.
6 Many people see the past through rose-tinted spectacles. *or* ... rose-coloured spectacles.
7 The thing about Adam that particularly stands out in my memory is his red hair.
8 I wish I were young again. *or* I wish I was young again.
9 I hope you'll keep in touch when you go back home.
10 I regret the day I decided to emigrate. *or* I regret deciding to emigrate.          10 marks

**80.2**
1 Things aren't what they used to be.
2 It's a shame you have to leave now.
3 Schooldays are the happiest days of your life.
4 They showed no sign of remorse for their behaviour.
5 They don't make cars like they used to.
6 I mourn the passing of time.
7 I'll never forget what happened next.
8 In the good old days things were different.
9 If only we could turn the clock back. *or* If only we could turn back the clock.
10 I often wonder what Richard ended up doing.
20 marks: 2 marks per sentence

**80.3**
| | |
|---|---|
| 1 disappointing | 6 days |
| 2 pity | 7 make |
| 3 remember | 8 wonder |
| 4 forget | 9 whatsisname |
| 5 good times | 10 disappointed |

10 marks

# Test 81

**81.1**  1 conform    2 tally    3 approve    4 coincide    5 concurs    10 marks: 2 marks per item

**81.2**  1 divisions    2 rift    3 split    4 dissent    5 discord    10 marks: 2 marks per item

**81.3**

| noun | verb |
|---|---|
| compromise | compromise |
| settlement | settle |
| difference | differ |
| concession | concede |
| division | divide |

5 marks

**81.4**  1 on    2 with    3 in    4 to    5 of    5 marks

**81.5**
1 I think we should exercise/show a little more discretion in this matter.
2 I think we have to agree to differ.
3 The boss made several concessions to the union leaders.
4 The two parties have come to/arrived at/reached/achieved a compromise in their dispute.
5 The employers and the unions have reached/arrived at/achieved/negotiated a settlement in their dispute over staffing levels.
10 marks: 2 marks per sentence

# Test 82

**82.1**  Jackman **advocates** a **somewhat** different approach to the subject. He **perceives** the main problem as being the lack of **empirical** data and argues that more **comprehensive** surveys are **crucial** before any **authoritative** conclusions can be drawn. **Notwithstanding**, he praises one study done by Braithwaite in the 1990s, arguing that it suggests a **coherent** method **whereby** larger scale studies could be carried out.    10 marks

**82.2**
| | |
|---|---|
| 1 distort | 6 widespread |
| 2 deduce | 7 ambiguous |
| 3 trigger | 8 the converse |
| 4 complement | 9 thereby |
| 5 incidence | 10 denote |

10 marks

**82.3**  
1 likewise   6 reside  
2 infer    7 demonstrate  
3 whereby   8 arbitrary  
4 sequence   9 deviate  
5 predominant  10 overlap

10 marks

**82.4**  
concept – conceive  
contradiction – contradict  
conversation – converse  
denotation – denote  
deviation – deviate  
distortion – distort  
negation – negate  
perception – perceive  
appendix – append  
residence – reside

10 marks

## Test 83

**83.1**  1 a   2 b   3 a   4 c   5 b

10 marks: 2 marks per item

**83.2**

12 marks: 2 marks per item

**83.3**  1 deal   2 upon   3 return   4 addressed   5 descending  
6 made   7 forced   8 ascending   9 account

18 marks: 2 marks per item

## Test 84

**84.1**  
1 CAMBRIDGE UNIVERSITY PRESS is written in upper case on the front cover of the book.  
2 a) round brackets   b) square brackets  (2 marks)  
3 a font *or* a typeface  
4 a) italics *or* italicised text   b) bold (text)  (2 marks)  
5 block  
6 bullet points *or* bullets  
7 single inverted commas and double inverted commas *or* single quotation marks and double quotation marks *or* single quotes and double quotes  
8 an asterisk

10 marks

**84.2**  
1 *To write something down* is to write something on a piece of paper, usually so you don't forget it, and *to write something up* is to make a proper written text out of notes you have made.  
2 *To scribble* is to write something down quickly, whereas *to doodle* is to draw little patterns or pictures while you are thinking or talking or because you are bored.

3 When you are word processing, you *cut and paste* a piece of text if you take it out of one place and put it in a different place in your document. If you *copy and paste* something, you copy a piece of text to put it somewhere else but you also leave it in its original position.

4 A *title* is the main title of a book and a *subtitle* is an extra or second title that provides more information about the title. For example, in *Grammar in Context: Grammar reference and practice*, 'Grammar in Context' is the title and 'Grammar reference and practice' is the subtitle.

5 *To jot something down* is more informal than *to make a note of something*, but they both mean to write something down in order to remember it.

6 *To print a document* means to make a printed copy of a document that is on the computer, whereas *to format a document* means to decide on font sizes, margins, etc. to make the document look good before printing it.

7 *To indent a line* means to position it so that the line starts further in from the margin and *to put a line in a shaded box* means to put it in something like this:

This line is in a shaded box.

This line is indented.

8 A *manuscript* is the orginal copy of a book or article before it is printed, whereas the *first draft* is the writer's first version of a piece of work.

9 *Upper case* letters are capitals or block letters, i.e. LETTERS, and *lower case* letters are small letters, i.e. letters.

10 A *chapter heading* is the main title of a chapter and *a sub-heading* is one of several smaller headings within a chapter or article. Sub-headings are usually found in articles or in academic books rather than novels.                                                     20 marks: 2 marks per item

**84.3**  1 Jane scribbled a note to her mum.
2 You should put all the headings in bold.
3 I copied out my lecture notes for Sam.
4 I'm hoping to submit the final draft soon.
5 Ben is writing up his thesis at the moment.
6 Let's all just jot down our first thoughts and then discuss them.
7 It'll save time if you copy and paste these sections of the document.
8 It's a good idea to indent every paragraph.
9 Don't forget to put single quotes round direct speech.
10 Make a note of your reference number.                                                      10 marks

## Test 85

**85.1**  1 We'd love to retire early, but the problem is we simply don't have the money.
2 I know it's a nuisance, but I wish she wouldn't make such a (big) fuss about it.
3 One of the subjects he touched on in his lecture was globalisation.
4 Those kids frighten old people and the police can't take any action. *or* … the police can't do anything about the matter/situation.
5 As the situation is at present, I cannot see the government funding such a project. *or* In the current situation, I … *or* As matters stand …
6 My belt is too tight. Where's that tool for making holes in leather?
7 He has a dislike of cats. He hates them coming into his garden. *or* He dislikes cats. He …
8 Firstly, I don't think it will work, and secondly it will be very costly. (2 marks)
9 I think we should get the matter/situation sorted out as soon as possible. *or* I think we should take action as soon as possible.                                                        10 marks

**85.2**  1 MANDY:  Well, he was, but he never got it together.
2 LUKE:    No, but if I can get him on his own for an hour or so tomorrow, I will.
3 KEN:     Sorry, I don't get it/that.
4 FRAN:    Well, we need to get these letters in(to) the post. *or* Well, we need to get these letters off. *or* Well, we need to get these letters to the post office.      8 marks: 2 marks per sentence

**85.3** 1 I've told you umpteen times not to do that. *or* I've told you not to do that umpteen times.
2 She hasn't done a scrap of work all day.
3 I had a touch of flu last week.
4 It took masses of bureaucracy and paperwork (*or* paperwork and bureaucracy) to get permission.
5 I hate teachers, present company excepted, of course.                    10 marks: 2 marks per sentence

**85.4** PAULA: I was talking to ~~whoisisname~~ *whatsisname* yesterday, oh, you know, Bill Knight. I've never met anyone so childlike, and I mean that in the ~~possible nice way~~ *nicest possible way*.

ERIK: Yes, I know what you mean. But a lot of people have a slightly childish side, except for you, of course.

PAULA: Well, no ~~intended offence~~ *offence intended*, but you can be very silly yourself at times, and you know it.

ERIK: Mm. I accept that up to ~~the~~ *a* point, but I wouldn't say I was childish.

PAULA: Well, I think we all are occasionally, ~~me including~~ *myself included or me included*. And ~~if you don't care me saying~~ *if you don't mind me/my saying (so)*, so are most of your friends.

ERIK: Hm. Well we're all silly and immature then.                    12 marks: 2 marks per mistake

# Test 86

**86.1** 1 They're trying to tease you, typically by pretending that something is true when it isn't.
2 They would say 'Thuthie' /θuːði/
3 They're more likely to be drunk.
4 They are more likely to shriek if they see a snake. A fly is not frightening or unusual enough to make most people shriek.
5 They are saying nasty things about them and are probably criticising them.
6 You'd be more likely to praise them because you want something from them.
7 You would probably ask them to speak more loudly and clearly.
8 They are more likely to mutter.
9 You probably don't like it if someone nags you because it means being constantly criticised for things you have done wrong or things you have not done.
10 You would say that they have a stammer or a stutter, or that they stammer or stutter.                    10 marks

**86.2** 1 murmur   Murmur is a soft way of speaking, whereas shout and yell are both loud.
2 roar   Roar is a loud way of speaking, whereas mumble and mutter are soft or quiet.
3 scream   Lisp and stammer are speech impediments, things that people cannot control about the way that they speak, whereas scream is something that we all do from time to time and it is to a certain extent under our control.
4 wind up   Whinge and nag are both types of complaining, whereas wind up is teasing and playful.
5 chatter away   Slag off and bicker are both negative, whereas chatter away suggests to talk for a long time about non-serious things with, for example, a friend. Of course, you could also have chosen bicker, as the other two are phrasal verbs.                    10 marks: 1 mark for identifying the odd one out, 1 mark for giving an appropriate reason

**86.3** 1 without    6 with
2 tongue     7 about
3 under      8 up
4 about      9 at
5 raise     10 above                    10 marks

**86.4**  1 butter up, slag off, whinge, wind up  (3 marks for any three of these possible answers)
2 roar, scream, shriek, yell  (2 marks for any two of these possible answers)
3 gossip, slag off  (2 marks)
4 bicker, mutter, nag, slag off, whinge, yell  (2 marks for any of these possible answers)
5 murmur  (1 mark)

10 marks

## Test 87

**87.1**  1 few                                5 give; take  (2 marks)
2 smattering                          6 so
3 in; region  (2 marks)             7 lines
4 in; of  (2 marks)

10 marks

**87.2**  1 It's always **a bit of** an effort explaining things to her.
2 I think you should just add a **dash** of olive oil to the spinach.
3 I put a **(large) dollop** of cream onto each bowl of strawberries.
4 If you want more information, send me an e-mail **or whatever**.
5 The apartment was nice, but it was **a bit on the** small **side**.
6 These buns are delicious served with **lashings** of jam on them.
7 He said, "I'll never resign," or words **to that effect**.
8 This **stuff** is excellent for removing stains caused by fruit juices.

16 marks: 2 marks per sentence

**87.3**  1 oodles  (2 marks)
2 a) about   b) approximately  (1 mark each)
3 -ish: She's thirtyish.  (2 marks)
4 b) with other types of expressions (e.g. *We've more or less finished; It's more or less ready.*)
5 b) an informal context
6 I've had some tests and interviews **and things like that / and suchlike / and the like.**
(1 mark per expression)
7 -(k)y: It was made of a plasticky material.

14 marks

## Test 88

**88.1**  1 throats    2 art    3 cold    4 see    5 block    6 thoughts
7 purposes    8 blue    9 foot    10 ice

10 marks

**88.2**  1 I'm afraid we're going to have to start again **from scratch**.
2 I like to be fashionable but **I draw the line at wearing** a mini skirt.
3 She turned up (completely) **out of the blue**.
4 Make sure you **keep an eye on** the children – they can be quite naughty.
5 Diane always behaves in a very **high and mighty** way.
6 There's a great restaurant **on our doorstep**.
7 Tony always **keeps his parents in the dark** about his girlfriends. *or* Tony **is a dark horse** about his girlfriends.
8 I'm **as blind as a bat** without my contact lenses.
9 Ron says he's feeling a bit **under the weather** today.

18 marks: 2 marks per sentence

**88.3**  make-believe
stumbling block
open-ended
nitty-gritty
half-hearted
long-winded

Note that open-hearted is also possible.

6 marks

**88.4**
1 long-winded
2 nitty-gritty
3 stumbling block
4 make-believe
5 half-hearted
6 open-ended

6 marks

## Test 89

**89.1**
1 After a bad year, fortunately, things are now **looking** up.
2 It was a great success. Everything ran like **clockwork**.
3 The government intervened to solve the problem at the **eleventh hour**.
4 Good news! Our plan worked like **a dream!**
5 We took six months to plan our website and now I'm pleased to say it's up **and running**.

10 marks: 2 marks per sentence

**89.2** 1 –    2 +    3 –    4 –    5 +    6 –

6 marks

**89.3**
1 You asked if I understand. No, sorry, I'm afraid **it's as clear as mud.**
2 Just when I thought we would never succeed, **everything fell into place.**
3 Sorry about the mix-up last night. **We got our wires crossed.**
4 It was all set up to make him admit his guilt. Luckily, **it went according to plan.**
5 I wasn't expecting her to say that. **It threw me completely.**
6 That company is totally disorganised. **It's a complete shambles.**

6 marks

**89.4**
1 bad dream (2 marks)
2 muddy (1 mark)
3 wood; trees (2 marks)
4 storm; teacup (2 marks)
5 brush; under; carpet (3 marks)

10 marks

**89.5**
1 needed *or* need
2 last thing
3 calm; storm
4 make; easier
5 mystery
6 lost
7 close
8 pain *or* palaver

8 marks

## Test 90

**90.1**
1 Paula only has eyes for Johnny.
2 Matthew is the man of her dreams.
3 Pat could talk the hind legs off a donkey.
4 Kay is one sandwich short of a picnic.
5 Gary certainly has the gift of the gab.
6 Jack and Fay fell head over heels in love.
7 Sam's arrogance really gets on my wick.
8 Gordon has got nothing between the ears.
9 Tony can be a bit slow on the uptake.
10 Helen is several bricks short of a load.

10 marks

**90.2**
1. soft
2. nobody's *or* no
3. information
4. knows
5. brains
6. world
7. hit
8. planks
9. foggiest *or* faintest (Note that 'slightest' or 'remotest' would also be possible, but are less common.)
10. back

10 marks

**90.3**

| sad | happy |
|-----|-------|
| down in the mouth<br>down in the dumps<br>as miserable as sin | walking on air<br>on cloud nine<br>in seventh heaven<br>in your element<br>over the moon<br>on top of the world<br>look like the cat that's got the cream |

10 marks

**90.4**
1. I'm getting a bit fed up with the way Myra raves on and on **about** her new job.
2. Charles is certainly bright but he upsets others by being such a **smart** aleck. (Note that you can also spell aleck 'alec'.)
3. The way Roger talks down to other people really **gets** on my nerves.
4. You really need to use your **grey** matter to solve cryptic crosswords.
5. Sue and Larry are the perfect couple; they're **made** for each other.
6. Mark's been in the business for years and he certainly knows what's **what**.
7. I'm sorry I told Emma your plans. I didn't mean to let the cat out of the **bag**.
8. If you come and see me after the meeting, I'll **put** you in the picture.
9. Tina's very bright – you'll never be able to pull the **wool** over her eyes.
10. Your dad wasn't born **yesterday** – he'll guess what you're up to.

10 marks

## Test 91

**91.1**
1. Suzanne surprised everyone by joining the army, but she's always been a bit of **a dark horse**.
2. That film was horrible. All the blood and violence just **turned my stomach**.
3. He never lets me finish what I'm saying. It **drives me nuts**.
4. I was so shocked by what she said that I found myself completely at **a loss for words**.
5. Jess is such a dreamer. He always seems to be in **a world of his own**. *or* He always seems to be in **his own world**.
6. My mother doesn't want me to have a motorbike but I know I can persuade my father. He's a (real) **soft touch**.
7. She could solve her career problems but she seems to lack the will. She's her **own worst enemy**.
8. Lucy is such a refined woman, but her new boyfriend is the complete opposite. He seems a bit of a **rough diamond**.
9. Oh I'm not surprised Aysha spoke so directly. She never **minces her words**.
10. I've tried everything. I simply don't know what to do. I'm at **the end of my tether**.

10 marks

**91.2**

**91.3**  1 give someone the benefit of the doubt
2 be your own person
3 be at loggerheads
4 rub someone up the wrong way
5 get the measure of someone
6 put a brave face on it

**91.4**  1 You feel very ashamed and embarrassed.
2 You are very tired or exhausted.
3 They are doing exactly what you want them to do. In other words you have persuaded them to do what you wanted.
4 You are lost or confused.
5 It is a negative relationship with a lot of disagreements.
6 They are experiencing extreme anger.
7 wrap *or* twist (1 mark per correct verb)

## Test 92

**92.1**  1 words    2 thumbs    3 cap *or* crown *or* top    4 learn    5 world
6 story    7 vu    8 minding    9 show    10 ends

**92.2**  1 All's well that ends well.
2 It's a small world.
3 I was minding my own business; I was twiddling my thumbs. (2 marks)
4 a feeling of déjà vu
5 You live and learn.
6 to cut a long story short
7 Famous last words.
8 to cap/crown/top it all
9 It just goes to show …

**92.3**  1 You can't win them all.
2 If you can't beat them, join them.
3 It was just one of those things.
4 One thing led to another.
5 Jane turned up out of the blue. *or* Up turned Jane out of the blue.
6 Then, to cap it all, I ran out of petrol.
7 I could feel it in my bones that something bad was about to happen.
8 Kyle started reorganising all my CDs without so much as a by-your-leave.
9 So far so good.
10 As luck would have it, I met my boss coming out of the restaurant.

## Test 93

**93.1**
1. George left the room and took off without saying goodbye to anybody.
2. The waiter removed the bad bottle of wine and said he would take 20% off the bill.
3. The plane taxied along the runway then took off into the sky.
4. She took off her jacket and helped us remove the table to give us room to dance.
5. When I got home, I removed the sweater from the bag, took off the label and tried it on. *or* ... took the label off and tried it on.

`10 marks: 2 marks per sentence`

**93.2**

| keep **off** the grass | stand **for** election as President |
|---|---|
| keep **up** your English | stand **by** your friends when they need you |
| keep the truth **from** somebody | stand somebody **up** on a date |
| keep **up with** somebody walking fast | stand **in for** a sick colleague at work |

`8 marks`

**93.3**
1. The flight took off on time.
2. The scandal blew over after a couple of weeks. *or* After a couple of weeks the scandal blew over.
3. The robbers took off when they heard a police car arriving.
4. I blew the photo up on my computer. *or* I blew up the photo on my computer.
5. The taxi pulled up outside the station.
6. Her father told her off because she came home late.

`6 marks`

**93.4**
1. It was a major operation, and she was seriously ill, but she **recovered**.
2. I find it difficult to **distinguish** crows **from** blackbirds.
3. When the truth came out, the Chairperson **resigned**.
4. I promised I wouldn't **betray** him if he cheated in the test.
5. The dentist had to **extract** three of her teeth after the accident.
6. His mother **scolded** him for not phoning to say where he was.
7. The train **stopped** at a small country station.
8. The storm **extinguished** our lamp and we were in complete darkness.
9. I'll take that photo of my mother and get it **enlarged**; it's such a nice one.
10. I'm convinced she's **concealing** something (from us).

`10 marks`

**93.5**  1 told  2 stand  3 pull  4 stood  5 blown  6 stand

`6 marks`

## Test 94

**94.1**
1. catch on – become popular
2. doze off – fall asleep
3. dumb down – make something less intellectually demanding
4. ease up – become less extreme
5. lay on – provide
6. play it down – make something seem less important
7. slog away – work hard
8. stick it out – persevere
9. tip off – pass on secret information
10. whittle away – gradually reduce or destroy

`10 marks`

**94.2**  Hi, Jean

How's things with you? It's been raining heavily here all day though it seems to be (1) **easing up** a bit now. We're both busy. Larry is (2) **slogging away** at his thesis. He keeps threatening to give up but I hope he'll (3) **stick it out**. I'm designing a new kids' toy. I just hope it (4) **catches on** (or **will catch on**) as our savings are being rapidly (5) **whittled away** at the moment. I try to (6) **play it down** for Larry as I don't want him to be worried about anything else but his thesis. He's been (7) **tipped off** that his external examiner is likely to be Prof Carr, who has a reputation for toughness. In the evenings I do what I can to (8) **lay on** nice meals to keep him going. We're both so tired after dinner that we just (9) **doze off** in front of the TV. They say the programmes are being (10) **dumbed down** but we never watch long enough to know whether that's true or not!

Nell                                                                              10 marks

**94.3**  1  down; up
        2  up; out
        3  on; on
        4  up; off
        5  away; out                                                              10 marks

**94.4**  1  Whenever I sit in that armchair beside the fire, I **doze off**.
        2  I'd have got home at 6 p.m. if a problem hadn't suddenly **cropped up** at work.
        3  It's **pelting down** in London at the moment.
        4  The boy got to this country by **stowing away** in the hold of a plane.
        5  Psychologists say it's better not to **bottle up** your feelings.
        6  I never expected DVDs to **catch on**.
        7  It always takes a few hours for a dental anaesthetic to **wear off**.
        8  Please **step on it** or we'll be late.
        9  I was planning to sing in the competition but I **bottled out**.
        10  We can **sort out** the final details later. *or* We can **sort** the final details **out** later.                 10 marks

# Test 95

**95.1**  1  up with *or* up on
        2  in for
        3  out on
        4  away with
        5  round to                                                    10 marks: 1 mark per word

**95.2**  1  Ben     2  Jason     3  Olivia     4  Millie     5  Rob     6  Penny
        7  Philip     8  Lorna                                                      8 marks

**95.3**  I had a bad week last week. First I fell ~~down~~ [out] with Carol – it was a stupid argument, then I came [down] ~~below~~ with a cold and had to stay in bed for two days. I felt very grumpy and took it ~~off~~ [out] on my sister, as if it was her fault. I decided I needed something to ~~happy~~ [cheer] me up so I invited another friend round and opened ~~out~~ [up] to her and told her my troubles. We just ~~cooled~~ [chilled] out listening to some new CDs she'd bought. She was bubbling ~~out~~ [over] with excitement; she'd just met a new man who she'd fallen madly in love with.                 14 marks: 1 mark for finding each mistake, 1 mark for correcting it

| 'weather' metaphor | 'high and low' metaphor | 'cooking' metaphor |
|---|---|---|
| chill out<br>be snowed under | fall out with<br>pick up<br>bottom out<br>come down with | simmer down<br>bubble over |

Note that 'chill out' could also be considered to be a cooking metaphor.

8 marks

## Test 96

**96.1**

Crossword grid:
- 1 (down) I
- 2 (across) INTERSTATE
- 3 (across) TRAIL
- 4 (across) FAUCET
- 5 (across) GROUND
- 6 (across) CROSSWALK
- 7 (across) OVERPASS
- 8 (across) BACKUP
- 9 (across) KITTYCORNER
- 10 (across) STOVE
- Down word: ITALIAN / STATION (I-T-A-L-I... column letters)

10 marks

**96.2**

1  American   We rented a house by the <u>creek</u> and spent the weekends exploring little <u>trails</u> nearby. (3 marks)
2  American   I'll wait in the <u>parking lot</u> while you load up the <u>shopping cart</u>. (3 marks)
3  British   We stopped at a <u>petrol station</u> just before joining the <u>motorway</u>. (3 marks)
4  British   There's a <u>frying pan</u> next to the <u>cooker</u>. (3 marks)
5  American   The flight will <u>deplane</u> <u>momentarily</u>. (3 marks)
6  American   <u>Coach class</u> passengers are only allowed one piece of <u>carry-on</u> baggage. (3 marks)
7  British   It's very expensive to rent a <u>skip</u>. (2 marks)

> 20 marks: 1 mark for identifying whether the speaker is British or American, 1 mark for identifying each of the underlined words

**96.3**

| | British English | American English | | | British English | American English |
|---|---|---|---|---|---|---|
| 1 | path | trail | | 6 | skip | dumpster |
| 2 | frying pan | skillet | | 7 | trolley | cart |
| 3 | turn left | take a left | | 8 | disembark | deplane |
| 4 | hand luggage | carry-on baggage | | 9 | shortly | momentarily |
| 5 | cooker | stove | | 10 | stream | creek |

10 marks

## Test 97

**97.1**   1 b   2 b   3 b   4 a   5 b

10 marks: 2 marks per item

**97.2**  1 The washroom's over there. – a Canadian
2 She has two lovely bairns. – a Scot
3 We shifted last week to a bigger house. – someone from Malaysia
4 I don't believe it, mate! – an Australian
5 It's okay. We pay at the shroff. – someone from Hong Kong    `10 marks: 2 marks per item`

**97.3**  1 Australia
2 b
3 bloke
4 c   You are most likely to find one in Australia.
5 a) Oz   b) beaut
6 the outback
7 the veld
8 b
9 b
10 true    `20 marks: 2 marks per item`

# Test 98

**98.1**  1 cleaner or cleaning person
2 Ms
3 supervisor
4 to staff an office
5 chair *or* chairperson
6 human resources
7 flight attendant *or* member of the cabin crew
8 spokesperson
9 nurse
10 working hours    `10 marks`

**98.2**

| negative | neutral | positive |
|----------|---------|----------|
| effeminate | female | manly |
| sissy | feminine | womanly |
| mannish | male | virile |
| butch | masculine | |
| | tomboy | |

`12 marks`

**98.3**  1 tomboy
2 male
3 sissy
4 masculine *or* feminine; feminine *or* masculine  (2 marks)
5 virile (Note that 'manly' would also be possible in this context.)
6 female
7 manly
8 butch *or* mannish
9 mannish *or* butch
10 womanly
11 effeminate    `12 marks`

**98.4**  1 They use it because it acknowledges that not all firefighters are men.
2 No, it is meant to include women as well.
3 humankind
4 She could be either but we don't know.
5 They disapprove.
6 handle roughly *or* treat roughly    `6 marks`

## Test 99

**99.1**

|  | hoi-polloi | plebby | posh | toff | oik |
|---|---|---|---|---|---|
| *higher* |  |  | ✓ | ✓ |  |
| *lower* | ✓ | ✓ |  |  | ✓ |

**99.2**    1 toff    2 hoi-polloi    3 plebby    4 posh    5 oiks

**99.3**
1 the upper crust
2 the chattering classes
3 They are people who have recently become rich and who spend money in a showy way.
4 stuck-up
5 snooty
6 luncheon
7 riff-raff
8 the middle class
9 lavatory, loo  (1 mark per word)

**99.4**
1 stuck-up          4 chattering classes
2 luncheon          5 bourgeois
3 riff-raff          6 new money

**99.5**    1 old    2 young    3 old    4 young    5 old    6 old

## Test 100

**100.1**
1 Something has happened at the monarch's residence or some kind of royal palace.
2 There was probably an explosion of some kind, for example a bomb or a gas explosion.
3 They are people who drop rubbish in public places.
4 There is a campaign to try to stop the problem, perhaps by fining people who drop rubbish on the streets.
5 Something has happened at a holiday resort in a sunny place.
6 A typhoon has caused serious damage there.
7 A Member of Parliament is in the news.
8 He or she is being surrounded or followed by journalists.
9 The police and some thugs (violent hooligans).
10 The 'cops' or police are carrying out a campaign focusing on dealing with the problem of thugs or violent hooligans in the city.

**100.2**
1 Car company cuts costs  (1 mark)
2 MP (Member of Parliament) and TV (television)  (2 marks)
3 terror and thug  (2 marks)
4 MP TO VISIT STATES  (1 mark)
5 A car company has cut (or is cutting) its costs.  (1 mark)
A television star has had a terrifying experience when on his/her own.  (1 mark)
A Member of Parliament is going to visit the United States.  (1 mark)
A teenage thug has been charged.  (1 mark)

**100.3**

| | headline | probable story | double meaning |
|---|---|---|---|
| 1 | Kids make nutritious snacks | Children prepare food for themselves. | Children are good to eat. |
| 2 | Local high school dropouts cut in half | Fewer students are now dropping out from a local high school. | The school is cutting or sawing its dropouts in half. |
| 3 | Stolen painting found by tree | A stolen painting was found beside a tree. | A tree found the stolen painting. |
| 4 | New study of obesity seeks larger test group | Scientists studying obesity are looking for more people to take part in the research. | Scientists studying obesity are looking for fatter people to take part in the research. |
| 5 | Pop star appeals to Pope | A pop star makes a formal request to the Pope. | The Pope finds a pop star attractive. |
| 6 | Milk drinkers turning to powder | People who drink milk are increasingly drinking powdered milk rather than natural milk. | People who drink milk are becoming or turning into powder. |
| 7 | British left waffles on public transport | The British left-wing party talks a lot about public transport without saying anything useful. | The British left behind some waffles [a kind of cake] on public transport. |
| 8 | Police begin campaign to run down illegal workers | The police start a campaign to stop illegal workers. | The police start a campaign to drive cars over illegal workers. |
| 9 | Drunks get nine months in violin case | Drunks who were involved in a legal case involving a violin are punished with nine months in prison. | Drunks are punished by having to spend nine months in a case that normally holds a violin. |
| 10 | Police head seeks arms | A head or chief of police is looking for weapons. | The head of a policeman is looking for some arms (as if it is gradually collecting body parts). |

20 marks: 1 mark for explaining each probable story, 1 mark for explaining the double meaning

# Personal diary

| Test | Word | Translation | Points to remember | Related words |
|------|------|-------------|--------------------|---------------|
|      |      |             |                    |               |

# Personal diary

| Test | Word | Translation | Points to remember | Related words |
|------|------|-------------|--------------------|---------------|
|      |      |             |                    |               |

# Also available:

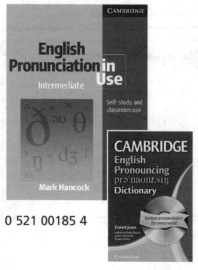

English Pronunciation in Use
Intermediate
Self-study and classroom use
Mark Hancock

0 521 00185 4

CAMBRIDGE
English Pronouncing Dictionary
Daniel Jones

0 521 01713 0

English Idioms in Use
60 units of vocabulary reference and practice
Self-study and classroom use
Michael McCarthy
Felicity O'Dell

0 521 78957 5

CAMBRIDGE
International Dictionary of Idioms

0 521 62567 X

English Phrasal Verbs in Use
70 units of vocabulary reference and practice
Michael McCarthy
Felicity O'Dell

0 521 52727 9

CAMBRIDGE
International Dictionary of Phrasal Verbs

0 521 56558 8

## Cambridge Advanced Learner's Dictionary
## Second Edition
### Upper intermediate to advanced

- Ideal for FCE, CAE, CPE and IELTS preparation.
- NEW up-to-date vocabulary.
- NEW 'mini-collocation' boxes.
- NEW frequency information.

The CD-ROM offers even more!
The whole paper dictionary plus:

- New interactive exam-related exercises.
- Thousands of new example sentences.
- Unique SMART Thesaurus.
- Audio recordings.
- Hundreds of interactive exercises.

CAMBRIDGE
Advanced Learner's Dictionary

NEW edition

CD-ROM Dictionary and thesaurus in one

New

SECOND EDITION
CAMBRIDGE

Paperback                     0 521 60498 2
Paperback with CD-ROM         0 521 60499 0
CD-ROM for Windows            0 521 60500 8